LL

ADAM'S FARM

COUNTRY**FILE**

ADAM'S FARM

My Life on the Land

By Adam Henson
with Cavan Scott

BOOKS

This book is published to accompany the television series
entitled *Countryfile*, first broadcast on BBC1.

Executive editor: Andrew Thorman
Series producer: Teresa Bogan
Producers: Andrew Tomlinson, Andrea Buffery and Barbara Lewis
Production manager: Hilary Jones

13 5 7 9 10 8 6 4 2

Published in 2011 by BBC Books, an imprint of Ebury Publishing.
A Random House Group Company

The Random House Group Limited Reg. No. 954009

Addresses for companies within the Random House Group can be found at
www.randomhouse.co.uk

A CIP catalogue record for this book is available from the British Library.

ISBN 978 1 849 90070 6

Mixed Sources
Product group from well-managed
forests and other controlled sources
www.fsc.org Cert no. TT-COC-2139
© 1996 Forest Stewardship Council

The Random House Group Limited supports the Forest Stewardship Council (FSC),
the leading international forest certification organisation. All our titles that are
printed on Greenpeace approved FSC certified paper carry the FSC logo. Our paper
procurement policy can be found at www.rbooks.co.uk/environment

Commissioning editor: Muna Reyal
Project editor: Laura Higginson
Copy editor: Bernice Davison
Production: Helen Everson

Designed and set by seagulls.net
Printed and bound in Great Britain by Clays

To buy books by your favourite authors and register for offers, visit
www.rbooks.co.uk

CONTENTS

WINTER

INTRODUCTION
MILLIE

Life doesn't get much better than this. I'm standing on one of the highest points of my farm on the top of the Cotswold hills, roughly 900 feet above sea level, the first rays of spring sunshine beating down on me. The field is empty save for half a dozen of some of my favourite sheep – the black-faced Norfolk Horn and the shaggy Cotswold Lion. At my feet is Maude, my top sheepdog and a constant companion for 11 years. I love working with Maude, but she's getting a bit long in the tooth now. The old Border collie is slowing up and gets tired quickly. She deserves a good retirement but that would leave me with a gap in my team of working dogs. My other main dog, Ronnie, isn't what you expect from a British sheepdog. Sleek and almost yellow in colour, she's an Australian kelpie, a favourite among shepherds the world over. Some claim that, due to their appearance, the kelpie is related to the dingo, but breeders believe that they are actually descendants of the English North Country collie. Whatever their origin, kelpies make brilliant sheepdogs, full of boundless energy and capable of working in the harshest of conditions. Ronnie's a great little worker, who can bark on command and moves both sheep and cattle well, but even she would struggle to handle all of our 600 sheep by herself. Maude does have a daughter – Pearl – but she's no help. Sadly, Pearl was run over when she was still a puppy and has never taken to training very well. I'd given Pearl to my daughter, Ella, to encourage Ella to work with sheepdogs and she was understandably devastated when the accident happened. In any other situation I would have put down Pearl, but that would have been the last straw as far as Ella was concerned. Instead, we spent a fortune on operations to insert pins and rods to rebuild Pearl's legs and she recovered well, although, if I'm honest, she is a bit rubbish when it comes to being a sheepdog. But I am extremely fond of her.

So the time has come to introduce a new working dog to my motley band. That's why I've come up here this afternoon. Straining on the leash and eager to get to work is Millie, a 14-month-old dog who is three-quarters collie and one-quarter kelpie. She's a sweet little dog with a beautiful tri-colour coat – black and white with a ginger tinge to her legs and eyebrows. She also has a lovely nature, and my first attempts at training her have gone well.

But today, our training session will be observed by the man who taught me just about everything I know about working dogs. My dad, Joe Henson, is perched on the drystone wall behind me, wearing his trademark cloth cap and leaning on his walking stick, taking in everything.

It was dad who took over the tenancy of Bemborough Farm, back in 1962. The place, which was originally owned by Corpus Christi College, Oxford, was just 400 acres. Nearly 40 years later, it has grown into a 1600-acre estate, a testament to dad's vision. Even though he looks every inch the farmer today, dad didn't come from an agricultural background. His family would have been more comfortable on stage rather than on a farm. My grandfather, Leslie Henson, was a famous comedian on the West End stage in the 1920s and 1930s. He spent the whole of the Second World War entertaining troops all over the world in ENSA – the Entertainments National Service Association – before returning to the West End theatre. Dad grew up as a child with stars visiting the house – Stanley Holloway, Heather Thatcher, Dickie Hearne, Nan Kenway and Douglas Young – but whereas dad's brother, my uncle Nicky, followed in Leslie's footsteps, dad's heart wasn't in the glitz and glamour of show business, but in the countryside. The bug had bitten him when he was a young lad. His mum used to take him to a farm up the road run along traditional lines. The 30 cows were hand-milked, the hens all free-range, while all the work in the fields was done by carthorses. He instantly fell in love with farming and every sixpence he could save was spent on a collection of lead animals. He's always quick to joke that if he still had these now highly collectable toys, they'd probably be worth much more than many of their real-life counterparts.

On leaving school, dad worked on farms for three years, striking out from London to work as herdsman of a herd of Jerseys in Somerset before winning a two-year place at the Royal Agricultural College in Cirencester. His first job was on a farm in Northwood, back on the outskirts of London, but at the age of

30 he ended up at Bemborough. When he took over the tenancy with his old school friend and business partner John Neave, the place was just a little Cotswold farm, near Bourton-on-the-Water. It's a bit different now.

When dad and John retired, the tenancy passed to me, as it will to my own children – if, that is, they want to farm like their old man. I hope they will. There's hardly a day that goes by when I don't wake up in the morning and realise how lucky I am to farm in the middle of such beautiful countryside. I honestly look forward to work every day. I get to work with one of my oldest friends – my business partner Duncan Andrews, whom I met during my time at Seale-Hayne Agricultural College down in Devon – and enjoy the variety of work on our farm. Unlike many places today, we're still a mixed farm, with 988 of our 1600 acres taken up with arable crops – mainly winter barley, wheat, oilseed rape and beans – which bring in most of our money, alongside our flock of commercial sheep to produce lamb for the table. We're perhaps best known, however, for our large collection of rare and heritage breed farm animals, which dad started to gather together back in the 1970s. Many of these amazing beasts are on display to the general public through our side venture, the Cotswold Farm Park, which attracts more than 70,000 visitors during the seven months of the year when it's open. Life is certainly never dull.

Under dad's expert gaze, I put Maude through her paces, hoping that Millie, who is still on the leash, will pick up the moves. The idea is that in a few minutes I will let Millie loose and see how she reacts. It'll be her first time working with sheep for me and, as with any new sheepdog, there is a risk involved. Will she be a natural, or instead run straight through the middle of the flock? Some rookie dogs even attack the sheep in all of the excitement. I don't think Millie will, but you can never be sure.

The moment of truth has come and I bring Maude back to me and let Millie off the leash. She's off like a shot, circling the sheep and sitting herself on the other side of the flock before I've even uttered a command. Dad and I exchange looks. That's a good sign.

I start giving commands – shouting 'Away' for Millie to go right, and 'By' for her to go left. Dad nods in appreciation. She's a fast dog and when I yell out 'Sit', she immediately drops to the ground. It's such a relief. Millie is a natural. OK, so she comes quite close to the sheep on the turn, still isn't too sure which way is left and which is right and is taking the sheep the way she thinks they should go rather than the way I want them to, but there's real potential here. All it will need is 15 minutes of training a day and in a few months' time Millie should be as good as Maude was in her heyday. The old girl can start enjoying a well-deserved retirement.

I can't help smiling as I bring Millie in and watch dad praise her. Shepherds have been working with sheepdogs for centuries, and for good reason. They're safe, efficient and, most importantly for a farmer, make complete economic sense. One dog can do the work of three men when it comes to moving sheep and, in these environmentally friendly days, is still the most ecologically sound way of handling sheep – far greener than a gas-guzzling quad bike.

But there's something else about working with your dog, something almost primeval. Man and beast working together for a common goal. Up here, on the hills where I ran as a child, I'm the alpha male of the pack, my dogs working to please me because they love me. There's nothing like seeing your dogs bringing in your flock. It's a timeless pleasure that I never tire of.

As I pop Milly and Maude up on to the back of my truck, ready to take them back to the farmhouse for a treat, I glance over my shoulder and take in the view. I can hear the ewes in the valley below and see the new crops swaying in the breeze. Soon, my kids will be returning home to the very farmhouse where I was born. OK, so not every day is like this. The sun isn't always shining and the work can break both your back and your heart, but I wouldn't change it for the world. This place is in my blood and I'd be lost without it.

My name is Adam and this is my story.

SPRING

CHAPTER 1

NEW ARRIVALS

March 2009. The lamb is in trouble. The ewe has started to give birth but something has gone wrong. Lambs are supposed to be born with their front legs first, followed by their nose. In this case the head is out but the legs are nowhere to be seen. There's no way the mother will be able to give birth with her baby in that position. I need to act fast. First, I check that the lamb is alive and, thankfully, he is. There's only one thing to do. I need to get him back into position so that nature can take its course – with a little helping hand from yours truly. The only snag is for that to happen I need to push the lamb back up into the mother. Then I will be able to manoeuvre him so that his feet are pointing forwards and I can pull him out. It's a difficult procedure but one I've done time and time again. Modern sheep breeds are huge compared to some of the rare, heritage breeds I also have on my farm. Modern sheep have been bred to produce as much meat as possible to be commercially viable, but their sheer bulk can cause difficult births like this one.

I slip on a rubber glove that keeps me reasonably clean and, more importantly, prevents me from introducing any infection to the ewe. After applying a little lubrication, it's down to work. Snatching up some string, I start to make a noose to slip around the lamb's head. This sounds extreme, but the last thing I need is for the head to flop back once I've got him back inside his mum. If that happens, it's game over – I'd never get him out. Carefully, I ease the noose over his head, tucking it around his ears and through his mouth. I don't want it to go around his neck for obvious reasons. He's still getting oxygen via the umbilical cord, but I don't want to crush his windpipe.

Once the noose is tight, I grip his head gently, but firmly, and begin to push him back inside. As you'd expect it's not an easy job. The poor ewe is having contractions and pushing back at me, desperate to give birth, so I pull her by her back legs, leaning her up against my body slightly so gravity, at least, is on my side. The head goes back in and I push deeper, gently easing the little lamb back into the depths of the ewe's womb. Once in place I finally have some space to try and find his legs. With some careful dexterity I wriggle my figures down the lamb's front, feeling my way through the glove. There's one leg, but where's the other? There. It's folded beneath him as if he's kneeling. I pull them both forward and, when I'm happy they're in place, begin to tug on the string to make sure that the head comes with them. My hand slips out, gripping one foot, which is closely followed by the other. I lean back slightly and the head makes a return performance. I quickly remove the noose and the lamb spills out of his mother on to the straw-covered floor, its twin sibling arriving seconds later.

Almost immediately, apparently unfazed by the drama, the ewe turns round and starts licking her lambs clean. Soon they will start nuzzling against her, finding her teats so they can start taking in her all-important first milk, full of antibodies which will bolster the lambs' immune systems. I stand and watch her, thankful that I had passed this way when I did. If I hadn't spotted that she was in difficulty, both lambs would have probably died, along with the mother. It's always a tragedy to lose lives during lambing, but you never get through the season without some deaths. No matter what we do, and how vigilant we are, around two per cent of the ewes and seven per cent of the lambs don't make it. It's a hard fact of farming life and one that also affects our bottom line. Those deaths equate to more than £5000 pounds of lost revenue.

Of course, at the time it isn't the money that's on your mind. Every new life is something special. When I'm in the lambing shed and helping to deliver a lamb, I'm not thinking this is forty or sixty quid in my hand. I'm thinking, I need to keep this little thing alive. There's a huge amount of emotion tied into each birth, especially when you've not really slept for days and are drop-dead tired. All you want is for each lamb to survive.

As the mother continues to lick her lambs, I set off to clean myself up. I don't mind admitting that I'm exhausted. Lambing is one of our busiest times and there's no such thing as nine to five. Last night, I was on the night shift, checking on the lambing sheds on the hour, every hour. It's a lonely job, and wasn't helped by the fact that it was chucking it down outside. But it's

3

also a good time to keep an eye on what's going on. By the middle
of the night, the sheep are usually very settled and it's easy to
spot one who's restless in the first stages of labour. Around 1
a.m., in the middle of one of the coldest April nights I can remember, I call it a night and grab a few hours' sleep, but am back in
the sheds at half-past five – albeit a little bleary-eyed – checking
on the girls once again.

The antisocial hours of lambing are just something you get
used to, but the one thing I hope I never become too blasé about
is the sheer wonder of new life around me. I've seen thousands
of lambs born here on the farm, but even after all this time, it's
still special.

Of course, there is one thing that's very different this year. As
I clean myself down after the difficult birth of the twin lambs, I
can't help but chuckle. It's a procedure I've carried out hundreds
of times before, and one that needs total concentration, but I've
never had to do it on camera, describing each step to millions of
viewers who will be tuning in to watch the activity in my lambing sheds in a couple of weeks. Today, *Countryfile* is on the farm.

I grew up used to television. I had to be. As I've said, my uncle
Nicky had taken after my grandfather and stepped into the lime-
light. You may have seen him in *Fawlty Towers* as the ladies' man
who causes Basil so much trouble in 'The Psychiatrist' episode or
more recently in *EastEnders* where he played Billy Mitchell's
father-in-law, Jack. When I was a kid he was married to his first
wife, Una Stubbs, Aunt Sally from the children's TV programme

Worzel Gummidge. Christmases were always a scream. We used to play charades with Nick and Una – and as Una was one of the team captains on *Give Us a Clue*, it was like having our very own version of the show in our lounge.

The Henson theatrical gene has also passed down to Nicky and Una's sons, Christian and Joe, who are both composers. After Nicky and Una split up, Nicky married Marguerite Porter, a prima ballerina who had danced with The Royal Ballet. Together they have a son, Keaton, named after my uncle's hero Buster Keaton.

Closer to home even dad got into the act. He may have chosen pig muck over greasepaint but the bright lights of showbiz still sparkled in him, even if it was just a case of spinning a yarn to keep everyone entertained. He's a born storyteller, adding in all kinds of embellishments to build up the action; he was a natural appearing in front of the farm park visitors. Pretty soon he was popping up regularly on the *Animal Magic* television show with Johnny Morris, as the show's resident farmer and even presented a precursor to *Countryfile* back in the early Eighties called *In the Country* with Angela Rippon and Phil Drabble. However, despite our family show business connections, I never dreamt that I too would become a TV farmer.

It all started back in 2001 when *Countryfile* put out a call for new presenters in a *X Factor* style contest. You had to send in a two-minute audition tape and wait to see if you would be lucky enough to be called up for the next stage, which would eventually see you facing the vote of a cross section of *Countryfile* viewers.

One of the girls who worked on the farm wanted to enter the competition but didn't have a camcorder, so she asked to borrow mine. It was the first I'd heard of the contest. Of course, I'd watched *Countryfile* from time to time and John Craven had even come to film on our farm, but I didn't think anything of it and simply handed over the camera. That night when I was talking about it over dinner, my partner Charlie – who works in the media – piped up, 'You should be going in for that.'

I dismissed the idea. I was a farmer – why would they want me to present a TV show? But the seed was sown and after a few days I found I couldn't get the idea out of my head. Why shouldn't I go for it as well? So, when the camera was returned, Charlie and I headed out into the yard to record my own audition. It was quite a laugh, but took us far too long, mainly because I kept cocking it up and having to do more takes. I'd also decided to share the screen with a goat kid and a huge bull. What's that about not working with children or animals? The kid, which I was holding, bleated its way through every one of my links and then, when I put it down, the bull had wandered off. Finally, once I'd got both of them to behave, I told the camera about the farm, my history and what I can do. Along the way, Charlie gave me a few pointers and – most importantly – a few home truths. Apparently I kept overacting. Me? A Henson? Too dramatic? Surely not! When it was in the can, Charlie edited it for me and I popped it in the post, ignoring the nagging voice at the back of my mind that kept reminding me that it was a bit rubbish and nothing would ever come of it. Now, when I think about the tape I can't help but cringe, but amazingly it seemed to do the trick. Out of the blue I received a call.

'We loved your tape,' said the voice on the other end of the phone, 'and would like to invite you on location in a couple of weeks' time.'

True enough, a few weeks later, I found myself in the middle of a crash course in presenting. A group of 20 of us had to go out on location, prepare for and then carry out an interview – with a member of the production team acting in the role of country expert. We also had to record some pieces to camera to top and tail the interview and then lay down some voice-overs. It was terrifying, but you didn't have enough time to be scared. You just had to get on with the job. Before I knew it, the ordeal was over and it was out of my hands. Unbeknown to me, the production crew had already whittled the twenty hopefuls down to a short-list of three and my report had scraped through. It would now face the *Countryfile* viewers. All I could do was play the waiting game again.

Looking back, I still can't believe that they voted for me. Out of 3500 hopefuls, I got the job. Amazing. Of course, right at the last minute it was nearly snatched from my hands. Just at the time I won the contest, the BBC broadcast a new series called *Castaway*, one of the very first reality TV shows on British tele-vision. In it, a group of people were sent over to the Isle of Taransay, off the west coast of Scotland. The series was an instant hit and those early reality TV stars included a certain young man called Ben Fogle. The BBC quite rightly realised that they had something special in Ben and offered him a presenting job on the *Countryfile* team. Apparently there was a lot of head-scratching in the production office in Birmingham. They'd only needed one new presenter and now they had two. The trouble was, one had quite a lot of experience of TV through *Castaway* and the other – me – was a complete novice.

The call came in.

'Congratulations, Adam, you've won the competition and we can offer you the prize – one day presenting with John Craven.'

My heart sank. A prize of just one day? I thought I'd been going after a proper job. I was pleasant enough on the phone, but was seething inside. All that effort for nothing. I put the receiver down and went to find dad to explain what had happened. He sat and listened, and when I'd finished my tale of woe just sat there, thinking about what I'd said.

'Well, Adam, the way I see it is this,' he finally said, wise as ever. 'Either you throw your toys out of the pram and lose everything, or you go along and enjoy the experience. You never know where it may lead anyway.'

He was right. I had done my best and it was out of my hands. Luckily, one of the producers saw some potential in me and the BBC were as good as their word and offered me the job at the same time as Ben started. I can still remember my first assignment. The call came from *Countryfile* saying they wanted me to head over to Wales to find out how to grow drugs.

I had to ask them to repeat that last bit. 'Growing drugs? On *Countryfile*?'

8

There was a laugh on the other end of the line.

'We're not exactly talking about class A here, Adam. It's a couple of Welsh sheep farmers who've found a unique way to diversify. They've started to grow herbs that can be used in all kinds of natural remedies. We thought it would be right up your street.'

When they rang off, I allowed myself a sigh of relief. Although I was glad I'd got the job, I'd been worrying about being sent off to do something completely new. It was bad enough that I had to learn a whole new trade on the hoof. At least my first report would be about farming, my own area of expertise.

So, with what felt like a whole swarm of butterflies in my stomach, I found myself climbing into my car a few days later and driving to Wales. The actual day of recording passed by in a blur. To be honest, I can't recall much about it now, except that I seemed to stumble over my words every five minutes and was worried about looking as stiff as a board on camera. Everyone kept telling me that it was going well and before I knew it we had everything in the can and I was setting off home.

Then came the next nail-biting moment. How would the veteran *Countryfile* team take to me, a farmer-boy from the West Country who had spent his life mucking out pigs and lambing rather than delivering witty pieces to camera? I must admit I was particularly worried about what John Craven would think. I didn't have long to wait. The production team had decided to make a bit of an event of my initial report. They had decided that on that particular week John would present the show from my farm. The viewer would see him welcoming me back home after completing my first interview.

As I crossed the border back into Gloucestershire, the butter-flies returned for another flight around my insides. It's fair to say that John is a bit of a legend. After all, I'd grown up watching him present *Newsround* and *Multi-Coloured Swap Shop*, for heaven's sake and now I'd be sharing a screen with him. I had already met him a couple of times when I was growing up – because of my dad's connections to the BBC in the past, he'd filmed on our farm a few times – but this would be different.

The production team met me at the gate and told me what would happen. I'd drive up, the cameras would be running and John would be delivering a piece to camera. Then I'd get out, shake his hand and he'd introduce me. I nodded, trying to look as confident as possible and set off. Inside, I was convinced I'd stall the car, or fluff my lines. My car bumped down the track and I could see him, in one of his trademark stripy jumpers, chatting away to the camera. Thankfully, everything went perfectly and I didn't muck up at all. Well, not much anyway. In any case, we did another take just to make sure.

Looking back now, I know I had nothing to worry about. John welcomed me to the show with open arms and soon took me under his wing. I've learned so much from him. Almost immediately he was giving me tips, letting me into the tricks of the trade and help-ing me every step of the way. He taught me how to make the scripts my own and how to get the best out of interviewees. And he still does today. Nearly ten years later, I have so much to thank him for. *Countryfile* was my first job in television and if I'd been stamped upon as soon as I'd walked into the programme's office, I would have soon come running back to the comfort of the farm. Thankfully, that never happened. John and the other presenters I've worked with over the years – including Michaela Strachan, Charlotte Smith, Miriam O'Reilly, and more recently Julia Bradbury, Matt Baker and Ellie Harrison – have all been fantastic.

For the first eight years on *Countryfile* I was often sent out and about as a roving reporter and got up to all kinds of crazy exploits that I would never have had a chance to experience otherwise. Some of them were so bizarre that when I talk about them now I worry that people think I'm making them up. Take the toe wrestling, for example. Yes, you did read that right. This toe-curling sport was devised back in the 1970s when a guy called George Burgess was fed up with England losing every sporting event imaginable. And so the World Toe Wrestling Championship was organised, held at Ye Olde Royal Oak pub in Wetton, Derbyshire. Surely an Englishman would be able to lift that trophy. Unfortunately for George, the inaugural championship was won by a visiting Canadian.

The idea of the contest is that you link toes with your opponent on the toedium (the people who organise these kinds of events are big on puns) and, like an arm wrestle, try to force each other's foot down. Now, I do have a quite a competitive streak so even though I couldn't quite believe what I was doing, I set about winning. Trying to keep as dignified as possible I lay down on the platform, slipping my big toe between that of my rival and twisted my foot. His ankle turned almost immediately and I couldn't resist a little whoop of triumph. OK, I realise that he was probably a little nervous to be on telly, but after this first taste of success I convinced myself that I would sail through this report and would end the day lifting the trophy. What's that they say about pride coming before a fall? At the beginning of the next round a great big, hairy man covered from head to foot in tattoos sat down opposite me. It was the feet that worried me. To say they ponged a bit was an understatement and I'm pretty sure that he had athlete's foot. Talk about sneaky tactics. I'm sure going into a competition like this with a fungal infection is a form of chemical warfare. The one thing I am sure about is that my rival had extremely sharp toenails. After he'd wiped the floor with me, and was pulling his foot away, he managed to cut the inside of my big toe with a jagged nail. Oh, the glamour of telly.

Thankfully not all the contests I covered for *Countryfile* were so stomach-turning, although most were equally wacky and, unsurprisingly, usually involved a pub. The Barley Mow Inn in Bonsall, near Matlock, is the venue for the World Hen Racing Championship. It may sound odd, but people have raced chickens – and bet on the winner – since before Tudor times, and the modern championships have been going since the Nineties. While I'd been a novice when it came to toe wrestling (thank heavens), at least I knew my poultry and so set about training a couple of our own hens, who I named Charlotte and Michaela after my fellow *Countryfile* presenters. Confident of victory, I headed off to Bonsall with my girls in tow. The rules are simple. You place your chickens at one end of a line and, on the signal, they race against each other. The first past the post wins. It's all down to the birds. If you're spotted helping your hen to head in the right direction by means of a friendly hand or a less than friendly boot, then you'll be disqualified. It was OK, I wouldn't have to cheat. Charlotte and Michaela wouldn't let me down. They took their places, clucking away happily as the crowd of spectators fell silent and then they were off. Unfortunately, they didn't win.

Of course, not all of my reports were quite as bonkers. The show gave me a chance to travel all over the UK and beyond. I went husky mushing in Scotland, watched minke whales off the Isle of Mull, headed to Italy for a Christmas special and even found myself in Australia on an amazing shoot where we traced Hereford cattle from their home county to the Outback.

And then there were those moments where we slipped easily from the sublime to the absolutely ridiculous. When I first sent off my audition tape, I never imagined I would be interviewed standing outside my cowshed dressed up like James Bond. Like so many of these madcap adventures, it had started with a phone call. It was the summer of 2007, and the show was celebrating its twentieth anniversary. By now, it was so popular that the BBC had launched a spin-off magazine and I soon became used to the magazine team phoning me up to arrange photoshoots on the farm. But this was different. To celebrate the anniversary, they wanted to gather the current roster of presenters together for some photos. It sounded great. The funny thing about *Countryfile* is that the presenters hardly ever get a chance to see each other. We're always shooting around filming here, there and everywhere, only ever bumping into each other when we head to the *Countryfile* studios in Birmingham to record voice-overs and links. Could they do the photos on my farm? Of course, I'd look forward to it.

'Excellent. There's just one other thing.'

The morning of the photoshoot came and the magazine team turned up to prepare for the shoot, armed with lights, cameras and costumes. Yes – costumes. They had thought it would be fun to add a little glamour to *Countryfile*. The boys – John Craven, Tom Heap and myself – would be wearing tuxedos, while the girls – Michaela Strachan, Juliet Morris, Charlotte Smith and Miriam O'Reilly – would be all glammed up in evening dresses. A chaise longue had been delivered to the middle of the field and we were all to complete our swanky outfits with welly boots; some of my animals would be used as further props.

It was one of the funniest days of my life. The TV crew had decided that it was too good an opportunity to pass up and so came along to film the shoot for the anniversary programme itself and we spent the day running around in the mud, lugging around pigs, chasing a particularly camera-shy chicken (who ended up perching on John Craven's shoulder in one of the shots) and even leading up a cow to be milked by Michaela while she was still wearing her shiny gold gown. It was hilarious.

Over the course of the day we all had individual shots taken as well. Mine was standing in front of one of my prize bulls, looking moodily off into the distance in my DJ. Daniel Craig, eat

14

your heart out. The only difference between me and 007 is that I bet Britain's best-loved spy never has to try and look rugged and mysterious while a bull slobbers down his shoulder. I dread to think what the costume-hire company thought when my tuxedo was returned the next day.

Of course, not every day was fun and laughter. I also did my fair share of farming news stories. It made sense; I knew what I was talking about and so wouldn't have to do as much research as non-farming presenters.

There was another benefit. By our very nature, farmers can be a fairly insular lot. We have to work long, unsocial hours and the world of TV crews, make-up artists, cameramen and presenters is completely alien to us. Many of the farmers that *Countryfile* interviewed didn't know how to relate to media types. It was different when I turned up on a shoot. While the camera team was setting up, I'd chat to the farmers about what was going on around their farm or chew the fat about the price of wheat, what DEFRA (the Department for the Environment, Food and Rural Affairs) had been getting up to, or one of the other thousand and one subjects that farmers end up discussing when they get together. They'd give me little tours around their farms to show me their operation and, nine times out of ten, I'd even learn a few new tricks along the way. Most importantly, I tried to put them at ease. Just as John and the team had helped me when I first stepped in front of the camera, I tried to help the guys I was interviewing.

I was given the opportunity to do things that most farmers would give their eye teeth for. One of the most satisfying was being given the chance to interview MP Elliot Morley who, as Agriculture Minister, had to cope with the foot-and-mouth disease outbreak that put a stranglehold on the countryside in 2001. Most farmers I know wanted to ask Mr Morley why there hadn't been enough vets available to handle the epidemic. Thanks to *Countryfile*, I was able to do it for them.

Not all of the stories were as satisfactory. In 2007, I was sent to the Continent to report on how a disease called bluetongue was affecting farmers in Belgium. Bluetongue is a particularly nasty, non-contagious virus that is spread by midges, usually in late summer and early autumn. It can strike deer, goats, cattle and, most severely, sheep. The first signs are ulcers around the mouth, nose and eyes. After a while the animal's head can swell and lameness, internal bleeding, breathing problems and death soon follow. It had been a serious problem in the European Union for a decade, killing 1.8 million animals in total, but had never been heard of in Britain. However, back in early 2007, scientists had started to worry that we'd soon see cases here. The midges could easily travel across the Channel to the UK if the weather conditions were right. So off I was sent to interview Belgian farmers whose animals had been struck down by the disease, and witnessed heartbreaking scenes of very poorly animals. Little did we know how important our short report would prove to be. On our return, the scientists were proved right; on 23 September, while at the Labour Party conference, Prime

Minister Gordon Brown was informed that the first case of blue-tongue on British soil had been found at a farm near Ipswich, Suffolk. The news soon hit the papers and every news service turned to *Countryfile*. My report, which showed the effects of bluetongue in vivid, and quite distressing, detail, turned up on the BBC's *News at Ten*, *News 24* and also on *Sky News*. Thankfully, the nightmare that the scientists predicted didn't fully materialise and British farmers' vaccination programme has kept the disease largely at bay for now, but there's always a fear that it might take hold.

And so my new-found career continued rolling along merrily and other opportunities began to pop up. Over the years, my work on *Countryfile* led to a number of auditions – including one memorable one for CBeebies, the BBC's pre-school channel, when I had to perform with a strange little puppet called Jelly – but nothing came of them. I did manage to swing a job on Jimmy Doherty's *Jimmy's Farming Heroes* series and spent a summer recording reports only to see them disappear in the final cut. I didn't really mind. Even though I wasn't under contract, the jobs for *Countryfile* kept coming in and the strings to my bow continued to grow. When *Countryfile* magazine launched, the editor even came to me to write a regular column. Me, a writer! I couldn't believe it. My English teacher back at school wouldn't have either.

Then in 2009, everything changed. After twenty years of being shown on Sunday morning, *Countryfile* was moved to a new Sunday evening slot and hasn't looked back since. On

Sunday mornings we used to pull in 2.5 million viewers on a good day, but now the show averages around 7 million.

The new time also brought in some new faces, including Julia and Matt, another farmer's boy who'd been brought up on a sheep farm in County Durham. When I heard about the shake-up, I did wonder if I'd be given the chop. After all, I'd had eight good years on *Countryfile*, and had even been given the chance to try my hand at radio for Radio 4's *On Your Farm*. All that time, I'd kept reminding myself that TV can be a fickle business: one day your face fits and the next day it doesn't. That's why I'd always kept on farming – not that I could ever have given it up. Farming is my first love – always has been, always will be.

And farming kept me in the new-look *Countryfile* too. When the powers-that-be at the BBC were looking for ways to refresh the programme, they wanted to find some new regular slots. John was staying on board and would now present weekly rural affairs reports, but what to do with this Adam Henson guy? After all, Matt was more than likely going to be taking on the mantle of action man. Then the production team had a bright idea. What if they came to my farm every week and showed the viewers what we get up to? I don't mind saying that I jumped at the chance. First of all, I would be working from home. No more long, arduous journeys around the country. All I would have to do is step outside my door.

But there was another reason. In the decade I'd been working on *Countryfile*, the public perception of farming had changed. Our doors had been blown wide open and suddenly the public was interested in finding out exactly how we worked, what methods we used and what the conditions on our farms were like. It was a good job too. Some areas of agriculture had fallen into some pretty bad habits and suddenly found themselves in a completely transparent world. People began to realise what had been going on; suddenly we were all accountable.

I saw the new 'Adam's Farm' slot on the programme as a great opportunity to show what farming was like to an audience that I was sure would be made up largely of people who lived in cities and towns. It would be a chance to put the farmer's story across – to present some of the most wonderful moments in the farming calendar but also to show some of the darker times.

There was something else I wanted to get across as well – the fact that, above all, farming is a business. Without farming, the countryside wouldn't look like it does now. Farmers have worked the land for thousands of years, forming the landscape we know today. We've made some mistakes along the way, but we've also fed the nation and, in most parts, looked after the local environment. But we also have to make money. I knew that early on in the run of Adam's Farm slots, I'd be inviting the cameras into the lambing shed to watch the miracle of new lambs being born and while I hoped that the magic would translate on screen, I also wanted to get across that every new lamb is worth around £60 when the time comes to send them to slaughter. They're a valuable commodity as well as a precious new life.

*

And back in the lambing sheds, as I enter my second night shift in a row, those precious lives are at the front of my mind. The rain has set in for another night of hammering on the shed roof, but tonight it's just me and the sheep. The *Countryfile* crew packed up and headed back to Birmingham around teatime and as the clock strikes eleven I'm standing feeding a tiny lamb from a bottle as I keep an eye on the rest of the flock. Sadly, this little fellow had been born to a ewe who didn't have a maternal bone in her body. This doesn't happen that often, but it's something every shepherd has to cope with from time to time.

When lambs are born they are covered in the birth fluids and unless they are licked clean can soon get cold. In this particular case the maternal instinct just didn't kick in. Instead of moving in to clean her newborn lamb, the ewe actually looked a bit scared of the little thing, backing away nervously. I tried to kick-start the process, laying the mother next to the shivering little lamb, rubbing the birth fluids around the ewe's mouth. Sometimes this makes them start licking and getting the taste of the newborn lamb, but she wasn't having a bit of it and struggled and kicked as I tried to move her near. Then, as she struggled, she gave birth to her second lamb, almost kicking the poor thing in the process. Try as I might, she showed no interest in them at all, even when we put the three of them in their own little pen. The lambs huddled together for warmth as the mother resolutely stood with her back to them, rejecting her offspring completely.

And so now they warm themselves under a hot lamp and are fed by hand. It's not ideal. Usually we try to adopt orphaned lambs straight on to another ewe. Most sheep give birth to twin lambs – although in some cases you can get triplets or even quads – but every now and then you get a ewe with only one lamb. Moving quickly, you take the lamb you want her to adopt and lay it under the lamb that has just been born, rubbing the birth fluids over both of them. The ewe then stands up, assumes they are both hers and licks them dry. In essence, you trick her into thinking that she's had two babies rather than just one.

Sometimes it doesn't work and she rejects the newcomer, so you try it again with another ewe that has just given birth. But if the lamb keeps on getting rejected then you're forced to bottle-feed. While I try never to complain when we have to hand-rear lambs, the businessman in every farmer can't help but do a few sums. The economics of bottle-feeding just doesn't stack up. Not only does bottle-feeding take a lot of valuable time and effort, but the powdered milk itself is very expensive – around £25 a bag – and needs to be supplemented with concentrate pellets to provide addition nutrients that the lambs would usually get from the mother. At the end of the day, milk produced by a ewe eating grass is far cheaper and the bonus is that the mother rears the lamb for you.

But that's a very cold-hearted way of looking at things. As I stand here, the little lamb happily guzzling away in my hand, I can't help but be moved. They're such adorable little creatures and, even though they are here to make you money, they manage to get under your skin. You never want them to suffer or go hungry.

All around me, ewes are sleeping, wandering around or feeding their own lambs. It's a sight that I've grown up with and one that hasn't really changed since my dad first started farming fifty years ago. We have 11 breeds on the farm and lamb around 750 ewes every year. The more primitive rare breeds such as North Ronaldsay, Soay or Castlemilk Moorit all lamb outside. They are hardy beasts that can easily look after themselves. The majority of our lambs, however, are born inside.

As lambing begins my stockman Mike Caunter and I will bring the pregnant ewes into the large pens that house between 40 to 50 ewes, where they have enough room to move about, but they're all close enough for us to keep an eye on. Then when the babies are born you move the ewe with her newborn into individual pens so they can get used to each other. Here the lambs will learn how to suckle properly and the little families can get used to each other, learning to distinguish how each other smells or sounds. This is vitally important because 24 hours later they'll be placed into nursery pens for a day or two, where they'll share the space with around 10 or 12 other families. This means that the lambs get used to being part of a flock, but more critically, learn how to find their mothers quickly in a crowd. It's a lesson that can literally become a matter of life or death. Once a ewe has bonded with its offspring, she will feed only her own lambs. If another cheeky lamb moves in for a quick snack, she'll give them a sniff and if they don't smell like hers, see them off with a harsh butt. On a cold wet night, a lost lamb with an empty belly will soon hit problems if it can't find sustenance from its mum in a field of 300 sheep. They haven't long to learn, as after one or two days in the nursery it's out to the fields. All the family units are given an individual number, spray-painted on their side, so we can tell who belongs to whom at a glance.

British shepherds have been lambing this way for as long as we've been farming our land. Of course there are some farmers who lamb outside. High on the hills of Wales and the North, lambing is a little different. Throughout Scotland, Yorkshire and the Lake District, shepherds will be bringing their pregnant ewes into the farm's inbye field, near the homestead. Once the lambs are born they are let into the intake fell, a walled pasture providing the same environment as our nursery. Once the lambs can recognise their mothers, the gate opens and they skip on to the hillside. Lambing outside certainly has its benefits. Life on grass can be healthier than a crowded straw yard but the threat of predators and bad weather is a constant worry.

Whether born inside or out, a lamb's fate is decided in August, where you begin to reap the rewards of all this hard work, and the lambs you're caring for now start going off for slaughter and the best of the ewe lambs are kept as flock replacements. For now, it's back to the sheds with more lambs to deliver. It'll be a few more weeks before the last lamb arrives and, until then, it's going to be incredibly busy around here.

CHAPTER 2

BREEDS APART

My dad's mates thought he had gone mad. He wanted to *what?* Invite tourists on to his farm? Why on earth would he want to do that? Many locals probably thought that their first instincts had been right. They'd welcomed Joe Henson into the Cotswold farming community even though he had been a townie from London. He'd seemed a good sort and, despite the fact that he didn't come from a farming family, had taken agriculture seriously. But now, rumours were circulating that he wanted to open up part of Bemborough Farm as some kind of zoo. Didn't he realise that farmers weren't supposed to do things like this? They were there to feed the nation, not entertain them. As time went on, and the rumours proved to be true, the grumbles turned to anger. Something had to be done. The last thing dad's neighbours wanted were hordes of sightseers clogging up the roads. After all, they argued, what did the Cotswolds want with tourism? Now it was dad's turn to hear rumours. Apparently a petition was being circulated to try and block his latest venture – the Cotswold Farm Park.

But why had dad wanted to open a farm park in the first place? It started with his fascination for ancient breeds of farm animals, beasts that rapidly seemed to be going out of fashion. Although arable crops really brought in the money at Bemborough, dad decided to buy in a few Cotswold sheep. Also sometimes known as the Cotswold Lion, this large, docile breed was probably introduced, along with other longwool sheep, by the Romans. Before then, British sheep were smaller, primitive creatures with wool that was either moulted or pulled off in clumps by hand. The new longwool breeds, however, had to be shorn, as the wool they produced was heavy, lustrous and, it turns out, worth a fortune. By the Middle Ages, there were around half a million Cotswolds living on the hills. In fact, the area was even named after them: a 'cote' was a sheep enclosure and 'wold' meant rolling hills.

By this time, wool was big business and medieval Britain was quite literally built on the wealth it generated. The money the wool brought in paid for the construction of our cathedrals and great houses. It was used to build roads and develop towns as well as financing wars and overseas conquests. Even then, the value of wool was noted, with parliamentary records naming it 'the jewel of the realm' and the wise barons of the land stating that half the kingdom's worth rode on the back of our sheep. To give you an idea of just how valuable wool was, when the Saracens captured Richard the Lionheart during the Crusades, the ransom demanded was 50,000 sacks of English wool. Even today, the Lord Speaker sits on a sack packed with wool in the House of Lords, symbolically recognising how important the humble sheep has been to our nation. Originally the woolsack was the perch of the Lord

Chancellor, but the symbolism was put to the test in 1938, when it was found not to be stuffed with wool, but with horsehair. The matter was soon put to rights and the sack was restuffed with 270 kilos of wool from the UK and Commonwealth countries.

It's no wonder that the wool of the Cotswold sheep became known as the Golden Fleece. Every year, thousands of packhorses laden with heavy wool bales trudged from Cotswold farms to the markets of London, where the fleeces were sold at exorbitant prices to merchants who shipped it over to the looms of Flanders and Lombardy. The merchants became rich and bought great tracts of lands, building the so-called wool churches, ostensibly to give thanks for their great fortunes, but in reality as a way of showing off just how wealthy they had become. The bigger the bank balance, the bigger the church. One of the most famous Cotswold merchants of all is still name-checked during every panto season. Sir Richard 'Dick' Whittington didn't need to go to London – where the 'streets are paved with gold' – to make his fortune. By the time he was made Lord Mayor of London – a position he held three times – he was already an extremely rich wool merchant who owned Stroud and much of the surrounding area. Whether Dick also owned a cat is, unfortunately, unknown.

So important was the wool industry that parliament came up with ingenious ways of making sure that people kept buying wool. One of the craziest stories I've heard is that the Burial in Woollen Acts of the 1660s made it illegal to bury someone wearing anything other than a woollen shroud. If you did otherwise you'd find yourself slapped with a £5 fine, which in those days was a lot of money.

Those too poor to buy woollen shrouds were buried naked. The only way you could escape the penalty was to prove that the departed had died from the plague. This bizarre piece of legislation stayed on the statute books until it was finally repealed in 1814.

The wool industry remained in quite fine fettle until the turn of the twentieth century. With the introduction of man-made fibres, wool started to fall from favour and so shepherds had to rely more and more on rearing lamb for the table to make ends meet. Unfortunately, the good old Cotswold isn't a particularly early maturing breed – they have a rangy carcass, which was mainly used for mutton, a dish that has all but disappeared from our tables – and so started to be abandoned in favour of more commercially viable sheep. Farmers chose more productive breeds that had shorter legs, more meat and less wool.

The same was happening with our other county breeds. Numbers of Gloucester cattle, for example, also started to plummet. My favourite breed of cattle, with their beautiful dark mahogany colour and a distinctive white tail and a white stripe running down their backs, Gloucesters were originally a triple-purpose breed used to produce milk, meat and also for draught work. A popular breed for centuries, a Gloucester cow called Blossom in 1796 provided the cowpox virus from which Sir Edward Jenner developed a vaccine against the more deadly smallpox. Today, they are probably best known for the cheese made from their milk. While the rest of the country enjoys Double Gloucester cheese, Single Gloucester is still a firm favourite in the Cotswolds. This single variety is protected by European law, meaning that it can only be made from pedigree Gloucester cattle from within their namesake county.

Yet, again, these animals – which have served the county well for more than 200 years – had begun to dwindle away, hastened in the early 1920s by modern dairy farming, which called for specialist single-purpose breeds that could churn out milk by the gallon. The old Gloucester girls just could not compete on a commercial basis with Friesians and Holsteins, the black-and-white milk-producing athletes of the cow world.

It was a story that, by the 1960s, was being repeated time after time all over the country. Between 1900 and 1973, 26 breeds of native livestock became extinct in the UK, including Lincolnshire curly-coated pigs, Goonhilly ponies and Sheeted Somerset cattle, along with a number of poultry varieties. Dad spotted this, and started to investigate how many traditional breeds were in danger of dying out completely. Feeling he wanted to do something, he brought in the Cotswolds, soon followed by a small herd of Gloucester Old Spot pigs and even a couple of shire horses. He wasn't alone. Around 1969, he was invited to join a working party of people who were worried about the declining numbers of these and other farm animals. Together they would go on to set up and launch the Rare Breed Survival Trust (RBST) in 1973, with dad as its founder chairman. The national charity still exists today and can be proud that no breed has become extinct since its inception. Around the world, at least one breed of farm animal is lost every single month. But not here. In the UK at least, the rot has been stopped.

And there's a good reason that the RBST still works hard to make sure that things stay that way. One of the first things the trust did was to set up a gene bank, collecting semen and embryos, stockpiling their genetic characteristics for future generations. When the British countryside was hit by the terrible 2001 outbreak of foot-and-mouth disease and huge numbers of animals across the country had to be destroyed, yet more rare bloodlines would have been lost without the gene bank to fall back on.

There's also another reason why this genetic record of heritage breeds is a good idea. Farming trends change over time, and the archive of genetics sometimes help farmers move with the times. This is happening already. These days there's a move back to conservation grazing in many areas of the countryside, where traditional farm animals help to keep down grasses and bracken in areas where machinery has trouble getting to. That means there's a need for the kind of sheep that are easy to look after, don't necessarily need shearing and can survive in inhospitable weather on remote hills. The gene bank suddenly comes into its own, backed up by those valuable flocks that have been tended by rare-breed enthusiasts who have flown in the face of conventional wisdom for so many years.

In 1970, dad's early collection was about to grow in numbers. For a while zoos had been one of the few places to keep rare-breed animals, and Whipsnade Zoo in Bedfordshire had a prize collection of five cattle and eight sheep breeds. They also had a problem. Nearby Woburn Zoo was growing in popularity and visitors were abandoning Whipsnade for Woburn's more exotic attractions.

Whipsnade needed to concentrate on acquiring and caring for more spectacular animals and make room for the new arrivals. The vote was cast and the decision made to get rid of the rare-breed farm animals. But what to do with them? Victor Manton, the zoo's veterinary surgeon curator, was under the impression that farming should be looking after its own and that the rare breeds belonged in the farmyard rather than in the zoo. Victor got on the phone to Christopher Dadd of the Royal Agricultural Society and gave a tongue-in-cheek, but still quite chilling warning. 'You ought to be looking after these creatures,' he said. 'If you don't come and take them away, I'm going to feed them to the lions.'

Dad gave him a call. Eventually, the majority of Whipsnade Zoo's rare-breed stock finally arrived at Bemborough Farm, to join our three county breeds, the Gloucester Old Spot, the Cotswold sheep and Gloucester cattle. Dad and his business partner John now had more mouths to feed than the farm's arable business could possibly support and, unlike today, there wasn't a constant stream of celebrity chefs on TV urging viewers to sample the delights of heritage meats. His rare-breed collection could soon have become a millstone around dad's neck. And then he had a clever idea. What had Victor said? The animals belonged in the farmyard. Now what if he could invite the public into the very same farmyard to see these rare animals, some of which were more endangered than the giant panda? Could he charge them for the privilege? If he could pull it off, then the unviable rare breeds could finally start to pay for themselves.

Today, farm diversification seems pretty second nature. All over Britain farmers are throwing open their gates to the public. Some offer luxury holiday accommodation, making use of previously run-down barns. Others have brought in unusual and exotic animals, farming bison, ostriches and even crocodiles in place of sheep, cattle and poultry. And every month, thousands of stag parties and thrill seekers head out to enterprising farms to go quad-biking, paintballing and even horseboarding – one of the latest crazes that sees adrenalin junkies riding on a hefty skateboard pulled by galloping horses. There are also now a large number of farm parks up and down the country where people can get on to a farm to look at, pet and, in some cases, feed farm animals. Looking back, it's funny to think that dad coined the name 'farm park'.

Back in the early 1970s such schemes were unheard of. No wonder that some of dad's neighbours took such a dislike to his plans. As he had heard on the grapevine, a petition was indeed circulated and dad came under a lot of criticism, but he was convinced he was on to a winner, set up a counter-petition with his farming friends and his planning application was passed. The Cotswold Farm Park opened its doors in 1971 to the sound of some locals still grumbling and hoping that the entire venture would fall flat on its face. Plenty of people wagged a warning finger at dad, declaring that it would never work.

They were wrong.

In the first six months dad welcomed 25,000 visitors through the gates. Over the next 40 years, as the arable work of the farm continued in the fields around the park, we have seen 2.5 million people come through the turnstiles. We are now seeing the grandchildren of some of those original visitors coming back to see what we've got on offer and the farm's animal collection has now swollen to over 50 breeds. Of course, it's a great way to subsidise the income, but I'm also very proud that it acts as a shop window to the important work that goes on to protect these vitally important creatures. Without places like this, the only place you'd be able to see Cotswold Lions or Gloucester cattle would be in the pages of history books.

As long as I can remember I wanted to be a farmer like dad. I used to follow him around the place like a shadow. We all did. I have three sisters – Elizabeth (or Libby as she's known in the family), Louise and Rebecca – all of whom grew up on Bemborough Farm. Libby, a geneticist and zoologist, still works in agriculture, advising breed societies and farmers how to keep track of their breed registrations through computer packages. Louise lives down the road in Moreton-in-Marsh and works for Forest Peoples Programme, a charity that helps secure the rights of indigenous people living in rainforests worldwide. Rebecca, my youngest sister, followed in the steps of my grandfather and uncle, forging a career in theatre and television. However, more recently, after losing her son to cancer, her life changed and she and her husband founded the charity Useful Vision, which she runs full time. It has become one of the lead providers of services for families with vision-impaired children in the North East.

Charlie and I are proud to be involved as trustee and patron, helping when we can.

Looking back, I have no idea how mum and dad did it. Charlie and I have two kids – Ella and Alfie – and we struggle sometimes to juggle everything. Mum and dad had four! Looking back, they were quite a typical farming family. Dad ran the farm with his business partner John, while mum – who was a school teacher by trade – did the cooking, washing, looked after us kids, did the books, sorted out the wages and, when the farm park opened, looked after the retail side of things and even made all the food for the café. I still remember mum and grandma standing in the kitchen making hundreds of sandwiches.

Ever since I was a kid I wanted to take over the farm from dad one day. When he took on the farm back in 1962 he had been lucky enough to be offered a three-generation tenancy. Even back then, these were becoming rarer. It meant that dad could pass the tenancy on to a child, who in turn could pass it to a third generation. After that it would return to the landlord. Today, such things are practically unheard of. Your average tenancy is much, much shorter, sometimes just 10 to 15 years.

It was by chance that dad ended up the tenant, rather than John. They were searching the country to find a farm that they could run 50/50 with two equal-sized farmhouses. It just so happened that dad was working locally and found Bemborough and so applied for the tenancy. It could easily have been the other way around and, as John had no children, the tenancy would have ended when he died in 2007.

John may not have had children of his own, but he was like a second dad to me. He worked incredibly hard in the background. Dad was always the front man. He worked with the animals and the rare breeds, and was the one who drummed up publicity, ran the demonstrations at the farm park and got himself on telly. John looked after the arable side of the business and was absolutely brilliant when it came to machines. He could fix just about anything and was always building fences, rabbit hutches and chicken coops. His practical skills saved the farm a shedload of money in the early days.

Although I'd always helped out on the farm, by the time I'd hit 16 dad started to pay me a fair wage. It was never a case of slave labour, which was a clever move on his part. And I worked hard. When I finally went to agricultural college in Devon in 1985 I never ran up an overdraft as I used to work hellish hours in the holidays back on the farm to give me enough cash for food, lodgings and, well, beer.

It was while I was at college that I met Duncan who hailed from the Scilly Isles and we soon become firm friends. It had to be said that Dunc always did better at college than me. His results were consistently better, but he was a good mate to have as he helped drag me through my revision and exams.

When we graduated we decided that before we got bogged down in our full-time work, we wanted to see the world and so, probably over a few beers, we hatched a scheme to travel for a year. It was harvest time so we both got ourselves jobs to take in crops on two different farms, scraped together the cash and bought around-the-world air tickets. We headed first to Kuala Lumpur, then on to Malaysia and finally Western Australia and New Zealand.

Even though we were on the other side of the world, we still had links to Bemborough Farm. We travelled our way down to Boyup Brook in Australia and met up with Colin McGregor, who had worked for dad as a student. He'd gone Down Under to run a shearing gang and he helped us get a few jobs, collecting fleeces from the shearers and planting tea, then on to a big arable and sheep station. We even managed to borrow a car from a lovely family called the Stanningforth-Smiths and word soon got around that there were these two Brits who were willing to work to finance their travels.

Farming in Australia sounds glamorous but it wasn't always. I remember one job, working for a farming family known as the Drewers, where I had to worm-drench 18,000 ewes in blistering, 40C (104F) degree heat with flies buzzing everywhere. It was all right for Duncan. He was driving around in a lovely air-conditioned combine while muggins here was out in the heat.

Still, I wouldn't have changed a moment of our trip for anything. In the end we stayed in Australia for eight months in total, but as time went by I was ready to think about coming home. As always, dad had been very clever. As he'd waved me off at the beginning of our adventure, dad had said, 'Adam, just remember. There's no pressure for you to come home. If you meet a gorgeous Australian or New Zealand girl and you want to stay, you do it. It's your future.'

Well, I did meet quite a few gorgeous Australian and New Zealand girls – although I won't go into the details. But there was never any question about me coming home. There was no place on Earth like the Cotswold hills.

So back I came, and was taken on as an employee at Bemborough Farm. I was bursting with ideas.

'Dad, we need to get a quad bike.'

'A what?'

'A quad bike. Everyone's using them in Australia to get about on farms. They're nippy, economical – you'll love them.'

'OK, Adam, we'll think about it.'

'Cool. We also need a mobile set of handling pens.'

'We do? Why?'

'Because we're still using wooden pens in the middle of the farm. Every time we have a job with the sheep we have to drive them for three or four miles to get them. If we get mobile pens, we can drag them to the sheep with the quad with the dogs on the back of the bike. Job done in half the time.'

'Well, that makes sense, but...'

'And speaking of dogs, did I tell you about the kelpies?'

At this point dad would be rolling his eyes, but chuckling to himself.

After a while we did get a quad bike and a mobile set of pens, but dad didn't just agree to everything. He loved the fact that I'd come home with so many ideas, but he wasn't about to let me do everything I wanted. However, he gave me enough free rein that I could experience making decisions and changes, some of which worked, some of which didn't. But he never said, I told you so. If he thought I was about to fall off a cliff, he'd hold me back, but he'd let me experience most things for myself. He was a great life coach. He still is.

And he let me have my kelpie. I'd fallen in love with the sleek sheepdogs while in Oz. They come in all kinds of colours – black, black and tan, red, red and tan and, occasionally yellow. They're wonderful workers who love exercise and can easily cover 40 miles a day while herding cattle or sheep in the harshest of Australian conditions. As soon as dad gave me the green light, I tracked down a lovely red kelpie bitch puppy that I named Bundy after Bundaberg rum, my favourite tipple while travelling in Australia. There were very few kelpies in the UK at the time so when she was of age I imported some Australian kelpie semen and put it to Bundy. She gave birth to 12 healthy pups. There was only one thing I wasn't prepared for. One of them was yellow. I'd never seen a yellow puppy before.

Confused, I phoned a mate in Australia and asked him about my strange yellow puppy.

'You got a yellow one, mate?' he said. 'Yeah, we have yellow ones here as well, but we shoot them.'

Shoot them? It turned out that Australian farmers don't tend to keep the yellow kelpies as their noses and pads are thought to be softer than the other colours. I wasn't about to shoot this little lass and decided to keep her for myself, naming her Ronnie (because she barked so much).

*

After a couple of years dad and John offered me the chance to buy into the business. They could see that I was serious about the farm. I'd been living in the farm bungalow with three other blokes since I'd got back, including Pete Drewer whom I'd met in Australia. Have you ever said to someone 'if you're ever in England you should give me a call while travelling'? I did that with Pete and not long after getting home got a phone call from Moreton-in-Marsh train station one afternoon.

'G'day Adam. It's Pete Drewer here. You said I could come and stay. Can you pick me up?'

Pete ended up staying nine months and worked on the farm with me. We bungalow boys may have partied and played rugby, but we also worked hard.

Of course, I didn't have the money to buy into a business the size of Bemborough, so dad helped me out, giving me a forward on his will – a forward I've been paying off ever since.

It soon became clear that when dad and John retired, as they were soon to do, I'd need some help. Around the same time I went to see Duncan with my girlfriend Charlie. I'd met Charlie while doing my A-Levels at Westwoods Grammar School in North Leach. We went out with each other for a bit, but eventually went in separate directions when I headed to agricultural college and she got a place on a photography course at art college in Plymouth. Over the years, we met up every now and then and stayed friends, and she ended up working in television. Then one weekend she came home, we got together again and have been together ever since, Charlie leaving the bright lights of the capital to return to the Cotswolds and a job in Bristol.

Duncan, meanwhile, had also gone home. He and his girl-friend had taken a tenancy back on the Isles of Scilly. They grew cut flowers and vegetables, kept chickens and Dunc, who's always been a bit of a handyman, had converted some of the barns into holiday lets. As Charlie and I didn't have a lot of money at the time, he offered us a week in one of the barns as long as I would shear his six Jacob sheep. It was the best shearing contract I'd ever taken. Half an hour's work for a luxurious week's holiday. While I was there I said, 'Look Dunc, I'm struggling to run everything at home, what with the farm, the farm park, all the breeding programmes and the arable. If you ever fancy educating your kids back on the mainland, give me a ring.'

Almost before I got home, Duncan had written up a business plan and sent it over to me. He came to visit and talk it through. In the October of 1997 he started to work for me and two years later, when dad and John retired, bought into the business. It was perfect, I was running the farm 50/50 with a great friend, just as dad had done.

Well, it was almost perfect. In the late Nineties, British farming was on its knees. The price of grain was at rock bottom, meat was down and even the farm park was going through the doldrums. In fact, countryside tourism on the whole was down. People were starting to go abroad, thanks to the arrival of cut-price airlines and a strong pound. The trouble was that at the same time, farm parks were opening up everywhere. We'd been unique for a while, but others had cottoned on and were opening similar attractions. There were three new ones in the Cotswolds alone and not so many tourists to go around.

Everything was on a downer. Usually farming doesn't happen like this, especially on a mixed farm like ours. When one department's down the other will be up. Not this time and we were haemorrhaging cash. Both Duncan and I had borrowed from our parents to buy into the business and now it looked like we were losing it all.

Looking back, part of the problem was that in the mid-Nineties I hadn't given the farm park the concentration it really needed and had been content to sit back on the laurels of its early success. All that time, people's perceptions of what constituted a good day out were changing. Just having a walk and seeing some animals wasn't enough any more. They needed to be entertained and they needed to be kept dry when it rained. Duncan and I looked at the bottom line and thought, well, we have two choices. We either close the place down or invest more to bring it up to date.

It was one of those situations in which, even though we were losing money, we needed to speculate to accumulate. So we borrowed more and ploughed considerable investment into the park. We hired a tourism consultant and built new display barns, put on shows and gave the punters more things to do than ever before. There were shearing demonstrations, a petting barn where kids (and adults) could hold new chicks and stroke new lambs. We even lambed live, in front of the public.

And it started to work. 1999 had been hard work but in 2000 we started to reap the benefit. The agricultural side of the business was still struggling, but if all went to plan then the farm park would keep us afloat. Numbers were up and we were getting good reviews. What could go wrong? Well, they could close the English countryside, I supposed, but that would never happen. Would it?

CHAPTER 3

TRIALS AND TRIBULATIONS

In 2001 the countryside was effectively closed. On 20 February, Britain's first outbreak of foot-and-mouth-disease for 20 years was discovered during a routine inspection of Cheale Meats abattoir near Brentwood, Essex. Twenty-eight pigs were diagnosed with the illness and all 300 animals at the abattoir were slaughtered immediately.

It was the beginning of a nightmare that would last until October and would strike a devastating blow to British farming.

To try and stop the spread of this dreadful disease, which affects all cloven-hoofed animals including cattle, sheep, pigs and goats, exclusion zones sprang up all across the countryside. Fox hunts were immediately banned, most of the countryside became no-go zones for walkers and bike and horse riders and farms, including our own, faced crippling movement restrictions that meant that you could not buy or sell animals. Then came the slaughters. With 2030 confirmed cases of the disease in Great Britain and Northern Ireland, around six million animals were put to death by the end of the year. Farming suffered losses of £900 million and, on a wider scale, the tourism and rural economy was hit by losses of £5 billion.

I hope that I never live through another time like that. We didn't have a single case of foot-and-mouth on our farm but found ourselves bang in the middle of a restricted area. Suddenly, we were forced to close the gates of the farm park and couldn't sell any of our stock. The crisis came at the worst possible time. We'd just lived through a couple of really bad years and were up to our necks in debt thanks to our improvements to the farm park. We couldn't afford to pay the rent and all of our assets were tied up in agricultural resources, from sheep to tractors. Usually, farms in our situation would have held farm sales to raise some capital, but with no one allowed on or off farms that just wasn't possible.

I still wince when I remember Duncan and I sitting around my kitchen table looking at each other over mugs of tea. Both of our families lived in rented houses on the farm and both the landlord and banks were on our back. We had a farm park we couldn't open and animals we couldn't sell. The future looked bleak and, if the business went down the drain, we'd be jobless and homeless.

Thankfully, when the restrictions were lifted, we could open for business once again. We scraped through by the skin of our teeth, thanks to the patience of our bank manager and landlord and a foot-and-mouth insurance policy that dad had been paying for since year dot. I'd always questioned whether we needed it but thankfully had never cancelled the cover. After

Duncan had carefully trawled through the small print, he discovered we were eligible for a payout. It was the break we needed and Bemborough Farm emerged the other side. Granted, we'd lost over £100,000 but we were still in business. Just. Needless to say, since those bleak days, we've both made sure we have investments in non-farming properties just in case the same thing happens again.

Our staff had all been amazing. As we couldn't open the farm park, the seasonal staff simply stood down. They didn't grumble or complain – and as they all had contracts, they could have kicked up a right fuss. But they didn't, they just walked away, ready to come back when we could reopen.

It was the same with our full-time staff on the farm. One by one they said, 'If you can't pay me, don't pay me. I'll work for six months with no pay if it helps.' Thankfully it didn't come to that.

There was a real Blitz spirit in the countryside at that point. We all knew what we were facing and we all buckled down to get through it. There was help of course. The church and charities rallied around. We even started to receive donations from local folk and regular visitors to the park. Every week some money would come through the post to help pay for animal feed. It was quite humbling.

Since the crisis has passed, the countryside has, by and large, bounced back. If anything good came from foot-and-mouth, it was that people realised the value of the countryside. You always realise how much you need something when it's taken away from you. When the restrictions were lifted, the public flooded back and businesses such as our farm park were certainly grateful for the money they brought back to the rural economy.

More people than ever are now heading out of the cities to walk, run and ride in the great outdoors – thanks mainly to the changes in our right to roam in the last decade – and rural businesses are reaping the benefits. Our farm park is now busier than ever, employing 35 seasonal staff in total. In fact tourism – both the park and our caravan site – brings in 40 per cent of the farm's income these days, with arable contributing 55 per cent and breeding bringing in the final 5 per cent. I love heading out to the park and seeing people's reactions to the animals. For many, it's the first real connection they've made to farming and where their food comes from. The lambing demonstrations are particularly powerful. I've seen people break into rounds of applause or burst into tears, sometimes both together. Some are shocked while others come back day after day to see how the lambs are doing.

The touch barn is one of my favourite places where we allow children to handle the animals – as long as they wash their hands afterwards of course. The adults usually can't resist picking up the animals too. I remember one elderly lady who'd been sitting for ages watching the children holding chicks and ducklings. I took a chick out of the incubator and took it over to her.

'Would you like to hold one?' I asked, and her eyes lit up as I placed it gently in her hands. She almost glowed with pleasure.

'Thank you,' she said as she handed the chick back, 'that's the first chick I've ever held and I'm 80, you know.'

It proves that it's never to late to have your first encounter with livestock.

I hope that we will always be able to give people this opportunity. In the last couple of years there have been cases of E.coli 0157 on some farm parks. This is a particularly nasty form of bacteria that lives in the intestines of some cattle, sheep and which can cause severe abdominal pain and sickness, especially in children. We've never had a problem, but it's forced us to be extra vigilant, ensuring that the public never walk where animals have relieved themselves and that hand-washing facilities are available across the park.

I dread the day that visitors aren't allowed to have contact with animals. The day we have to put our livestock behind glass is the day I close the farm park. As long as visitors – and farmers – are aware of the threats and are responsible then there shouldn't be a problem. Just sticking your head in the ground and saying, well I played out in the fields when I was a kid and I never caught anything like E.coli 0157 just isn't enough. That particular strain only came into the country in the early Eighties. It's still relatively new. We just have to be aware that bugs exist and are mutating all the time. Just because we got away with things in the past, doesn't mean it's going to stay that way.

Unfortunately, for my cattle, and for thousands of other cattle farms around the countryside, there's another sickness that is hanging over us like a permanently black cloud, something almost as devastating as foot-and-mouth.

A couple of years ago, our local vet, Gill Allen, arrived on the farm to give our cattle their latest compulsory tuberculosis test. Mycobacterium bovis, or bovine tuberculosis, is a chronic, debilitating and highly infectious lung disease. By law, every cattle farm has to undergo regular testing to check whether its herd is infected. My worst fears became reality. Gill arrived and started the procedure, injecting every member of the herd with a couple of shots of a TB inoculum in the neck. Three days later she returned to see if any lumps had formed in the places where the needles went in. If they had, and the bottom lump was larger than the top, then the animal was classed as a reactor – it had TB and faced compulsory slaughter. Sadly, a reactor was found. It was official. We had TB.

But that wasn't the worst of it. As soon as TB is detected on your farm, you are effectively closed down. You aren't allowed to move cattle on or off the farm, unless you're rearing your cattle for beef – in those cases you are still allowed to send cattle direct to the abattoir for slaughter.

For breeders, such as ourselves, this is a complete nightmare. Our rare breeds just can't compete on a commercial basis when it comes to producing meat, so we make our money by rearing – and selling – quality breeding stock. But, as we're currently still closed down, two years later there's nothing we can do. Take our White Park cattle for example. Like the Cotswolds, these striking animals with their white bodies and black ears, nose and eyes were probably introduced by the Romans. When the Romans departed from Britain in the fifth century, they left herds of

White Parks behind, roaming the forests of England. Eventually, these wild cattle were enclosed within five large deer parks and hunted on horseback by the Plantagenet monarchs until well into the thirteenth century. The breed is also connected to the legend about a monarch knighting a cut of beef. White Park marbled meat is deliciously lean and, at one time, any local lord worth his salt would have served it to honoured guests. This is what is said to have happened when Henry VIII dined with the Abbot of Reading. The monarch was so enamoured with his plate of delicious meat that he immediately called for the loin of beef to be brought before him. The meat was duly presented and the king whipped out his sword, promptly knighting the side of beef. From that day on, he declared, the meat of the White Park would be known as 'Sir Loin'. Whether this is really how sirloin steaks really got their names is a matter of debate – certainly there are also similar legends that say it was James I or Elizabeth I who wielded the sword. All I know is that the cows make great mothers and are very self-sufficient, rearing calves on their own with ease. A three-year-old White Park heifer that is in calf is worth an awful lot of money, but when you're closed down there's nothing you can do. They can't leave the farm so you can't sell them. It's heartbreaking.

The only way to have the restrictions lifted is to pass two consecutive TB tests, held 60 days apart. If you manage to get through them with no reactors at all, you're immediately free to start moving cattle and taking them to market. Since July 2007 we'd gone through the test every other month. The problem was that every time we tested we picked up more and more reactors. Gill's told me on numerous occasions that one of the worst days of her career came in December 2007 when she had to tell me that we didn't just have one reactor. We had 12. Twelve cases of TB and twelve animals that needed to be slaughtered. I still get a knot in my stomach when I recall that day. How was I to know that we'd still be in the same boat nearly 18 months later?

So you can imagine how I feel, on this bright April morning, as I watch Gill drive into the farmyard for our latest round of testing. My heart has been in my mouth from the moment I woke up. Two months ago we'd been given a clear bill of health for the first time in seven months. Not a single reactor. If the same happens today, we'll be home and dry. But there's no point getting ahead of myself. We aren't out of the woods just yet.

The day starts by bringing in the first bunch of our 76 cows and 5 breeding bulls. We head out and gather them together. I can't help but worry for a couple of Gloucesters who come in with the first batch. For a while, they'd been looking increasingly skinny and sickly no matter what we try with them. Is it TB? I prayed that it's not.

Just getting the cows in to be tested is stressful enough. They had already been rounded up a few days ago to be injected with the initial inoculums and aren't too keen to be sent in again. Today, they are more jittery than ever, and keep trying to make a break for it as we walk along behind, holding our arms out wide to make ourselves look as large as possible.

Sometimes you can use dogs to help herd cattle in, but my rookie sheepdog Millie isn't quite ready to give a hand. She's still getting too near to the sheep and I dread to think what would happen if she got too near to a spooked cow and got kicked. I probably shouldn't have brought her with me but wanted her to get experience of being around this many cows.

Suddenly one bolts from the herd and I'm off like a shot, running around her to try and make sure she doesn't run off. In the heat of the moment, Millie's lead slips out of my hand and she's off, right into the path of a pair of running White Parks. I scream out her name and feel my heart skip a beat as Millie crouches to the ground right in front of the cows. At first, I can't make out what has happened. Has she been trampled? Please God no, not on today of all days – that will be too much to take. I call out her name as I run towards her and finally breathe again as she looks up and darts back to me. The cow's hooves have missed her, but only by a whisker. That was a close one. Too close.

Nothing stresses me out as much as TB testing time. Every year DEFRA spends £100 million testing cattle for TB and shelling out compensation for cattle that have to be destroyed, all of which comes out of the taxpayer's pocket. The ministry pays for Gill's time, but it takes three of us working all day to get in all of the cattle so she can look at them. That's a lot of manpower.

There are other worries too. Sometimes you're bringing in cows that are heavily pregnant. If the TB test is stressful for the farmer, just think what it's like for the cow. They are herded back to the farm where they are manhandled into a cage known as a cattle crush to restrict their movements. Then they are either injected or examined. Accidents happen and pregnant cows can abort during the process. It's very rare that you get through an entire day of testing without some kind of drama.

Even as we try to manoeuvre the first cow into the crush, I'm already wound up. It's a Gloucester, weighing around half a ton and there's no way it wants to get into the crush. We push and pull, giving it encouraging slaps on the rump, but she rears up, digging her hooves into the ground. Finally, grabbing both sides of the cage I put my full weight behind her and, begrudgingly, she steps forward so we can slam the doors behind her. Then it's heart in the mouth time as Gill moves in to check for telltale lumps. If she finds a lump, she'll measure it with callipers to see if it has been caused by TB. As the first animal is cleared, I realise that I've been holding my breath. One down, 80 to go. The gates at the front of the crush are opened and the cow happily clatters out.

After a while it's the turn of one of the sickly cows that I've been keeping an eye on. Gill rubs her hand over its dark black neck.

'No reaction, Adam,' she announces, 'no TB.' What a relief. Of course we still don't know what's wrong with it, but Gill takes a dung sample and some blood for further tests to see if there's another problem. Despite the seriousness of the situation, I can't help but try to lighten the mood as the vet draws out the blood, pointing out that if you were in a doctor's surgery giving blood you'd get a warm cup of tea and a lie down. No such luxury for these girls. Mike, my stockman who tends the animals, wonders if they'd like a nice chocolate biscuit. We laugh, but the tension is still there, underlying everything we're doing. Mike is a great companion on days like today. He's been with us four years now. A farmer's son from Devon, he left farming when he started work, moving up to Cheltenham to get into marketing and business development. But like so many folk from a farming background, a life behind a desk soon got on top of him and he started looking for outdoor work. As luck would have it, we were looking for a general farm worker and Mike fitted the bill perfectly. When our old stockman left to take up his own tenancy, Mike was the obvious choice to replace him. He'd already shown how great he was with livestock and had proved himself to be competent with all the paperwork that comes with pedigree breeding. As we've got so many different breeds on the farm, keeping on top of all the registrations and records is quite a task. Back in the old days, dad used to do it by quill pen, but now it is mostly logged online. Mike has a real eye for detail and so is ideal. He's also incredibly calm and patient. Nothing ever seems to faze him, which is good on days like today.

The first half of the herd is cleared by lunchtime so I head out with my eldest sheepdog Maude to bring in the rest. While I'm pleased that nothing has come up so far, my insides are still churning. As this is such a big day for the farm, the *Countryfile* crew has arrived to film the test and I try to describe what I'm feeling to camera. It is too much. How can I concentrate on filming when I have so much riding on today? I'm not reporting on someone else's farm. This is mine. These are my animals. These are my people, stressed to the limit. All around me the sounds of the farm are deafening, building into a cacophony. The clank of neck braces, the mournful call of cows separated from their calves, the bellowing roar of bulls being moved near to each other when usually they'll be kept apart, pawing at the ground and snorting because they want to charge against each other. In the end, all my training from John, and years of delivering scripts, fails me and I stumble on my words before trailing off, shaking my head and walking away. The moment stays in the final cut. It sums up how I'm feeling far more than any throwaway line.

Thankfully, the afternoon goes without any incident. I'd had fears about a beautiful little White Park calf, but she passes with flying colours as do our entire herd of Highland cattle with their shaggy, rust-coloured coats and distinctive long, curved horns. The Highlands are probably the nearest we get to the giant wild auroch cattle found on Neolithic cave paintings all over the world. Jumping into my buggy I happily guide them back to their field. Not long to go now. We're so close. Could this really be a second clear test?

Then disaster strikes. The moment I've been dreading happens. A White Park is in the crush and isn't looking good.

'There's some thickening,' Gill says, feeling against its side. Out come those callipers. Gill measures the two lumps. If the one at the bottom is a fraction larger than the one at the top we've got a reactor on our hands.

'Fifteen on the top,' Gill announces, leaning in close to double-check. Now the lower one. I run my hand over my mouth, if only to stop me shouting out in frustration. This can't be happening.

Not again.

'And 13 on the bottom.' Gill gives the cow a hearty pat on the shoulder. 'This one passes.'

The rest of the afternoon passes in a haze. There are no more scares and I'm overjoyed when my magnificent Belted Galloway bull goes clear.

Before I know it, we're down to the last animal. The fate of my business for the next few months relies on the next result, a two-year-old bull that, all things being equal, I would be taking to shows and thinking of selling privately. Usually he'd be worth a couple of grand. With TB on the farm, he's pretty worthless at the moment. Almost as if he realises how stressed we are, he walks happily into the crush and doesn't complain as Gill runs her hands over his flank and neck. It's the moment of truth.

'Adam,' Gill begins, and for a second it is as if time freezes. Everyone in the yard is hanging on Gill's every word.

'I'm delighted to say you've got a clear test.'

I don't care that the cameras are there. I jump in the air. I cheer. I wave my hands like an idiot. And last, but no means least, I wrap my arms around Gill and almost lift her off the ground in a bear hug.

I'm over the moon. That's it. We've beaten TB. We can start selling cattle again.

CHAPTER 4

STARS IN THEIR EYES

A few months later, that's exactly what we're doing. Dad takes Bemborough Alfie, one of our Gloucester bulls, down to market. We've been working hard on him, making sure that he's halter-trained so that he'll perform in the ring and follow his handler well. This morning we've given that gorgeous dark brown coat a deep shampoo and even polished up his horns. He's never looked so clean and tidy. We want him to get a good price.

Even though the guinea coin hasn't been legal tender in the UK since 1816, when it was replaced with the pound, it's still the currency of livestock and racing horse auctions. One guinea is worth £1.05 so if an animal sells for 100 guineas, the buyer pays £105. The seller gets £100 and the five quid difference goes to the auctioneer in commission. We've put a reserve on Alfie, a minimum price that the auctioneer will have to reach before he can sell the lot. If you don't do this, then you can easily not make enough, or even worse, your animal can be sold at a cut price to a butcher and killed for beef. That would break dad's heart, as he's taken a real shine to Alfie. There's another, more practical reason to place a reserve price. There has to be a recognition of quality in livestock sales. If you let an animal go cheap then it means that other breeders could be forced to sell at the same cut-down prices. Over time the entire breed is devalued. In my opinion, £1500 still isn't enough in real terms. In Perth, I've seen big commercial bulls sell for the equivalent of £30,000. Of course, the important word there is commercial. Mine are rare breeds. Because there are fewer of them you would think each would be worth more, but that isn't the case. There's less demand for these old breeds and so they can't command the same prices.

So, with a reserve of 1500 guineas, Alfie is led into the ring.

Five minutes later, back on the farm my mobile rings. It's dad, and it's not great news. Alfie hasn't sold. The auction ended at 1300 guineas, just shy of our reserve. However, there is a silver lining.

'He was champion cattle animal, though,' dad tells me proudly, 'beat all other breeds.' Before the auction there had been a show and Alfie had picked up the rosette for overall champion over all the other cattle there. So the outing hasn't been a waste. Alfie is coming home with more awards to his name, which only helps raise the profile of our stock. And he won't be idle. Alfie's got some good wives in the fields, so we'll put him out with them and let nature run its course. Next year, we may even think about putting him up for sale again. At least, we can think about doing such things now. With TB gone, it is business as usual. At last.

There's another reason that I'm glad we can finally start moving cattle about. It means that I won't have to let down Ridley Scott.

Yes, you read that right. Ridley Scott, the director of *Blade Runner, Thelma & Louise* and *Gladiator*, is in need of my services. He's currently starting work on a new *Robin Hood* film starring Russell Crowe and Cate Blanchett. He has his stars, he has his locations – from Sherwood Forest in Nottinghamshire to various sites in Pembrokeshire – but there is one thing he hasn't got: animals.

The problem with modern breeds is that they look so out of place in period dramas. The commoners of Robin Hood's time wouldn't have tended these kinds of animals. This is where our collection of rare breeds comes into its own once again. We have examples of just about every farm animal that has walked and snuffled its way across Great Britain since Neolithic times. If you're after a sheep that looks like it would be at home on a Bronze Age farm you can have one of our North Ronaldsays or a Shetland at a push (although, technically, the latter is more suited to the Iron Age). Got a bunch of marauding Vikings ready to pillage and plunder? Then, you'll be wanting some of our Manx Loaghtan or Hebridean sheep in the background. Need a pig to complete your realistic Victorian farm? No problem. A Gloucester Old Spot will be just the ticket, and you could throw in a few Castlemilk Moorit sheep and Belted Galloway cattle for good measure. I like to think that there isn't a period of British history that we can't handle.

Over the years, we've made a healthy little sideline in animal actors, supplying rare breed animals to feature film productions, TV shows, commercials and photo shoots. This was another of dad's clever ideas back in the Seventies, a way his heritage rare breeds could earn their keep. As I've said, dad's from a show-business family and around this time regularly popped up himself on *Animal Magic*. He'd kept his ear to the ground and soon worked out there was a gap in the market, a gap he was more than happy to fill. Since then our animals have appeared in hundreds of different productions from the kind you'd expect – sharing the screen with the likes of Gwyneth Paltrow and Mel Gibson in period films such as *Emma* and *Braveheart* – and a few you'd wouldn't: some of our animals even turned up on a distant prison planet in *Alien 3*. On the small screen they've also appeared in historic dramas such as the BBC's *Middlemarch*, become the stars of high-profile David Attenborough documentaries and brought history to life in Tony Robinson's *Time Team*. It's an interesting and rewarding side to our business, supplying animals for something other than meat. I've even got in on the act myself. Look very carefully in *Braveheart* and you can spot me as a grubby peasant leading oxen across the screen, drawing William Wallace's dead father back from battle on a cart.

While the fees we can demand for our animals are hardly going to break box-office records, they still bring in a tidy sum. Even a humble chicken can earn anything between £50 to £100 per day, while a flock of sheep, filmed for a day on the farm, will bring in a couple of hundred quid. Of course, if we have to take them off the farm then the price goes up, as we have to pay for transport and handling, so a day's shooting with a ram in Surrey will cost the same as the entire flock at home.

It has to be said that providing animals for films isn't for everyone. You're at the whim of a fickle director who can change his mind in a second. So, you could be told to turn up at 4 a.m. for an eight o'clock call. That doesn't mean it's going to work like that. It could be four o'clock in the afternoon before you're actually needed.

You also have to be firm. Directors have a very strong idea about what they want to achieve, but they don't always think about the animals. There was one film I was working on where the director had a horse and carriage racing over a bridge. The idea was that it would barge through my flock of sheep. The trouble was there wasn't enough room for the sheep to get out of the way. They would end up under the wheels. I had to step in and say, sorry, you're not doing that, my animals will be in danger. Directors are used to getting their own way and this one wasn't used to people saying no. But I had to stand firm and not be starstruck. The good thing is that because our animals are so used to being handled and are calm, we can work around most problems. Plus, with my background, I'm used to how the business works. It's meant I've now been able to share my insight with Mike as he goes off to do filming jobs.

You wouldn't believe some of the requests we get. Back in the 1990s, the phone rang and I was excited to realise that it was someone from Walt Disney on the other end of the line.

'We're trying to find a pig that can sit on cue,' they asked, 'and aren't having much luck. You wouldn't happen to have one, would you?'

'We don't,' I had to admit, 'but when do you need it by? I'm sure we can train one up for you.'

As soon as I'd put the phone down I wondered if I had just bitten off more than I could chew. Pigs are incredibly intelligent creatures – after all, these are the creatures that prompted Sir Winston Churchill to say, 'I like pigs. Dogs look up to us. Cats look down on us. Pigs treat us as equals.' – and if they don't want to do something it can be terribly difficult to train them to do otherwise. So, with a firm deadline set by the House of Mouse, we set to work. We chose Princess, one of our Gloucester Old Spot sows to be our star-in-the-making as she had a particularly agreeable temperament and, armed with buckets of food, tried to persuade her to sit whenever a certain command was given. The problem is that pigs don't naturally sit like a dog. They can't lift their heads up as they have such great thick necks, used to rootling up the ground. So we tried taking an apple, which we held by Princess's nose. She would immediately try and reach it. If we'd lift the apple higher, she would plonk down her bum so she could stretch up. As pigs are as clever as dogs, she'd start to associate the trick with a command to sit. After a while you wouldn't even need an apple, she'd do it as soon as she heard the word.

That was the theory at least.

At first, the results were laughable, and after a week of Princess stubbornly refusing to play ball, I was ready to phone up my contact at Disney and tell them that they'd better have a plan B in place. Then, right at the last minute, when I'd just about given up hope, I gave it one more go. Sighing, I held my hand above Princess's snout and wearily told her to sit.

Amazingly, Princess sat happily, her nose in the air. Was that a fluke? I tried again, just to make sure. She did it again. A star was born.

Excitedly, I phoned Disney.

'We're on,' I blurted out almost as soon as the phone was picked up, 'we've got a Gloucester Old Spot who will take direction beautifully. By the way, what kind of floor will she be sitting on? Is it in a studio or on location?'

'That's excellent news. She'll be required on location,' came the reply, 'but your pig won't be sitting on the floor. She'll be sitting on one of the cast.'

'Really? Anyone famous?' I asked, not really expecting the answer to be yes.

'Just Glenn Close,' my contact said calmly.

Just Glenn Close? I immediately started to hope that Princess didn't sit down too hard. But sure enough, the following year I sat and watched Princess pin the evil Cruella De Vil to the ground in *101 Dalmatians*.

Another one of our porkers had a close brush with fame in a bizarre little film called *The Hour of the Pig*. Directed by Leslie Megahey it starred Colin Firth alongside Ian Holm and Donald Pleasence. Colin Firth plays Richard Courtois, a fifteenth-century lawyer who escapes from the hustle and bustle of Parisian life to the countryside, only to find that he must defend a pig in court; a pig charged with murder. It sounds mad but, amazingly, is based on a number of true cases. Animal trials were a normal part of life for country folk across Europe from the mid thirteenth century. They were still happening as late as the 1800s. Farm animals, pets and even caterpillars and flies were put in the dock for all kinds of crimes. In the sixteenth century a French lawyer by the name of Bartholomew Chassenée was forced to defend rats put on trial for destroying the local harvest of barley, while earlier, in 1457, a sow was successfully convicted of murder. Her punishment was to be 'hanged by the hind feet from a gallows tree'. Her piglets almost faced the drop too. As they had been found splattered with blood, they were accused of being accomplices to her crime. However, as they were so young and impressionable, the judge decided that they should be acquitted and they avoided being strung up. I've heard the law called an ass before, but this is ridiculous.

The sow we provided for *The Hour of the Pig* was a friendly little Tamworth wild boar cross that went by the name of Guinevere. Now, you often hear of on-set romances, where actors meet the partner of their dreams while filming a movie. That's what happened with Guinevere. All it took was one look and Guinevere fell head over trotters in love with the dashing Mr Firth. She would follow him around the set like a love-struck teenager and even bit the poor actor who was playing the pig man, just because he wasn't Colin. But pigs are fickle creatures, and as soon as she was back on the farm she didn't seem to give the love of her life a second thought. We know that Colin didn't forget her though. When Guinevere had her next litter of piglets, Colin sent her a congratulations card.

With thoughts of these past cinematic glories we load the first of our Sherwood Forest-bound animals on the trailer. The production crew had ordered two Tamworth pigs, one of our most primitive surviving breeds. Descended from European wild boar, this boisterous breed has a distinctive ginger coat that makes it ideal for warmer countries as it hardly ever suffers from sunburn. By the Seventies the Tamworth had all but died out in the UK, but by chance, when working on a BBC TV show in Australia, dad visited a herd of the pigs in Woorak, New South Wales. He was amazed to see more Tamworths in that one herd than we had in the whole of the country back home. He immediately phoned the Rare Breeds Trust and came home with three boars to re-establish them here. Most importantly for Ridley Scott's production, the Tamworth best resembles the kind of pig that would have been kept by medieval swineherds.

The Tamworths are to be accompanied by a friendly Bagot goat, one of our rarest animals with less than 100 adults alive today, and, my personal favourite, a North Ronaldsay ram. These creatures have a very special place in my heart. They are one of the most primitive sheep kept on the farm. DNA tests have shown that my flock is very similar to remains found in the Stone Age settlements of Skara Brae in the Orkneys. That means the sheep is almost identical to the kind of animals kept by our ancestors more than 5000 years ago. It's a small but lively sheep that comes in a variety of colours. Its coarse wool can be white, grey, moorit (a shade of brown) or black and can literally be pulled off by the handful, no shearing required. The rams can boast an impressive beard and even more spectacular horns. The ewes may be horned, polled (meaning that they have no horns at all) or skurred (meaning that they have bumps where the horns would be).

Until the early 1970s, the entire population was kept beyond the sea wall of the Orkney island of North Ronaldsay and so had developed a real liking for seaweed. All it would have taken was disease or a disaster like an oil slick and the breed could have been wiped out forever. So in 1974, at the tender age of eight, I was bundled into a car by dad, and we drove up to Scotland where we caught a very choppy ferry to the remote island. It was my first experience of saving a rare breed. They're incredibly nippy little sheep when they want to be and I remember us slipping and sliding across the wet rocks as we tried to usher them into pens. Our trip was a success. We caught 178 North Ronaldsays in one day and shipped them off the island. Most were taken to the nearby island of Lingaholm while some were transported back to the mainland to be found new homes across the country. Of course, dad couldn't go to all this trouble and not bring some home to the Cotswolds. That foundation flock are the ancestors of the North Ronaldsays that I'm proud to breed to this day. They are still classed as endangered by the RBST, meaning that there are fewer than 500 surviving animals in the UK, and they are never likely to be commercially viable. While their meat is lean and flavoursome, North Ronaldsays take at least 15 months to mature and then you're only left with a very small carcass. Thankfully, film jobs such as these mean that my North Ronaldsays can still bring in some welcome cash.

As Mike's truck pulls away I make my way across the farmyard. The *Robin Hood* crew have made one more request, one I would not have been able to fulfil before the TB test. I reach the sheds to find dad waiting for me. I'm glad he's here. Today, we're going to begin training two of our Longhorn steers as oxen so that, in a few months' time, they can travel to the film location and pull carts in Scott's version of 'merry olde England'. An ox is a castrated bull, usually over four years of age, and can be from any breed of cattle. Dad's been training them for years and I can still remember watching him on *Animal Magic* being pulled along on a wooden sleigh behind a team of oxen that he had trained using traditional methods. It made good children's TV, but also helped explain how important oxen were to agriculture in days gone by.

For centuries, long before the tractor, oxen ploughed the fields, pulled sleds full of rocks to clear agricultural land and transported entire tree trunks from forest to timber yard. Many even favoured them over horses, and for good reason. They didn't cost as much to keep – there was no need for the expensive oats that working horses ate. The oxen just chewed down on the same fodder as any other cattle, simple straw and grass, and were about half as expensive to buy in the first place, although a good ox would still cost a peasant more than their average annual salary. To spread the cost, communities used to band together to buy a number of oxen, which they would share across their farms.

All of this isn't to say that the horse didn't have its merit. A single horse could produce the pulling power of two oxen and could often work faster than the cattle, but what oxen lacked in speed, they made up for in dogged resolution and brute force. The oxen would keep on trudging along until the work was done. Also, their lower speeds made them ideal for thicker, stonier ground. If a horse-drawn plough, moving at a faster rate, hit a large stone hidden in the soil, there was more chance the equipment could be damaged.

The oxen remained the draught animal of choice until the early to mid-1800s. The Industrial Revolution had brought with it a need for speed and greater productivity. Around the same time, the General Enclosure Act of 1801 meant that the old days of open-field farming were behind us and the countryside was being carved up into smaller fields. In late medieval times, it would have been quite common to see six, or even eight, oxen harnessed in rows pulling massive ploughs. Such huge plough teams just didn't fit into smaller fields and so the more powerful horse began to grow in popularity and oxen were phased out. You would have still occasionally seen pairs of oxen working the fields, pulling heavy ploughs or even, in some rare cases, pulling the colourful caravans of travelling folk, but in the main, the age of the ox was well and truly over.

Our farming ancestors chose their oxen carefully. They almost always worked in pairs and so the partners needed to be carefully matched. You'd need them to be pretty equal in strength, otherwise one would dominate the other and pull the plough off course and they also needed to be around the same height. Whereas horses were harnessed using an individual body harness and padded collar, the strength of the two oxen would be tamed with a yoke, a heavy wooden beam, that was fitted over their muscular necks, just in front of the shoulders and held in place by a U-shaped oxbow that curved underneath the head.

Once paired, the oxen would stay together for life, working and resting in each other's company. Some historical records show that even their names were carefully chosen. Tradition dictated that one of the oxen would be given a short, single-syllable name, such as Quick, while the other's was two-syllable, such as Nimble. It's a custom we've kept happily alive with our two oxen in training, naming them Butch and Sundance.

We're joined by Vicki, one of the newest recruits on the farm, who is going to help us yoke them up for the first time. That's if we can even get them out of their sheds. Both Butch and Sundance have been fitted with simple rope harnesses to help us lead them into the yard, but there's nothing simple about persuading 300 kilo steers to walk behind you if they don't want to budge.

Taking one ox each, Vicki and I put our weight behind it and after a little bit of yanking, Butch and Sundance begin to follow us into the sunlight. They are unsure at first and have a habit of stopping sharply, which is enough to pull you off your feet. I notice the smile on dad's face. His days of pulling oxen may be behind him but he can still remember how difficult it can be.

'The trick, Adam,' he advises, 'is to start them young when you are as strong as they are.'

I glance back at Vicki who is trying to get Sundance through a gate. Sundance, meanwhile, has other ideas and is refusing to budge.

'Are you feeling as strong as Sundance, Vicki?' I ask with a grin, finally getting Butch to follow me.

'Not quite,' she admits. Thankfully, Sundance suddenly seems to decide he's caused Vicki enough grief and begins to trudge, albeit a little reluctantly, after her. We stand them by a strong wooden fence, tying their ropes to the post so they don't wander off, and prepare to put them in the yoke. I've no idea how they'll cope with this. I'm hoping that they won't freak out. While they're still a little on the stubborn side, they're pretty docile and I'm sure that if we can break them in, they will make smashing oxen.

Vicki helps me place the yoke on top of their necks. So far, so good. Butch and Sundance don't even flinch.

'How tight does it need to be, Dad?' I ask, ready to connect the U-shaped wooden oxbows with chain links at the ends.

'It wants to be tight enough so they can't get their head out,' he explains. 'If they think they can slip their head out of the yoke, they'll have a go, which you don't want while they're walking along.'

The chains are linked to the yoke. Dad's right. The oxbows are designed in such a way that there is no risk of strangling them, there's still bags of room, but it's close enough to convince them that there's no point trying to wriggle out. Grabbing the ropes I lead them across the yard, testing how they walk yoked together. There are a couple of worrying moments, when they try to reassert their strength and kick up to the right, almost pulling me off my feet, but after a while they get the knack and seem to be quite happy walking behind me, helped along by the odd, light slap on the rump from dad.

But the final test will be how they take to the cart. It's one thing having them wandering around in the yoke but if they won't pull a cart, it's all been a waste of time. I get hold of their ropes and stand facing them. Vicki and dad have connected the cart so it's time for me to walk backward, taking the strain and encouraging them to take the first step.

'Walk on then.'

At first there is nothing. Both Butch and Sundance stand firm, bucking their heads slightly as I lean back on the ropes. Then, ever so slowly, they begin to follow me. Dad is at the rear, his walking stick held up over them to make himself bigger and encourage them forward. Vicki, meanwhile, is behind the cart, making sure that the wheels turn true. That's it. They're doing it. In fact they're doing it faster than I thought they would. At one point I find myself with Sundance's head pressed against my chest, and in danger of being pushed over.

We get a few metres out of the yard and the boys are taking to the cart as if they've been pulling one for years. 'That's brilliant, Adam,' dad exclaims as we bring them to rest, before warning me not to push it. 'I'd get them off the cart now. You don't want to wear them out or frighten them.' As always, he's right. We let them off, drop the cart and walk them back to the yard.

All in all it's been a successful day. In a few weeks, with just a little more training, they'll be ready for the silver screen and they'll earn their keep and be an attraction for the public. We lead them back into the shed for some well-deserved cattle nuts. Well, you have to look after movie stars, don't you?

CHAPTER 5

PREPARING
THE LAND

When most people think of my farm these days they think of the livestock. It's not really surprising. Our animals are so prominent, what with our work with rare breeds and the high profile of the farm park. But the bread and butter of our operation is still what dominated Bemborough Farm long before dad bought in his first Cotswold sheep – our arable crops. And, just as the animals in the sheds are constantly tended and cared for, we have to look after our wheat, beans, oilseed rape and barley to make sure that we get the best harvest at the end of the season and can demand the best prices.

Back in March we started to prepare the land. While I love farming in these beautiful surroundings, our free-draining soil can be troublesome. It is known as Cotswold brash, and is very stony. It does bring some benefits. If we're hit with a very wet winter, then the brash will very quickly dry out. This is especially useful after a heavy frost, or snow. Whereas a lot of farmers will be left with soggy, soft ground, ours will recover quickly meaning that it will be hard enough to take the heavy machinery we'll be using to prepare the soil for planting.

However, at other times of year these same traits can be problematic. The soil doesn't retain water at all, so if you don't get much rain you can soon end up with near-drought conditions, which can be disastrous for spring-sown crops.

Luckily this year wasn't that bad and we were able to get out nice and early. The first job is to muck the fields using the manure from our own animal sheds, which has been rotting away in big compost heaps over the last twelve months. It's potent stuff and a great start, proving essential energy that is transferred into the soil through natural nitrogen – which all plants need to grow – as well as phosphates and potash. It takes two days for all the muck from our sheds to be spread by a contractor using a front-end loader with a spreader on the back. I'd love the manure to provide all the nutrients we need – after all, it's a free by-product of our livestock – but unfortunately it's not as simple as that. Not only do we not have enough of the stuff, but also to produce the kind of yields we need to survive in the commercial market we have to rely on artificial fertilisers.

Many people still think that farmers are out in their fields spraying chemicals willy-nilly, smothering the land in all kinds of weird and wonderful concoctions. While we obviously do use artificial sprays, there's no way we'd apply any more than we need. First of all, we're not that irresponsible and, as you'd expect, there are strict environmental regulations governing the use of chemicals. Secondly, and more importantly to the bottom line, we're not that rich. Artificial fertilisers are hideously expensive so you don't want to use any more than you actually need. It just doesn't make financial sense.

To find out just how many additional nutrients we need, farmers spend time at the beginning of the year testing the ground. In the old days, this was done manually. To save time you found the part of your field that was in the poorest condition and worked out how much fertiliser you needed to add to bring it up to scratch. That was it. The entire field was then treated at that flat rate, whether it needed additional help or not. This, of course, meant that there were some areas that received far too much and you'd be left with a build-up of chemicals.

Thanks to modern farming technology this is no longer a problem. In March we hire someone to run up and down our fields driving a quad bike. It sounds fun, but he isn't larking about. Guided by a GPS system, he stops regularly, sampling the soil at various points along a computer-generated grid, building up a full nutrient map of our fields. This data is vital. Fertiliser spreaders are incredibly sophisticated pieces of kit these days. Each is fitted with the kind of onboard computer that would have seemed like science fiction when my dad started farming. I don't mind admitting that they seem a bit like science fiction to me today as well. Gone are the days when any Tom, Dick or Harry could hop on a tractor and set off. Today, the ability to drive the machinery is almost secondary – in fact there are some spreaders available that are able to drive themselves – the real work comes in knowing how to handle the computer systems. I couldn't do it, so I'm happy to leave it to the professionals.

Before spreading starts, the computer works out the exact amount of fertiliser that is needed for every section of the grid. It knows that this bit needs more, whereas that bit needs a little less. Then the engine is turned on and the mechanical beast starts trundling up and down the same lanes that the quad bike followed, adding more fertiliser to the weaker points, less to soil already high in nutrients and ignoring the area where no help is required. Unbelievably this GPS mapping system is accurate to just 10 cm. There's no way the old method could compete with that. When the engine is finally turned off again, not only do you have a field that has been given a consistent spread of nutrients, you've also saved money on unnecessary wastage. Plus, there are obvious environmental benefits – the risk of excess fertiliser running off into watercourses has been significantly reduced. Being responsible makes sense for both our pockets and the planet.

A hundred years ago, farmers would have sowed seed by hand, throwing it out from a bag or using a weird and wonderful device known as the seed fiddle. A box, containing a canvas bag, would hang to one side of you from a shoulder strap. You'd hold the box in one hand and a long bow that threaded through the device with the other. With every step you'd take, you'd push the bow in and out, thus turning a disc inside the box, which regulated the amount of seed that dropped from the bag inside. After the seeds were sown, you'd scratch it into the soil using a simple horse-drawn device.

By the time dad started farming, the mechanical drill ruled the roost. Tractors would pull the drill, a landwheel turning cogs that released the seeds down pipes to the ground at a regular rate.

Today, in a similar way to the fertiliser, everything is computerised. The modern drill is six metres wide and uses radar to deliver just the right amount of seed as the tractor trundles on. Fans blow the seed down the pipes from a big hopper on the back of the tractor on to the ground, where it will be rolled in on another pass.

Whereas, in the past, drilling seed was labour-intensive, it now takes one man with a tractor and a satellite navigation system to work out the most economical way to drill the fields, managing to cover about a hundred acres in a day. If the tractor is moving in a straight line, it will even self-steer!

After our crops have been planted and are starting to grow, more chemicals comes into play and once again it's always a case of less is best. Every couple of weeks we invite an independent agronomist to the farm to walk the fields. He's here to examine our weed-burden, the sheer volume of weeds that have been springing up between the wheat, barley and rape. He also checks how much, if any, fungus is growing on the plant. After his visit, we'll receive a report letting us know how much risk he feels there is to the crops. If it's considerable, he'll recommend a suitable cocktail of chemicals to spray. This will continue throughout the growing season to ensure that we have the best harvest later in the year.

*

Elsewhere on the farm we look for other ways to save money. As you can imagine, feeding around 2000 animals every day is a real expense, but there's no way I want to cut corners when it comes to the quality of the food I use. Just like our crops, the nutrition of our animals is vitally important. I have to make sure that I'm keeping them well fed, healthy and that they have a good balanced diet.

One of my little secrets is apple pulp, which is mainly fed to my pigs. I'm really proud of how we've integrated the pulp into our feeding systems. It comes from Bean Benson, a mate of mine who lives nearby. He's a traditional juicer and every autumn presses thousands of English apples to make high-quality juice and lollies. I love going to watch him work. The apples are poured into a machine that chops them up – skin, flesh, pips and all. They are then wrapped in cloth and slowly pressed together so that the tasty nectar flows out. One of the other reasons I enjoy going to his farm is that I usually get a glass or two of the freshly-squeezed juice. There's nothing like it.

My animals get what's left over once all the juice is wrung out. It's a brilliant example of how farmers can work together to help each other out. For Bean, the pulp is nothing more than a waste product that he'd need to find some way of getting rid of, but to me it's a valuable foodstuff, which saves me money. It's not just the pigs that enjoy it. In the winter, it also helps feed my cattle, replacing the expensive 16 per cent concentrate nuts that we used to feed them. So throughout the autumn I nip back and forth to Bean's place, picking up pulp by the crateful.

Back on the farm we don't just chuck the pulp out to the pigs and hope for the best. Before I head out into the fields with buckets full of the stuff, we work out the mineral and protein content of the apples. If there's a shortfall, I make it up with a blend of nuts. And the pigs absolutely love it. Even before I'm through the gates, they start trotting towards the concrete pad where their food is thrown so that it doesn't get lost in the mud and mess of the field. It's hardly out of the bucket before they're jostling each other to get to the tasty pulp.

I watch them tuck in and take a minute to appraise how they're doing. This morning I'm feeding my Gloucester Old Spots, a breed that hopefully will soon be making some extra money for the farm.

I've quite literally grown up with Gloucester Old Spots. Dad first introduced them to the farm when I was only three years old and we've been breeding them ever since. Alongside the Cotswold sheep and the Gloucester cow, they complete our roster of three county breeds, but that's not the reason why they're my favourite pigs of all. They are possibly some of the most docile and self-sufficient pigs you'll ever farm and yet are as tough as old boots, happy to be out in all elements. The sows happily give birth outside – or farrow as it's known with pigs – producing wonderful litters of at least ten piglets each. They make great mothers too, which is why so many first-time smallholders are now starting out by rearing Old Spots.

The white pig with its trademark black spot is one of the world's oldest pedigree pig breeds in the world. The first records were made in 1885, and the Gloucester Old Spots Breed Society was officially formed in 1913. Before this time, the pig was still suffering from a poor public image. Cattle, horses and even sheep were the animals of kings and lords, whereas the humble porker was a poor man's beast that wallowed in the mud and scavenged for roots. It is thought that the Gloucester Old Spots were actually first bred around Berkeley Vale, on the banks of the River Severn. Originally known as the orchard or cottager's pig, they were kept in the vast cider apple and pear orchards that stretched across the West Country as well as on dairy farms, growing fat on windfall fruit and the whey of Gloucester cheese. In fact, if you listen to one of the many old wives' tales that still flourish around here, those distinctive blotches started out as bruises formed by falling apples from the orchards. Somehow I find that a little hard to believe.

It also beggars belief that these lovely, floppy-eared creatures almost became extinct in the twentieth century. The problem – as with all heritage breeds – is that they couldn't cope with modern intensive methods, hating being kept inside. They also naturally run to fat and, fantastic mothers or not, just don't produce enough piglets. For a while it looked as if the breed was doomed.

That was until a Worcestershire farmer by the name of George Styles stepped in. By the 1950s, George was so alarmed at the falling numbers of Gloucester Old Spots that he single-handedly attempted to save them, breeding them on his farm. It worked. George is known affectionately as the grandfather of the breed, and the Gloucester Old Spot, although it's still listed as a minority on the RBST watchlist, is one of the most popular rare breed pigs farmed today, with around 600 breeding females kept around the country. In fact, there are now more Old Spots registered than any other pig on the RBST books. George would be beaming if he could see how well they are doing these days.

The Gloucester Old Spots not only have a special place in my heart, they also have a place in *The Guinness Book of Records*. The most expensive pig in British history was an Old Spot by the name of Foston Sambo the 21st, who fetched the grand sum of 4000 guineas (£4200) when he was sold at auction in 1994. While I'd love my Old Spots to bring me that kind of money, I'm not holding my breath, but there is a way that they can help pay their way.

It may sound odd, but most of the time, the best way to help save rare breed farm animals is to eat them. Around half the young animals born – be they calves, lambs or piglets – will be male. The problem is that you don't need many males. One ram will mate with 50 to 80 ewes, one boar with 20 sows and one bull with 20 cows. That means that whatever you do, you always get a surplus of males. If you can't sell them the breed become unviable and the farmer will consider abandoning them for a more profitable beast.

However, as more people demand their meat, the more commercially viable they become. It helps, now people are becoming more aware of the plight of rare breed animals, that they are also realising how tasty they are. Our Gloucester cattle, for example, have become a bit of a delicacy in certain London restaurants and these days you can't turn on a TV without hearing some celebrity chef or other wax lyrical about this breed or that.

In the case of the Gloucester Old Spot, once someone has tasted their meat, you don't usually have to wait too long for them to come back for more. All that fat means amazing flavour and, if you're so inclined, crackling to die for. You just need to be able to sell enough to make them pay for themselves. The difficulty with pigs is that they eat so much. Whereas sheep and cows happily graze on grass, which is cheap to grow, with pigs you need to feed them a cereal-based diet every day. And they eat a lot.

There's another problem too. As Gloucester Old Spot meat is becoming so popular, a lot of farmers are starting to cash in. Farmers in other areas are buying the pigs – which is great for the breed – but some unscrupulous folk are passing off other breeds as proper Old Spot. It's quite sickening really.

To try and combat this, the Old Spot Pig Breeders' Club is campaigning for the breed to be given protective status by the European Union. The EU Protected Food Name scheme first came into force in 1993 and aims to protect food names depending on geographical location or the use of a traditional recipe. It's supposed to protect those awarded designation from imitation throughout Europe.

There are three main types of status protection currently recognised in Europe. The first is a PDO (Protected Designation of Origin), which is the most common and means that a foodstuff has been produced, processed and prepared in a certain

My dad, Joe Henson, feeding a Golden Guernsey goat in the Farm Park.

With my business partner Duncan at the opening of the Wildlife Walk at the Farm Park. We first met at Agricultural College in Devon.

Millie and I pose for a picture.

Having a well-earned rest with Maude.

Me with *Adam's Farm* producers Sam Bailey and Dan Davis.

'The name's Henson, Adam Henson.' Celebrating *Countryfile*'s 20th anniversary in style on my farm!

My favourite cattle and sheep breeds – the Gloucester (above) and Cotswold (right).

Lambing Live 2010 – Kate Humble helps me through my first taste of live telly.

Warming new-born lambs, which must be hand reared, under a hot lamp.

My own unique method of shearing. I just wish the fleeces were worth more!

The combine takes advantage of a break in the clouds to bring in the winter wheat.

Bringing in the grain calls for some precision tractor driving.

Making straw bales, which are used for bedding, while the sun shines – a rare occasion this year unfortunately ...

Rolling one of the hay bales into an animal feeder.

The grain stores are full –
but after all that rain, is
the barley up to scratch?

Martin Parkinson, my
arable manager, and
contractor James Arkell
check the ground for
dropped grain after the
combine has passed over.

geographical area. Foods that have PDOs include Italy's Parma ham, Greece's feta cheese and the UK's very own Melton Mowbray Pork Pie.

The second level of certification comes with the PGI (Protected Geographical Indication) that proves that the produce is made in a certain place but uses raw materials that are sent in from another area, a designation the Cornish Pasty Association is currently trying to achieve for their famous snack.

In the case of Gloucester Old Spots, the hopes are being pinned on the third tier – a TSG (Traditional Speciality Guaranteed) award. If the breeders' club is successful, the Old Spot will be only the second British product to gain TSG accreditation after Traditional Farmfresh Turkey was awarded the status a decade ago. The TSG means that producers will only be able to market their pork as Gloucester Old Spot if it comes from pedigree Gloucester pigs using the traditional farming methods unique to the county.

I for one will be pleased if they're successful, as this will help me sell my pork, but in the meantime, if I want to increase my herd I need to find a new outlet for my Old Spot sausages. We've been making them for years in small numbers, selling them through the odd farm shop and the Rare Breed Survival Trust rare meat scheme, but never in the numbers I've wanted. And so I've charged Mike with a new task. We'd never really encouraged local butchers to take rare breed meats. It was too good an opportunity to miss. Could Mike go out and find some shops willing to give our meat a try?

*

A few days later, I come into the office to find Mike on the phone to Lambournes Butchers in Stow-on-the-Wold. There has been a butcher on the site in the middle of town for as long as I can remember, but in 2005 it was taken over by Bob Preston and his wife Karen. Bob's been butchering for 30 years now. He started young, picking up a job at Oxford's covered market when he was just 13 years old. Over the years, he worked as a freelance butcher, providing holiday cover in various shops across Oxfordshire and Gloucestershire, picking up tips and tricks of the trade along the way. What he doesn't know about sausages isn't worth knowing. It's always a treat seeing what bangers he has on offer as he changes his selection regularly, coming up with all kinds of weird and wonderful concoctions. When Wimbledon is on, his pork and strawberry sausages go down a treat, while during the last Cheltenham Races he dug out an old Irish recipe that used Guinness, black pudding, loads of herbs and – and this is where it got interesting – Gloucester Old Spot pig.

From what I could gather, Bob is interested but isn't sure. As I listen to Mike having his conversation I can guess what Bob is saying. It's not just sausages. To make it work they'll have to shift the rest of the carcass as well and the trouble is that Old Spots have a habit of running to fat and are therefore difficult to shift.

But Mike keeps badgering away and in the end Bob agrees that we can take some meat in to show him. He isn't making any promises though.

*

And so we're soon rounding up a few of the pigs to take over to Checketts abattoir at Long Compton. We use two local abattoirs, as I never like the idea of the pigs travelling too far. I've also decided to take them in myself today and, as always, you do find yourself being ever so slightly conflicted on abattoir runs.

It's not that I'm squeamish in any way about killing our animals for food. That's just the way of life we lead. I've always seen animals killed on the farm. Dad used to kill the odd rabbit or chicken, and we've always had animals hung up in the food store next to where we keep the animal feed. We even used to kill our own turkeys for Christmas and I've no problem wringing a chicken's neck for the Sunday roast.

Even so, going to the slaughter is an odd time. There's no easy way around it. If you want to rear livestock for food, they've got to be killed. There's nothing nice or romantic about it. It's just the way it is. As a farmer you work very hard to keep your animals alive. You spend a huge amount of energy making sure that they're looked after and reared in the right way. Without getting sentimental about them, because that would never do on a farm, you can't help but put in a lot of love too. They're living creatures and some of course take much more care than others. There are always problem animals that take up your time, such as weak or poorly babies. It's especially true of sheep. Dad always reminds me that 10 per cent of your flock takes up 90 per cent of your work. He's right of course. But with so many sheep on the farm, you don't get so attached to the animals and usually can't tell them apart. Pigs are different. Because we have so few, we get to know them as individuals.

So, after so much time working with them, when the inevitable day comes, and you take them for slaughter, you want to give them the best death you can. You don't want it to be long or drawn out or rough. You want it to be clean and respectful.

As well as saving on transport costs, we like to deliver the animals to slaughter ourselves. If I can see it's done right, I can sleep easy at night. I'm proud of our animals and the way we treat them, from the moment they're born to the moment they die. This morning I have volunteered to do the journey so Mike can get on with jobs back on the farm.

Arriving at the abattoir I back up the trailer to the ramp and we let the pigs out. After even a short journey in the car they're happy to get out and scramble down a corridor into a holding pen. While they're there it's time to hit the paperwork. As you'd expect there's quite a lot of legislation to get through. There's the movement licence, and medicine licence, plus the declaration that they haven't had any antibiotics recently. It's a lot of work, but it's all very important. In Britain, we can quite rightly claim some of the best food standards and traceability in the world. No corners should ever be cut.

Once you've jumped through the red tape, it's time for the pigs to move through the process. From the holding pen, they're taken to another area where there's a sliding door. The door opens and you usher a pig through. A guy is waiting on the other side, ready to stun them. A device is placed behind the pig's ear and the charge is released. The animal hits the floor unconscious, after which it is hung up and its throat is cut.

It's never easy and even today, after all of this time, I steel myself slightly before I encourage my pigs to trot through the door with a friendly little tap. One minute you're encouraging them, the next, they're gone.

But it's what needs to be done. After being prepared, the carcasses will make their way to Bob. That will be the ultimate test. What will he think of the meat? Will it sell? If it does, then this process will be worth it – the pigs will have had a good life, a respectful death and will have lived up to their purpose. I know some question this way of life, and are against the rearing and slaughtering of animals for meat, but at the end of the day, the truth of the matter is this; if we didn't want to eat animals like the Gloucester Old Spot, then they would simply be extinct by now. Farmers take pride in breeding good quality livestock to produce fantastic meat.

SUMMER

CHAPTER 6

BOARISH BEHAVIOUR

It's June and I'm back in the car, pulling the pig trailer behind me. This time, however, I'm not taking pigs for slaughter. I'm heading to Coventry to start building up my pig herd.

The good news is that Bob Preston had been impressed with the first load of pig carcasses that had come to him from Checketts. They were smaller than he'd usually take, but I promised that we would try and get the pigs bigger next time. The deal had been done and he'd agreed to take two pigs a week. Soon word had got around and our sausages and chops began flying off his shelves almost as soon as he'd prepared them. The last time I went in to see how we were doing I was amazed by the result.

'You're not going to believe this, Adam,' said Bob, 'but last week we had a woman who had driven over from Wales to buy your sausages. Luckily we still had some in stock.'

I was gobsmacked. Of course, I'm the first to admit that being a TV farmer isn't going to hurt my business, but at the end of the day, my level of – and I hate to use the word – celebrity will only get people to pick up my goods once. If they're not up to scratch then it's doubtful they would come back for more. It actually means we have to work harder to make sure what we sell is second to none. The fame game just raises everyone's expectations.

Thankfully, the Old Spot bangers had so far lived up to their reputation and people were coming back – including, it appeared, our visitor from Wales. Bob was certainly happy with the business. Then came the bad news.

'I'm going to have to up my order. I'll need around six pigs a week, I reckon.'

I know. That doesn't seem like bad news, but the truth of the matter was that I'd never be able to provide that kind of number.

At least this is a good problem to have and why I'm off to Coventry today. I'm on the way to Malcolm Hicks's farm in Balsall Common. Malcolm's dad first came to South View Farm when he was two years old. The family has been there ever since, the farm passing from father to son, three generations down to Malcolm. When he meets me in the yard, Malcolm's oldest son William is on hand to lend a hand. Looks like history is going to repeat itself once again.

Malcolm is one of the country's most celebrated Gloucester Old Spot breeders and is the proud owner of the biggest herd in the country. I'm here to buy a boar to replace the father of my six female Old Spots (or gilts, as we call young girl pigs who have yet to mate or give birth). I can't have them breeding with their dad, so it's time to bring in a new bloodline.

Malcolm has three boars lined up for me, but before we get there I want to have a look at Josephine, a 300-kilo pedigree

Gloucester Old Spot sow which Malcolm hopes will win him the Champion of Champions trophy at the upcoming Royal Show in a month's time. It's a trophy he's brought home from the Royal for the last couple of years and is prestigious, to say the least. To even qualify you have to win one best of breed at a regional show and then join the other winners from around the country to be judged against each other – it's the FA cup of the Gloucester Old Spot world. The massive silver cup is pretty much the same size as the famous football trophy as well. Malcolm hopes that Josephine's name will soon be engraved alongside past champions and so is already planning her training and preparation regime. She's to be given a good scrub twice a week, and will receive a good application of pig oil to make sure her skin is supple and shiny. Then, she'll be trained to walk well around a ring. Unlike cattle you can't lead a pig with a lead, so you have to rely on a pig board and stick. A pig will never walk in a direction it can't see so you use the board to block its vision and guide it in the way you want it to go. The board also comes in handy every now and then as pigs who don't know each other can often fight. I've witnessed the odd scrap at shows over the years as competitors take chunks out of each other. Thankfully it's never happened to me, or to Malcolm for that matter.

This year's Royal – the 160th in its history – is going to be a bittersweet time, as it will be the last. Which is why Malcolm is even more determined to win some silverware this year. It will be his last journey to the show grounds at Stoneleigh Park to nab a Royal trophy.

'I'm really sad about it,' he confides in me. 'We're only 10 minutes' drive away from Stoneleigh so for all intents and purposes, it's our local show. And to win the Royal? Well, it's the pinnacle, isn't it? The ultimate prize. We've been showing the pigs there for the last seven years, but I've been going my entire life. It's not right thinking that my boys won't be growing up with the Royal as part of their life.'

Talking about William, he's desperate to show off his dad's prize boars, so we head over to their pens. They are lovely beasts and it's a really difficult decision. Which one am I going to choose? When buying Old Spots you want a nice flat back with good broad shoulders. You're also looking for big hams, the thigh and rump of the pig's haunch, plus a nice strong underline, that is the row of teats. Females will need to feed between 12 to 14 piglets, so you want two rows of seven teats evenly spaced, so when they're lying down the piglets can easily feed off her. Watching piglets scrabble to choose their teats for the first time can be hysterical. They actually set out a pecking order and once they've fought over the best seat in the house will stick with that self-same teat for as long as they are taking milk from their mother.

Malcolm gives me some more tips. It's nothing I don't know, but I don't mind taking advice from a champion of his stature. Besides, there really isn't much between these boys.

'Look at the heads when you're comparing boars. You need a good wide head and ears that come together at the end of its nose,' he tells me, as I walk from boar to boar. 'Also, check out their tails. If the tail is nicely curled up, you've got yourself a happy and healthy pig. If it's hanging down there's something amiss.'

In the end I go for a gorgeous 10-month-old boar that sets me back three hundred quid, but is a fantastic example of the breed.

As I pull away from South View Farm with my new boar safely tucked up in the trailer I can't help but think about what Malcolm said about the Royal Show's demise. He's right. It's always sad when a tradition dies, but in the case of the Royal it's been a long, drawn-out death and no one is really that surprised.

The Royal Show was originally a reaction from a group of Victorian agricultural giants, writers and landowners wanting to jump-start the English countryside after 20 years of decline and strife. In 1815, when the Battle of Waterloo ended the Napoleonic war, thousands of soldiers found themselves demobbed and out of work. They turned to the countryside for labour but found that positions were few and far between. The trouble was that while they had been away, agriculture had moved on and a whole host of new-fangled threshing machines had been invented to do the work of many, many men. Angry and starving, the out-of-work war veterans turned on the machines, sabotaging all they could find. In the city there were great Luddite uprisings, but in the rural areas of the south of England the situation got out of hand. On 28 August 1830, after over a decade of unemployment and the bad luck of three consecutive bad harvests, a threshing machine in Orpington, Kent was destroyed. Six weeks later the tally of wrecked machines throughout Kent had reached 100 and other counties were following suit. The riots continued well into 1831 and all the time farm owners, parsons and magistrates received threatening letters signed by an enigmatic individual who went by the name of 'Swing'. Most people took the choice of name to be a barely disguised threat of hanging. No one knows if Captain Swing, as he became known, was a real individual or an imaginary figurehead created to unite the protestors.

After the Swing Riots had died out, 19 rioters were executed and 644 found themselves imprisoned, while more than 500 were transported to Australia. The countryside, meanwhile, hit rock bottom and food production faltered. In 1838, the year of Queen Victoria's coronation, landowners formed the Agricultural Society, with a mandate to breathe new life into agricultural science. One of the society's first decisions was to hold an inaugural agricultural show in 1839. It took place in Oxford and was an immediate success, attended by 111,916 visitors. In honour of its achievement Victoria issued a royal charter the following year. The rest, as they say, is history.

We used to show sheep at the Royal and regularly showed at both the Rare Breed show, also held at Stoneleigh, and at the Three Counties show at Malvern. The latter is probably my favourite show, where farmers from the counties of Herefordshire, Worcestershire and Gloucestershire compete against each other.

Dad has always been keen on showing and used to judge at the Royal. At a very basic level, it's a fantastic way of letting people know that your stock is the best it possibly can be and a great way to advertise your farm to fellow breeders. One of my first reports for *Countryfile* saw me taking a Longhorn cow to the Three Counties. I was glad. While I was still new to this tele-vision lark, I knew what I was doing at a show, and winning the rare breed champion rosette on national TV wasn't bad either.

What was slightly more daunting was that I was also due to slip on my tie and jacket and do a spot of judging myself later in the day. Judging itself doesn't worry me. Dad's been doing it for years and my eldest sister is a rare breed judge who has judged on both sides of the Atlantic, so I knew what I was looking for. Like pigs, there are certain general characteristics, although each rare breed also has its own guidelines distinct to the breed, such as the right shaped ears, eyes or the colour of the face. On that particu-lar day I was judging sheep, both Soay and Hebridean, so I was looking for good strong teeth, a nice firm udder and the right frame. It's easier if they've got something really wrong, such as a twisted foot, small testicles or poor-quality wool, but if they're all pretty much perfect then it's incredibly difficult to put them into order. In the end you have to just go on what catches your eye. This is second nature to me, but this time was different. Suddenly I wasn't just Joe Henson's boy, I was that bloke off the telly. It was like being in a goldfish bowl, everyone peering in to see if I'd get things wrong. Judging can be highly pressured enough as it is – after all, it's a competitive world and everyone wants to win. There you stand in the middle of a field, with ten animals walking around you, every farmer dressed up in their white coat, all think-ing that their animal is the best. It's your job to say 'actually, yours didn't quite come up to scratch'. My new-found fame only intensified the pressure. Luckily everyone seemed to agree with my decisions and the Three Counties has asked me back many times over the last few years. It's still always nerve-racking though. I remember judging Belted Galloway cattle a couple of years ago. It was between two animals. There was a cow in calf that was really lovely and a bull that was absolutely magnificent. As a judge, I knew that whoever won would have to go on to the interbreed champion stage, to go against all the other cattle at the show. I had to think ahead and try and work out which one would stand out among the other champions. I chose the bull over the cow. As I was walking away, a few people came up to me and said, 'I wouldn't have gone for that bull, you know. He had a bit of a dip in his back.' Brilliant. I was in half a mind as it was. I still don't know to this day if I was right or wrong, but in those situations you have to stick to your guns and be confident.

One thing I am sure about is that agricultural shows are absolutely essential. They are one of the best ways for the general public to get a good insight into British agriculture. They can see the very best of livestock, get up close to the animals and are able to talk to the farmers and find out where their food comes from.

For the rural industry, not only do they give you the chance to show your stock, they're also a fantastic social event, a good excuse to see your mates and catch up. In fact, I'd go so far as to say they're pretty much vital when it comes to building a good community in farming. We are notoriously bad at giving ourselves time off, so for many farming families the local show is an event that forces people to get together and let your hair down a bit. Quite often an entire clan will take caravans, camp or stay at a nearby B&B. The adults will all enjoy a drink after the public has gone home, while the Young Farmers' Club will probably be as far away from their parents as possible. When I was a kid I used to love going to the rare breed show and sale that was held at Stoneleigh every year. It was a big family event. Mum and dad used to take a caravan and a lorryload of stock. Me and my sisters would earn a little extra pocket money helping out, leading animals in different rings all over the show. It was always exciting but always hard work.

The local Young Farmers' Club (YFC) took up a lot of my time when I was a teenager. There are 662 YFCs across England and Wales boasting 25,000 members, all aged between 10 and 26. You don't actually have to be from a farming family, but need to live in the countryside and the entire thing is organised to keep young people excited about rural life so that the next generation can be built up. There are weekly meetings and a lot of socialising but you also learn a lot of rural skills along the way from flower-arranging to woodwork and stock-judging to knowing how to gut, dress and get a chicken ready for the oven. Needless to say I was always terrible at flower-arranging, but could prepare a mean bird for the pot.

The indications are that local shows such as the Three Counties continue to do well, where the Royal itself has faltered. There are at least 24 other annual shows in the UK's farming calendar and many are booming. The largest two-day show, the Royal Norfolk, has already announced that from next year it's going to add an extra day to its timetable and the Royal Welsh

Agricultural show, founded a mere 105 years ago, attracted 236,000 visitors and raked in the cash, despite the rain.

And then there's the Royal Highland Show in Scotland, a four-day event that has been held for 225 years. The organisers expect more than 50,000 people through the gates every single day this year.

So, what went wrong with the Royal at Stoneleigh? According to the Royal Agricultural Society of England (RASE), the organisers of the show, support has dwindled over the last ten years. In 2001 the show was cancelled thanks to foot-and-mouth – something unheard of other than in times of war – and the recent batch of bad summers we've suffered in the UK didn't help. I can still remember the muddy scenes as the torrential rains of 2007 forced the show to close a day early after its car parks had been transformed into one massive, hazardous quagmire. It wasn't an easy decision and one only made after 30 acres of barley had been prematurely mown down to create emergency car parks. Unfortunately, it just wasn't enough.

A year later, bluetongue restrictions hit meaning yawning gaps in the cattle sheds. Usually you'd expect 1200 head of cattle and 1600 sheep on show. Instead they struggled to get 200 cattle and 400 sheep in the pens. No wonder so many people stayed away. Less than 100,000 visitors walked through the gates, amounting to a £200,000 loss in ticket sales alone. In its heyday, back in the 1980s, the Royal attracted well over 250,000.

Many reasons have been given for its decline, including the disease and weather problems I've already mentioned. RASE maintains that as there are fewer farms and fewer farmers, fewer people attend events such as this, while the credit crunch was the last nail in the Royal's coffin. Personally, I think the problems ran deeper than this. Granted, money did play its part, but I don't think for the reasons that have been given. In my opinion the Royal lost its way, becoming more about shopping than agriculture as the years went by. That's why fewer farmers went along. With fewer animals on show, RASE tried all kinds of stunts to keep people coming, the events in the grand ring becoming more and more elaborate. Anyone who's been to an agricultural show knows that the grand ring is always the home of some pretty amazing displays and the Royal was no exception. I've stood watching the Royal Horse Artillery or the marching Gurkha bands there; absolutely stunning but very, very expensive to book. And with dwindling crowds, the only way to recoup your money is to start hiking up the ticket price and the cost for farmers to show their animals. It became a vicious circle. Prices rose to cope with falling numbers and more people were put off making the trip as it became an increasingly expensive day out.

Another part of the downfall is that while at one time everyone went to a general agricultural show, there are now a whole host of specialist shows throughout the year. There are dairy and livestock shows, pig and poultry shows, the cereals show and tillage events for tractors. The list is endless. While these have less appeal for the general public, they're ideal for farmers and also for the all-important exhibitors. Why spend money on exhibiting at a general interest show when you know your customers are going to be somewhere else? It seems that even someone at RASE has finally taken notice. The Royal may be dead, but a series of year-round events has been planned in its wake, including an annual Festival of the Horse. There's also talk of Royal livestock competitions. Malcolm Hicks will be pleased. He's probably still got a little bit of space left in his trophy cabinet.

But, as dad said when he heard about the axing of the Royal, it's not our farmers and our business we have to worry about. It's Britain's standing in the international farming community. 'The Royal Show was our shop window, Adam,' he said on the day the news of its demise broke. 'Our own farmers will just go to their local shows, but we'll lose the international visitors. The Royal wasn't competing with the Three Counties – at least it shouldn't have been. It was competing with the Paris show. People who came over to Britain to look at pedigree livestock will now stop off in France instead.'

One good British farmer I know is Richard Barter who runs Berrow Farm in Ashleworth, Gloucestershire where he produces goats' milk. I love going to Berrow Farm because it's such a fantastic operation. Richard has 11,000 goats on the farm producing 725,000 litres of milk every year, most of which is sold to supermarkets. Every time I come by I pick up a new trick of the trade. This time is no different. As we walk through the goat sheds there is a line of goats poking their heads through the feeder and munching away merrily at their TMR – total measured ration.

'This looks like dairy cow feed,' I comment, scooping up a handful of the stuff.

'It's maize silage,' he explains, 'in essence, corn on the cob. The entire maize plant is chopped up and red clover, whole oats and soya added.'

'Well, they do say that goats eat anything.'

'If only that were true, Adam. Come back here tomorrow morning and all you'll find is the centre of the cob but they would have spent most of their time picking out the soya and tasty grains first. Saying goats will eat anything is a bit of an old wives' tale. They'll chew anything, but they're picky about what they eat.'

Talking of which, the reason I've stopped by is waiting for me in the next shed – or perhaps that should that be reasons. Just over a year ago I sold Richard two Old Spot gilts. The girls – which he named Itchy and Scratchy – were pets for the family, but ultimately were destined to end up in the family's larder.

'We couldn't do it, Adam,' Richard admits when I asked him why Itchy and Scratchy were still alive and well 15 months later. 'I mean, they're pedigree registered stock. Too good to go to the freezer.'

'And it's nothing to do with the fact that you fell in love with them and you're an old softy?'

He gives me a look that lets me know that's nearer the truth. But I don't mind. As my gilts back home are only six months old, they are not really ready to go to my new boar. I've therefore offered to buy Itchy and Scratchy back. It helps Richard and suits me. The pigs are my bloodline and look in fantastic condition. They're ready to breed and will speed up production quite a bit. I give him £250 and he helps me load the girls back on to the trailer.

It isn't until we get back to the farm that I introduce the boar to his new wives. It has to be said that it's not exactly love at first sight. The boar sniffs around them, grunting well and showing all the signs of dominance. Sometimes, there is a worry that when you introduce a new boar to sows they'll turn on him and beat him up, taking him down a peg or two. There isn't any danger of that here. Itchy and Scratchy give him one look and wander off to explore their new home. No interest at all.

Hopefully, love will be in the air any day soon.

CHAPTER 7

GOING TO WORK ON AN EGG

We have always had chickens scratching around on the farm, but they've been even more of a hobby than our porkers. We do keep some chickens to show on the farm park and also to produce chicks for our young visitors to fuss over and hold come the spring, but it's never gone further than that. Some of the rare breeds are really attractive birds. Scots Dumpies, for example, are an ancient native breed. Archaeologists reckon there have been Dumpies north of the border for 700 years, known by a multitude of names including bakies, hoodies, daidies and – best of all – creepies, thanks to their stubby little legs. They come in a variety of colours, but are known mainly for their black and cuckoo fineries, the latter being a mottled mix of black and white. While Dumpies were a regular sight at poultry and country shows in the second half of the nineteenth century, they had all but died out by 1970, when a band of Dumpie fanciers worked hard to re-establish them.

Another of my favourite breeds isn't actually a native to these shores, but was introduced to Britain in 1928. The hen of the

Welsummer breed – named after the village of Welsum in Holland – is a pretty golden-brown bird with a long copper and yellow neck. But it's the cockerel that's the most impressive, with its bright red wattle and comb, golden neck and red-brown shoulders. The rest of its body and tail are covered with glossy black feathers with the slightest hint of green sheen. It's like every cockerel you've ever seen in a storybook.

While no one can answer the question of whether the chicken came before the egg, Charles Darwin maintained that every domestic chicken in the world is descended from the red jungle fowl, a bird found in the Far East. Recent research from the University of Uppsala in Sweden indicates that the author of *On the Origin of Species* was partly right. Most of the genes in domesticated fowls do come from the red jungle fowl, although at some point, early on in chicken farming, it was crossed with the grey jungle fowl, giving modern chickens their yellow legs.

Either way, in Britain chickens only became destined for the pot in Roman times. Before that they were used either in rituals by the Celts or, more often than not, for cockfights. Now they are one of our favourite meals. Fifty years ago, they were still a treat for most people and your average man on the street would eat less than a kilo of chicken meat every single year. Today, we eat double that in a month, around 23 kilos a year on average.

And then of course, there are eggs. We love eggs in this country, boiling, frying, poaching and scrambling our way through 29 million eggs per day. That's a staggering figure. You might even say eggs-traordinary (sorry, I won't do that again, I promise).

However, producing the sheer number of eggs needed to satisfy that demand is certainly no joke. Britain is home to approximately 29 million laying hens. At present, just to meet demand, 24 million of Britain's egg-layers are battery hens, producing 72 per cent of our eggs and living out their life in cramped conditions in rows and rows of cages. Usually four or five birds are crammed in one cage, unable to follow their natural instincts to perch, dust-bathe or even flap their wings.

At the moment, under current legislation, a single shed can contain up to 30,000 birds and, as egg-laying is prompted by sunlight, artificial lighting is kept blazing away for around 17 hours a day to increase production. Food and water are delivered automatically, again to ensure that as many eggs as possible are laid.

And it works. These battery hens are egg-laying machines, some even producing 300 eggs per year. That's even more staggering when you consider that their wild ancestors would have only produced between 12 and 20 eggs a year. The young hens are kept in intensive conditions until they are ready to start producing eggs – when they are between 18 to 20 weeks – before they are transferred to the cages, ready to live out their lives in an area roughly the size of an A4 sheet of paper.

Although it is something I haven't been brought up with, and is poles away from the way we keep our rare breeds, I totally understand the need for intensive farming. To feed a growing world population, food grown on a massive scale is a necessity and the UK can boast the highest welfare standards in the world.

OK, so some intensive systems may not be perfect, but they're getting better all the time.

In recent years the situation for chickens has been changing. Intensively reared chickens, both meat birds – known as broilers – and egg-layers, have hardly been out of the news recently. A number of celebrity chefs, including Hugh Fearnley-Whittingstall and Jamie Oliver, have taken to heart the plight of these birds and have run high-profile campaigns to promote better welfare conditions.

Keeping chickens has also become fashionable. All over the country, chicken coops started appearing in back gardens, even in the city. Omlet, a firm that makes trendy henhouses, reckons that every year sees its sales double. It is selling more than 15,000 houses every 12 months, with 70 per cent apparently going into urban gardens. Do-it-yourself chain B&Q reports that sales of its own coops are rising 25 per cent year on year. No wonder that membership of the Henkeepers' Association is booming – it has seen record growth, with 8000 new members in just four years. Britain has gone chicken-crazy.

One charity had been keeping an eye on this trend and realised that it could use the nation's new-found love of fowl to help battery hens. The British Hen Welfare Trust – formally known as the Battery Hen Welfare Trust – was founded by Jane Howarth in 2003. She'd long been concerned about the ultimate fate of battery hens after watching a BBC *Panorama* programme back in the 1970s called 'Down on Factory Farm'. She learned about the poor conditions of the birds, and also their eventual fate. Chickens can live for around six years, but after just 12 months of laying, the ability of battery hens to produce eggs starts to fall. In a battery system you need every hen laying as many eggs as possible and so, after 12 months in the cages, the birds are killed. As they've never put on much weight, they can't be eaten in the conventional way and so they are minced up for processed food. Jane was horrified and began writing to any MP she thought would listen to see if she could help. The most heartbreaking thing for her was that she couldn't do anything personally. She would have loved to save some battery hens from the chop but didn't herself have the space. That changed when she moved to Devon and started to take in hens, rescued from battery farms. She started with a handful, but still wanted to do more, so in 2003 persuaded a battery farmer to give her 200 of his old hens and these she successfully rehomed around the country. The trust has now rescued 60,000 hens from slaughter by finding them homes as pets through a network of 25 regional centres. I really like Jane's attitude. In interviews she is always keen to support British farmers rather than attack them – trust me, this sometimes feels like a novel approach – and has even said that she'd rather we had caged birds in the UK than started to import caged eggs from overseas. It's a refreshing change.

My partner Charlie knew about Jane's work, as Charlie's sister had already taken in some former battery hens. Then one day she asked if we could get some. At first, I have to admit I wasn't too keen. 'If you want some nice hens in the garden, why not get some lovely rare breed ones?' I said, pointing out that we still had quite a lot of chickens on the farm. Then an idea struck me. We do use an awful lot of eggs on the farm and in the farm park. Perhaps getting some more chickens wouldn't be such a bad thing. If we could get 50 or so ex-battery hens then they might be able to lay enough eggs for baking in the farm park kitchen or to sell to people staying on our campsite. So the call was made and Charlie and I were soon on the way to our local trust centre to pick up our battery veterans.

I have to say nothing had prepared me for the state of the birds that volunteers Molly and Ian showed us. To say they were in a sorry state is a complete understatement. The rescued birds are straggly and almost naked, their feathers rubbed off by the bars of the cage. When we arrived Molly was carefully clipping their talons, which had grown to an astounding length. The reason she gave was actually quite sickening, 'They've never stood on a solid floor before, so they've never had the chance to wear their claws down.'

As a farmer it's difficult to come to terms with such things. I hate seeing animals kept in such poor conditions, but can see how we've ended up here. Our demand for millions of cheap eggs every year has led to birds being kept in these cages. It's business, pure and simple – but it doesn't sit easily with me.

Nor does it seem to sit well with the European Union. Conventional battery cages will be banned across Europe from 2012, although that doesn't mean the end of cages completely. New 'enriched' cages will become the norm. Instead of having 450 sq cm of space, each bird will have 600 sq cm, plus a nest box, a scratching area and a perch raised seven centimetres from the floor of the cage. Some campaigners say that this isn't enough, and have called for the government to ban the use of any cage but the poultry industry has pointed out that if this happens, the supermarkets will simply look elsewhere for cheap eggs. British farmers won't be able to compete. Plus, more and more of us are eating free-range eggs. Ten years ago, less than five per cent of the eggs in our shopping baskets were free-range. Today that figure stands at around 23 per cent. Free-range hens are housed in barns, but have access to the great outdoors. While this is all very well – and it's exactly how I want my hens to live – the price of free-range eggs can easily double by the time they hit the supermarket shelves. Better conditions cost money and the question is whether we're happy to say goodbye to our cheap eggs.

Hopefully, it's not a choice I'm going to have to worry about from now on. As soon as Charlie and I got our former battery hens back to the farm we popped them in one of our old chicken runs. It's just a temporary home until I get something better but for the moment that doesn't matter. When rehousing battery hens you need to keep them inside at first and away from other birds so they don't get too stressed. There's a lot of work to be done, but I can't help but feel satisfied that we've given these scraggly birds a new start in life.

All that happened this morning, and this evening I'm going to be picking up even more hens, but for the moment I'm at a neighbouring farm. Just after I made sure our latest arrivals were safe in their new home I received a call from Duncan, my business partner. He's at a farm sale trying to shift our old gear and has spotted something that might help me with my new egg venture, so I go along to have a look.

Farm sales are a bargain hunter's delight. They usually happen when farmers are selling up or wanting to make some extra cash. It's a way of auctioning off their old equipment to recoup some money and I love pottering around them to see what I can pick up. Occasionally, the host farm will allow other farmers to take kit along for sale. It makes sense. The more gear you have for sale, the more chance you've got of attracting larger crowds and pushing up the prices.

Duncan is here as we're trying to shift some of our old stuff. We've not brought a lot to sell, just some odds and ends really, but the thing we want shot of is our old red Kuhn fertiliser spreader. Although it's a bit rusty in places, it's in pretty good nick and works perfectly. Dunc's put a reserve of £750 on it to ensure that we're not just giving it away and, if it sells, the money raised will help offset its replacement.

But before the auctioneer starts the bidding the place is full of people wandering here and there, looking at the agricultural treasures arranged around the field. The spreader seems to be attracting a lot of interest, which is good, but I'm here to look at Duncan's find.

'It's over here, Adam,' he says, leading me past an old horse-drawn plough that looks like it came straight off the Ark and a pile of buckets and tubs. 'There you are...'

Dunc is right. He has found something unusual. It's a large, grey nest box that will be ideal for my new chickens. Ten chickens sit in little plastic nest cubbyholes, five at the top and five at the bottom. Once the eggs are laid, they roll to the back of the box where they collect in little trays ready to be collected. It's a clever little system that will keep everything nice and clean.

With still some time before the auction, Dunc and I have a walk around, seeing if there's anything else we want and catching up with old mates. These auctions are little social events in themselves, and we allow ourselves a break to chat with friends in the sunshine. Well, it can't always be work, work, work you know. Everywhere I look there are old rugby mates and neighbouring farmers dressed in their old overalls and work boots. It'll be straight back to everyone's farm when the sale is over.

As soon as the auctioneer announces that the sale is about to commence, it's every man for himself. We've all got our eyes on something or other, and there's plenty of friendly banter to put each other off. You need to concentrate to get what you want for the right price.

Our fertiliser spreader is soon up and so I wander over to lurk in the background and see how it goes.

The auctioneer starts at £600 but no-one bites, so he tries £500. Still no bids. I hope this isn't a bad sign. As we've put a reserve of £750 on it, the auctioneer won't sell it for anything less, but I'd rather we weren't carting it home again later on. £450? Nothing. £400. Yes, one of the farmers standing around nods ever so slightly. The auctioneer sees it and acknowledges the bid. Well, it's a start. Soon the price starts to rise as the farmers get into a mini-bidding war. £450. £500. £600. Nearly there. £750. Yes, we've done it – that's a sale. But then it keeps going. £800. £850. Getting better by the second. All eyes are now on the auctioneer.

'Do I hear £900? No? £875? Yes, £875. Any other bids. Done then.'

When the auctioneer slaps his walking stick down on his list of lots the auction comes to an end. £875, that's a better result than I expected. I'm happy with that.

The auctioneer walks from lot to lot taking the crowd of eager bidders with him. Eventually we get to lot 221, the chicken nest box I'm after. Hopefully this won't go too high. Whenever you're doing an auction, it's good to decide how far you're willing to go in bidding. The trick then is to stick to it. In this case, I'm only really willing to pay a maximum of fifty quid, but even though this isn't a lot of money it's all too easy to get carried away and end up paying over the odds if someone's bidding against you.

We gather around the rectangular metal box.

'OK,' starts the auctioneer, 'what are we going to say for this? £30?'

It's under what I'm willing to pay but you never go for the first price called. If you do, you could end up paying more than you need to, or have it escalate so it goes over your highest offer.

'£20?' the auctioneer continues, '£10?'

Right, that's a better starting price. I nod at the auctioneer. I'd definitely take it for a tenner.

Not that I'll get the chance. It's soon obvious I'm not the only person after the box. A tall chap in a rugby top and green coat standing beside me seems to have also taken a fancy to it. He put's in a bid for £12 and I counter with £18. This is hardly big money, but it's fun.

The bidding goes quickly. After all, this is only a little lot and the auctioneer doesn't want to waste too much time on it. It's amazing how exciting it is to bid for something. At that precise moment in time, all you can think of is winning.

It's between me and Mr Rugby Top. It's £22 now, then £25. £28? Yes, I give a nod. £30? I can see out of the corner of my eye that my rival has stopped bidding. I've got it then.

'Going at £28?' concludes the auctioneer, before slapping down his stick once again. 'Selling and done then. Henson and Andrews. Thank you, Adam.'

Once the clerk has noted down our company name and marked us as the winner, the crowd bustles off to lot 222. I'm chuffed though. It's an absolute bargain. Fantastic.

A good afternoon all round then, but I can't wait about. There are more chickens to pick up.

It's not just battery hens that reach the end of their commercial life – it happens to organic chickens too. On the way back to the farm I take a slight detour to Abbey Home Farm near Cirencester. Abbey Home is a 1600-acre farm run by tenant farmers Will and Hilary Chester-Master and their farm manager John Newman who's been here since 1992. Like us, Abbey Home is a mixed farm with both livestock and arable crops but unlike

Bemborough, they're organic. They have a small dairy herd of 25 Shorthorn cows plus a pedigree herd of good old Gloucester cattle for beef. As well as sheep and pigs they have 740 acres of cereal – mainly wheat, oats and barley – and 37 acres of 80 different varieties of vegetables. It's quite an impressive set-up.

But I'm here for the chickens. Farm manager John is doing me a little deal and once I've tracked him down I clamber over an elaborate fox-proof double fence system to meet my new birds. John starts passing them over to me to pop in my crate. I'm picking up two breeds. First up are Silver Links. They are beautiful cream birds at the best of times, but I can't get over how healthy they look compared to the scruffy battery hens I picked up earlier today. Talk about chalk and cheese. The only real similarity is that the Silver Links are also prolific layers, which can produce around 300 lovely brown eggs a year at their peak.

'They're around two years old now,' he tells me as we crate them up, 'and they're starting to slow down egg-wise. They'll still produce enough for someone who wants to keep chickens in their back garden or yourself but they don't quite produce enough now to meet our needs. We need to move them on to make room for some younger birds.' It's a numbers game and with tight margins, optimum production is critical, even in an organic set-up like this.

I'm also taking some Black Rock chickens, which is Abbey Home Farm's main breed. These are bigger hens; almost jet black save for a little chestnut around the neck. They are slightly less prolific than the Silver Links and are expected to produce around 230-odd eggs a year.

Just when I've got most of the hens in the crate, one Black Rock makes a bid for freedom and flaps out of my hand. This prompts a good few minutes of chasing around trying to capture it, but I've soon got her and she doesn't complain when I put her in with the rest. Poor old girl. She obviously doesn't want to leave. I can't blame her; Abbey Home is a lovely, calming place.

But I hope the hens will enjoy their new home back at our farm. We won't be keeping them as organic as we don't operate under an organic scheme, but they'll definitely be free-range, allowed to wander with not a cage in sight. I'm determined that they'll be happy hens with us and I'm certainly looking forward to all the eggs.

Back at Bemborough, I release the Silver Links and Black Rocks into their field. For now, I'm using another of our old coops, but am going to do some work to make the field even more suitable for them, getting some more huts and, of course, installing my new egg nest box from the auction.

At the moment, we're keeping the birds from Abbey Home separate from the battery hens. Chicken communities have quite severe pecking orders – it's where we get the phrase from – and each hen has to fight it out for their place in the grand scheme of things. We're not talking bloodshed here or all-out war, but if a chicken puts a claw out of place, they'll receive a short, sharp jab of the beak so that they soon remember their place. A chicken at the bottom of the pecking order usually has to let everyone else eat first. Some resort to running in and trying to steal some food, but, again, they risk the wrath of their superiors.

With this in mind I don't want to put the weaker ex-battery hens in there. They just won't be able to compete at the moment, and they've had a harsh enough life already. I don't want to add bullying to their woes. It won't last forever, and once their feathers have grown out and they've put on a little weight I'm hoping that they'll all live happily together.

Talking of which, it's time to give the battery hens their first real taste of freedom. Walking around the other side of the farmhouse, I find them all quite happy sat inside their coop. But the moment has come. I undo the door and stand back. At first, they sit inside looking at me and then slowly, one by one they start venturing out into the great big world. I sit back on a post and do what people who keep chickens have done for centuries. It is possible to lose hours watching chickens meander about. The amazing thing about these particular birds is that they've been shut inside cages all their life, and yet here they are doing everything a chicken should – scratching, pecking, exploring the great wide world. It's phenomenal, watching them exert their natural instincts; instincts that have been repressed for so long.

CHAPTER 8

LAMBS TO THE SLAUGHTER

It seems like only yesterday that the lambing sheds were full of pregnant ewes, but time marches on and as it's now mid-July the first are being sent off for slaughter. No matter how cute they were when they were born, this is no time for sentimentality. It's time for business so I'm out with three of my dogs, rounding the lambs into pens to check which ones will make the grade. Working with three dogs is quite tricky, especially with Milly still being so inexperienced, but they seem to be going OK and it's good to give them a run.

After a while you can pretty much tell whether a lamb is ready for the abattoir by just looking at them. You're after a live weight – quite literally the weight it is when it's still alive – of around 40 kilos. Our lambs usually reach 40 kilos within four months of being born and we'll continue going through this process until December when the last lambs of last spring will be rounded up and sold.

Like all things on the farm, there's a knack to choosing the right lamb. With a group of them all in front of me, both commercial and a few rare breeds, I cast an eye over the flock. Right at the front there's a male who looks about right so I go over to him and start feeling over his back. You work your hands along the spinal recesses to see how many bumps you can feel. Ideally you'll pick one with a good covering of meat, meaning that you can't really feel the individual vertebrae of the spine. This one isn't ready yet. As soon as I press against him I can feel his backbone and ribs. He hasn't got enough meat cover so he's no good this time. That's the trouble with all this long wool. Sometimes looks can be deceiving.

The lamb next to him is a different story however. I check his back, shoulders and dock – his tail. This is more like it. I can hardly feel any bones and his meat is solid to the touch, not too fatty at all. Double-checking on the scales, I discover that he's pretty much bang on 40 kilos. Perfect. He's off to the abattoir then.

At the moment the price of lamb is pretty good. This fellow is worth about £3.80 a kilo dead weight. When a lamb is slaughtered, skinned and gutted it loses about 50 per cent of its weight. So a 40-kilo live lamb will be 20 kilos once it's dead and prepared. If you're getting around £4 a kilo dead weight it means you'll receive around £80 per carcass.

This price isn't constant throughout the year and varies depending on availability. As you'd expect, if there isn't much lamb on the market the price is high, dropping off as the markets flood. This is why some farmers try to lamb as early as possible. It usually depends on when the grass grows. People in the south, say Devon and Cornwall, start lambing earlier as it's slightly warmer down there and as you move up the country the lambing season gets later and later. In Scotland they won't start lambing until late April.

Of course there are always exceptions to the rule. As I've mentioned, my new colleague on *Countryfile*, former *Blue Peter* presenter Matt Baker, also comes from a sheep-farming family. His parents farm up in the beautiful Durham dales and keep Hampshire Down ewes that come into season early. While most of us are sitting down to our Christmas dinner, Matt's folks are in the lambing sheds with newborns popping out here, there and everywhere. He's told me quite a few stories about opening Christmas presents when he was young while sitting on hay bales so his mum and dad could keep an eye on pregnant ewes.

So why go to so much trouble to lamb three months before the rest of us? Simple really – economics. At the time when I'm gathering the ewes into the lambing sheds, the shepherds in Devon (and Matt's parents too) will be almost ready to send their lambs to market. As meat will be thin on the ground then, they'll clean up, demanding more money. Some will even be ready to slaughter when the rest of us haven't started. They are so ahead of the trade they'll get a fantastic price, although they will be spending much more on feed to get the lambs through the cold weather. Around now, when the lambs that arrived on our farm are ready to go, there will be a glut of lambs so prices, while not exactly rock bottom, will be lower. The lambs I'm weighing today will face a lot of competition.

Once they get to the abattoir and are slaughtered they'll face even more tests. Each slaughterhouse has an independent grader who examines the carcasses. There are two types of grades. The first is for fatness and is graded from one to five. One is very skinny and five is far too fat. Hopefully most of today's lambs will be about three – the optimum grade.

The second grade is the conformation, which relates to the shape of the carcass its general build and form. It has all to do with the sheep's skeleton and the depth and distribution of its fat. Just sorting out the sheep today I can see which will do well in conformation grading. Ideally you're looking for short, stocky legs and strong, thick loins. The back must be well rounded and the width of the breast and shoulder around the same as the depth of the chest. The final sign is a short, plump neck. It's all about symmetry, and in layman's terms, if you've got a lamb with good conformation you're going to get a good load of chops and cuts from the carcass.

Conformation is all down to the breeding. I look at the two lambs I've just weighed. One is a Texel, a breed that hails from the Frisian island of Texel, one of the most westerly islands off the Dutch coast. Introduced to Britain in the last 50 years, the Texel is hardy enough to survive harsh winters but has been bred specifically for meat. At the minute it's standing next to a Romney lamb. Whereas the Texel was bred for meat, the Romney was bred for its lustrous long wool. Originally introduced to Kent by the Romans, the Romney was exported to New Zealand in 1853, where it's still incredibly popular thanks to its wool, which is used in blankets, knitting yarn and carpets. But like many wool breeds it's not known for its meat. You can eat it, but its conformation doesn't stack up, thanks to its narrow back end and shoulders. In this case, I'm going to keep this Romney for breeding as the breed is very prolific.

On the whole, lamb prices are pretty fair at the moment. It's been a very long time coming but, finally, if you can lamb efficiently you can make good money. To improve our chances we don't go it alone. A farm our size would never produce enough meat to supply a supermarket, so we've teamed up with a number of different farmers in the area to create a cooperative. The Cotswold Lamb Group has more than 100 members and between us we produce around 150,000 lambs every year. These are sold together under the Cotswold Quality Lamb brand and means that we're dealing with the kind of numbers you need to be a player in the supermarket system. Being a member of a cooperative also means we can buy our veterinary medicines or sheep feed concentrate together. Bulk orders mean better deals so it's a lot cheaper than going it alone.

Our lamb group isn't unique. There are other similar set-ups elsewhere in the country, but it's still not as common as it could have been. The French, on the other hand, are exceptionally good at schemes such as this in ways that British farmers generally aren't.

It's probably because we're used to our farms being more self-contained and competitive. There's a completely different system in France. When a French father gives up his farm, he breaks it up into smaller concerns between his children. Over here only the eldest usually gets it, or the child who's shown the most interest in farming. That means that in France there are simply more people involved in agriculture. And they like to make themselves heard. There have been a number of cases where farmers have marched on central Paris when prices have fallen. I've read of straw bales dumped over all over the Champs Élysées, or hundreds of thousands of gallons of milk poured on to fields next to Normandy's Mont Saint-Michel. While I'm not about to glamorise such protests or suggest we submerge Parliament Hill under gallons of the white stuff, it just goes to show that French farmers are used to being heard.

In the UK, it's the opposite, mainly because we've shut ourselves off. Farming has quite a small voice and if we ever want people to start listening the only way we'll do it is to join forces and work together.

There is, however, one thing that sheep farmers should be fighting for – British wool. As I wrote earlier in this book, Britain's riches were built on our wool trade but sadly those days are long gone.

We're now bang in the middle of the shearing season. It starts around May, although we have been giving the sheep a little trim for a while now. About a couple weeks before shearing starts we start crutching the sheep – which means cleaning up their back end. As the grass gets lusher in spring, the sheep eat more of it and what goes in, must come out. As they pass more dung, the long wool around their bums starts to get clogged up as the muck sticks to the fibres. You need to keep on top of this for two main reasons. First is simple cleanliness. When you get the sheep into the shearing pens you don't want the muck spread all over the floor, getting in the fleeces and all over you. Then there's a health issue. Unsurprisingly, the muck around the rear end attracts blowflies. The little pests think Christmas has come early and lay their eggs in mess. When the eggs hatch into maggots they begin eating the sheep alive in a very sensitive spot. Not nice at all.

The best way to deal with this is to clip the dags – the lumps of muck-encrusted wool – from around the bum. It also gives us the chance to give the sheep a once-over before shearing, checking their feet for foot rot, a fiercely contagious infection which does exactly what it says, literally rotting away the area between the sheep's toes. If it's found, the animal is given a quick toe-trim and some antibiotics. A haircut and a manicure in one day. Can't be bad.

Our ancient ancestors had no need to shear sheep. The breeds they reared simply moulted every year and the farmer's family would wander around picking it up. Then the wool industry began to grow and farmers realised the value of wool and began to selectively breed sheep that hung on to their wool. Eventually they'd bred out the ability to moult. Instead, shepherds had to start shearing, clipping the wool from the animal's skin. The more the industry grew and the more money the merchants made, the more sheep were bred to produce more wool. It was simple supply and demand. And then, over years, the wool market dwindled away and we were left with these huge, cumbersome fleeces. We couldn't just leave them on the sheep. In the summer sun the sheep would simply expire in the heat, and the fleece itself could become infested with parasites. Again, blowflies could lay their eggs in the fleece, which would lead to maggot problems.

The main problem is that a sheep fleece is pretty much worthless these days. In days gone by, every wardrobe in the land was bursting with good old woolly jumpers. Not any more. These days our clothes are made from nylon, polyester, Lycra and – if you're after a touch of luxury – maybe some cashmere. The golden fleece of yesteryear has fallen out of favour. Even though we live in a country that paid for its great houses and waged war on the proceeds of the wool trade, you're lucky if you can get two quid for a whole fleece. And that's on a good day. The mad thing is that it often costs more to shear a single sheep.

There's certainly no shortage of help. Gangs of sheep-shearers travel the country, moving from farm to farm although you'll be hard pushed to meet a British shearer. Most are from Down Under, Australians and Kiwis. These lads and lasses travel all over the world, shearing as they go. They'll be here for a few months and then they'll work their way through Europe or the States on their way back Down Under. It's good money but back-breaking work, which is the real reason that there are hardly any British shearers any more. The job's just not attractive enough. The guys from Australia and New Zealand don't seem to mind. They've turned it into a kind of sport and have massive sheep-shearing tournaments back home.

Sheep-shearers get paid per sheep so the more they get through, the more they earn. At the moment the going rate is about £1.20 per animal and a professional shearer can get through a lot of sheep in a day. Back in the 1930s, using hand clippers, you could expect to shear around eight sheep an hour, about 64 sheep per day. When mechanical clippers appeared on the market, the rate increased.

When I was about 16, I was taught to shear by an old boy who used to come to our farm to shear our sheep. I can't remember his surname as we only used to know him as Bob the Cider Drinker. Living up to his nickname, Bob taught me how to drink cider and shear sheep – but not necessarily in that order. His style was quite old fashioned, doing the belly and neck first, going round and round, a bit like peeling an apple. Today the methods have changed quite a lot and the Bowen method – developed unsurprisingly by a New Zealander – means that you shear a sheep much quicker. The idea is to use as few blows (a blow being one movement of the clippers) as possible. You work in a certain order, covering the belly and crotch first, then the left hind leg and rump before moving up to the throat and left side, the back and the head and finally the right side.

My style is probably a mixture of both methods, but I can still remove a fleece in about two and a half minutes, which is pretty good going and means I can get through about a hundred in a day. That's nothing compared to the shearing gangs. A single guy can work his way through up to 400 sheep in a day. It's staggering to watch. But at over a pound a pop, if you've got a large flock shearing is an expensive time of year, especially as at the moment wool is only worth around 60p a kilo. If you consider that you only get a couple of kilos off the back of most of the sheep on our farm, you can see that sometimes the price of the wool doesn't even stretch as far as paying for it to be shorn. Ever heard the term fleeced? Well, that's how most sheep farmers feel about their wool. And we're not as badly hit as some farmers. In Cumbria it's almost impossible to shift the Herdwick's coarse fleece. And most of the wool merchants are so far away they'd never recoup the cost of the diesel used in transporting the fleeces, so you hear stories of wool being bundled up and set alight. That can't be easy, as wool is naturally flame-retardant.

On our farm, we cut down this expense by shearing our own sheep. Mike and Andy, our stockmen, do most of the work, although I help out when I can. We stretch it over six weeks so that we can shear in front of the public at the farm park. At least that way we can try to teach them how great British wool is.

And that's what really gets my goat. We should be championing British wool far more than we do. It's worked with local food, why not wool? First of all, unlike man-made fibres, it's not made from oil meaning that it isn't drawing on our ever-dwindling natural resources. It's also such a high-quality product. If you scrunch wool up in your hand and let it go, it will always spring back to its original shape because of the way the fibres work. Those same fibres also mean that breathable wool can keep you warm in winter but cool in spring. And I challenge anyone to prove to me that a carpet made from man-made fibres is anywhere near as hard-wearing as a wool one. The same goes for suits. A wool suit simply lasts longer and doesn't go thin and shiny over time. They can still be made of fine wool if you're after a summer suit.

Of course, the one thing wool can't do is compete with the cheaper alternatives on the high street. There's no way the British wool industry can cope with cheap, mass-produced clothes from China and the Far East. We've gone too far down that route to turn back now, but in just the same way as customers are willing to pay that little bit extra for organic food, we need to convince fashion-lovers to do the same for wool. There's a corny saying that local food campaigners have been using for years; if you want to keep the countryside looking the way it does you need to eat the view, buying British food to support the farmers who maintain the landscape. I think that we should be telling people to wear the view for the same reason. If you want to see sheep dotted around our hills, grazing merrily away, then you need to buy the wool off their back.

Thankfully, there does seem to be some movement in the right direction. Most of the wool produced in this country is sold to the British Wool Marketing Board. You roll up your fleeces, bung them in woolsacks, send it off to the board and wait for your cheque to arrive in the post. Most of the white wool from the commercial flock goes to the board, although we have started to export more and more of it to Ireland, which is an up-and-coming market. They pay more than the wool board, anyway.

Our rare breed wool is a different case. Most of it is coloured and wouldn't be touched by the wool board, so we sell it to spinners and weavers who enjoy working with its different textures and shades. Thank heavens the trend for white wool in the twentieth century didn't completely kill off rare multi-coloured fleeces and further remove the variety in Britain's flocks. The Wensleydale is a lovely sheep that was originally bred for milk, from which Wensleydale cheese was made. Its fleece, which is long and lustrous, can be either black or creamy white, while the traditional knitted shawls that are made from Shetland wool are said to be so fine that they can be pulled through a wedding ring.

There are good signs that this side of the market, however niche, is starting to grow. Earlier in the year we struck up a deal with the Natural Fibre Company down in Launceston, Cornwall. They've been spinning wool since they were set up in Lampeter in Wales in 1991 but after moving to Cornwall in 2005 they have really increased production, spinning high-quality yarn in ten different colours as well as their own range of blankets, cushions and scarves.

They get our best rare-breed fleeces, the result of the first year of a lamb's life. New lambs aren't shorn until they are at least 18 months old. Up to this point they've had nothing to do except eat grass and grow wool. That year-old fleece – known as the teg year– is the best quality a lamb will ever produce. Once they've started having lambs, they'll start getting a little stressed and the wool suffers. At the moment, the partnership is working well for us, although my first visit to MD Sue Blacker's office was a little tense when she noticed that we use spray markers on our sheep. While the dye is supposed to be able to be washed out, Sue said it takes far too much scouring. So she doesn't use that bit of the fleece, but I don't mind. I'm just happy that our wool is being used, one way or another. In the back of my mind, I have plans to sell scarves and jumpers made with our wool direct from the farm park, but one step at a time.

CHAPTER 9

RAIN, RAIN GO AWAY

In days gone by, every farmer would have turned his head to the skies on 15 July. The reason is found in an old, traditional rhyme,

> *St Swithin's day if thou dost rain*
> *For forty days it will remain*
> *St Swithin's day if thou be fair*
> *For forty days 'twill rain nae mair*

Saint Swithin was a Saxon bishop who died on 2 July 862. His dying wish was that he would be laid to rest in a humble grave in the grounds of Winchester Cathedral, so that his beloved flock could walk across it. However on 15 July 971 the then bishop decided that the saint needed a grander memorial. His bones were dug up and transferred to an elaborate shrine in the cathedral. However, a fierce storm broke over Winchester as soon as his body was removed from its original grave and didn't subside for 40 days and 40 nights. Locals feared it was the spirit of the saint showing his displeasure that his final wishes had been ignored.

This story gave rise to the myth that if it rains on the 15 July – St Swithin's feast day – it will rain solidly for 40 days.

Today, of course, we rely on more scientific means to predict the weather – although the results aren't always reliable. Back in April, I opened the paper to find the Met Office saying we were 'odds on for a barbecue summer'. According to the chief meteorologist, Ewen McCallum, we could expect summer temperatures in Britain to be warmer than average and the levels of rainfall near or below average.

It sounded too good to be true. The last couple of summers had been quite literally a washout and the promise of a hot, dry summer was music to my ears.

While we obviously need some water to give the crops a drink, the summer is the time of year when we need the sun to definitely have his hat on. Harvest starts in late July, when we bring in the first of our arable crops, oilseed rape, and we'll also be making hay.

To make hay, you allow your grass to flower and run to seed. You cut it and then spread it out in the fields to dry in the heat of the sun. You need to get three or four days of uninterrupted sunshine to dry it out completely. Get it right and there's no need to wrap it in plastic to protect it. It'll be so dry that once baled, it can be stored for a year or two. But if it gets wet, the feed value is reduced. If it stays wet for a few days it can be ruined.

We don't grow hay just for the animals; we also grow silage. This is less mature grass that is cut in late May or early June. Once it's been cut, the silage is left to wilt slightly before it is collected in huge plastic-covered bales. Some farmers still go for the old method of making silage. They cart the cut grass back to the farmyard where it is piled into a heap known as a clamp. Once it's all off the field a tractor will be repeatedly driven over the clamp to compress the grass. After it's been rolled, the silage is covered with plastic and weighed down, usually with hundreds of old car tyres. In either case, the grass must be kept airtight until it's needed. You're trying to create perfect anaerobic conditions, removing all of the air so the grass starts to ferment in its own juices. It's the equivalent of making jam or pickling vegetables to eat in the middle of winter. Silage is our own preserve, and a valuable feed for livestock, stored for the winter when grass is scarce on the ground. The entire process is quite an art. You need to cut the crops at just the right time so that it contains the exact sugar levels you need for your cows. In a dairy system they will scientifically test the sugar levels in the sap of the plant, but for us it all boils down to experience. We look for when the grass is flowering, when there's enough leaf on it, but it hasn't bolted and run to seed, because at that point it would be too woody and would contain fewer nutrients and less sugar.

Dairy farmers replant their silage fields – or leys as they are called – every two or three years, making sure that there's plenty of ryegrass and clover in the mix. These fast-growing grasses are packed with the sugar you need to keep your cows milking until spring. As a traditional sheep and beef farm, we use longer-term pastures as we farm within an environmentally sensitive area scheme, the Cotswold Hills ESA. As part of this, we took some of our worst land out of arable production and returned it to old

Cotswold grassland, full of ancient varieties, distinctive to this area. As we are 800 to 1000 feet above sea-level, our soil is quite thin and grass doesn't grow as well as it does down in dairy land where the soil is deeper, retains the moisture and produces lusher grass. But our grassland has a real benefit for wildlife, as the grasses attract rare butterflies and insects. The pastures may not be so productive, as they mature quite late and can't compete with the modern, high-protein, high-sugared varieties used in dairy systems, but the scheme pays out a subsidy to make it worthwhile.

While our silage doesn't yield so much, or isn't such good quality as dairy fodder, it does the trick for our animals, so at the end of the cutting period I was pleased we'd managed to make up 220 silage bales. If the Met Office was right, and we were heading for a cracking summer, then everything would work out perfectly.

When I was young dad once told me that if something seems too good to be true it usually is.

On 15 July, it poured down. Of course the weather experts were quick to point out that the curse of St Swithin was nothing more than a myth. Records showed, we were told, that since 1861 there had never been 40 consecutive rainy days following a wet St Swithin's Day. The only time we came close was in 1985 when Luton suffered 30 days of rain. The weathermen stuck to their guns. June had been warmer than usual and even though there had been rain in the first fortnight of July, we should still all be dusting off the barbecues.

By the end of July, it was obvious that the rain wasn't going anywhere. The Met Office had to swallow humble pie and scrapped their early forecast. August, they now said, would see rainfall that was near or above average for a British summer.

Sadly, this time they weren't wrong.

The alarm goes off and I can't help groaning. Surely it can't be that time already? I force my eyes open and look at the clock's display. Monday 3 August. 5 a.m. I drag myself out of bed, trying not to wake Charlie, and fire up the computer. Outside, the weather is already looking good, but will it hold? A quick check of the forecast says yes, and so it's time to hit the phone. Our combine contractors are standing by and it's all systems go.

The rains of the 'barbecue summer' have already had a serious effect on the farm. My hopes for good hay and silage have – literally – had cold water thrown on them. The haymaking itself was an absolute disaster. I'd planned to produce a couple of hundred acres of hay but it got so wet we ended up having to turn two-thirds of it into extra silage. That probably doesn't sound so bad – after all, it's all still food for the animals – but silage costs a lot more than hay thanks to all that plastic you need to wrap it in. Not only do you need to fork out for the stuff in the first place, when it's been opened you have to pay for it to be sent off for recycling. Gone are the days when you burn or bury whole heaps of the black and green plastic. That practice is now illegal – and rightly so – but I know that come February or March next year there will be piles of the stuff all around the farm waiting to be sent off.

By mid-July we were ready to start bringing in the oilseed rape, but there was no way we could start the harvest. To send in the combine harvesters, you need a dry crop otherwise the blades will get jammed with the wet straw. Plus, the soil needs to be solid enough to support the weight of one of those mighty machines.

And so the combines stayed silent as the rains continued, the oilseed rape remained in the fields and our moods began to blacken.

We've grown rape here for as long as I can remember, although it is still a relatively new crop to British agriculture. It was first widely planted in 1973, after Britain entered the European Community. Suddenly, there were new grants available and fields of stark yellow started popping up across the countryside. Some campaigners weren't happy about this, saying it was changing the way the countryside looks, but their complaints fell on deaf ears. I'm glad they did – I sometimes wonder if these people forget that the beloved countryside they want to preserve in aspic is a working environment. It's OK to expect farmers to be stewards of the countryside, but we have to earn a living too. And rape certainly allows you to do that. It's now Britain's third most widely grown arable crop, after wheat and barley, covering around half a million hectares in total. The crop has even proved to be environmentally beneficial as well. Ten years ago it was discovered by the RSPB that the linnet, a bird that had been in catastrophic decline in the UK, had started to recover thanks to rape. In 1987 new varieties of rape were planted without the glucosinolates and erucic acid that had previously been present in high levels in the plant. This meant that rapeseed oil, previously used mainly for fuel, candles, soaps and plastics, was now fit for human consumption. At that exact point, records showed that linnet numbers stopped falling off and started rising. It appears that the linnets swooped upon the new crops and today around 80 per cent of their diet is made up of rape seeds.

Our rape seed is either crushed to extract the oil that is used to make margarine or turned into biofuel. Our neighbour, Hamish Campbell, who also grows rape, sells his for frying and as an alternative to olive oil – lovely on salads.

The crop itself has a skinny little bean pod that contains little seeds. When it turns brown and tinder-dry you know it's time to bring it in. The seeds themselves are like teeny-weeny black ball bearings, but, as with all things, you can hit problems if they repeatedly get wet. If the plant gets damp, then dries out, gets wet and dries again, the pods can shatter, scattering the seeds on the ground. Once out, there's no way of picking them up. As the rains continued, I heard about loads of other farmers being hit by the same problem. Fields of rape that just go overnight. As we struggled to find a dry spell to bring in our harvest, I was worried that the same thing was going to happen to us. For a while, it was touch and go. Every day I'd come in and check with Duncan and Martin Parkinson, our arable manager, who would be out driving around the fields checking on the moisture content. Usually, he'd be waiting for the crops to be dry enough to send in the combines. This year, the worry was that the moisture levels would be rising constantly. It should be an exciting time. Even though I don't really get involved in the day-to-day running of the harvest operation, I obviously want to know how we're getting on. It's the moment of truth after a year of caring for the crop and keeping it in condition. How well have we grown it, and what financial return will we be getting?

The last week of July saw a break in the weather and so the combine was out as soon as the ground was dry enough for it to run. Eight days later, 297 acres of rape had been harvested and, Duncan was happy to report, looked in pretty good nick. The rain hadn't seemed to have affected the quality, at all. At least that was a result.

However, the fact that we were a week late brought its own problems. Rape is one of the crops that we sell straight off the combine. As it's coming in, we usually have people standing by on the farm, ready to take it immediately away. This year we missed the boat, literally. Most of the crop had been destined to be exported, but by the time it was finally in, our customer had lost his slot on the boat. Duncan had been receiving phone call after phone call from traders reminding us that they had lorries standing by to collect our grain and all the time it was still standing in the fields. Both Dunc and Martin were pulling their hair out every time the phone rang.

'Have you done it yet?'

'Is it in yet?'

Then of course, when we did manage to get it in, it was our turn to chase the traders.

'We've got your grain,' Duncan would announce when he got through on the phone. 'Can you come and get it?'

'Sorry, Duncan, the lorries are busy with other people now.'

And so the rape is now in storage, which is causing even more grief for Duncan. Today we start bringing in the first of the barley and need the stores to be empty, not full of the last of the oilseed rape, which came in yesterday. One missed deadline and everything goes up the wall. Luckily, we did manage to get one shipment off a couple of days ago and more lorries will be arriving soon. Thank heavens that we'd hired extra staff for harvest this year. It's going to be a mad week.

As I enter the office, Dunc is already on the phone to the combine contractor telling them we're ready to bring the harvest in. Up to now, there's no way that a farm our size could justify owning our own combine harvesters. Brand new, they can cost around £250,000 and even second-hand you'd be lucky to find one for under £100,000. You'd shell out all that money and the combine works for ten weeks of the year, then sits in a shed until next summer. As we want to be up to date we've always gone for a contractor, who designates a combine and driver just for us. With 1000 acres of arable, we're big enough for the contractor to know it's worth keeping a combine standing by until we're ready. That being said, we have just learned that he's about to put his prices up. The increase is enough to make us think twice and Duncan has started to talk to our neighbour Hamish about the possibility of our two farms pooling their resources to buy a combine between us. Like us, Hamish has got 1000 acres of arable so we can justify the expense of, say, leasing our own combine on a per-acre basis, two-year-deal and hiring an operator. This kind of joint venture farming was always the norm in the past. Some farmers couldn't even afford a plough so they bought shares in one and shared it between them. As time has passed we've become more and more hopeless at cooperative farming. British farmers really stress about it, worrying that they need to be self-sufficient and own everything themselves. It's nonsense. Once again, the French are so much better at this kind of thing than us. I really believe we'll have to learn quickly if we want to survive.

It's early afternoon before I watch the first combine drive on to the barley fields. As I see the driver get ready to start, I can't resist checking some of the grain between my teeth. Yeah, it's definitely hard enough to combine, although I've spotted some in another field which is looking decidedly dodgy. I just hope we get a clear run at this crop and can get on to the wheat as soon as possible.

The combine starts to run down its line, the great blades at the front cutting through the stalks. Unlike the rape we got in a week or so ago, barley has quite a short stalk. The blades of the combine have to be kept quite low so that the all-important heads don't end up on the floor. That sounds easy enough, but when you're cutting that low you're in danger of scuffing the floor and dragging stones and rocks into the front of the machine. You soon know when that's happened, as the rocks shoot through the workings and can do an incredible amount of damage in hardly any time at all. That's another reason I'm happy to bring in experienced combine drivers. They know exactly what they're doing and there's less chance of a disaster happening.

Even so, almost as soon as the combine is off, it hits a problem that not even our veteran combiner could have foreseen. A mole had dug up a massive pile of earth that was hidden in the stalks of barley and before we know it the front of the combine is clogged up. It's amazing to think that such a tiny creature can cause such havoc to such a huge piece of technology. Talk about David and Goliath.

At times like this there's only one thing for it. The combine is stopped, the blades motionless, and I dart in front of the monstrosity and move the offending earth by hand. You try not to think too much about what those blades could do to you as you crouch in front of the combine, picking lumps of mud out of its wicked teeth by hand. There have been many tragic accidents with farm machinery, but even though time is of the essence we take no risks. The mechanism is all turned off by the driver before I venture in.

The obstruction is cleared and the combine is off again. I'm glad that I'm now behind it, standing in its wake as it continues down the field. All around me is the straw that has been belched out of the rear of the machine. Barley is incredibly itchy when it's in the air, but the straw is valuable stuff in its own right. After the harvest has come in we'll be baling it up and either selling it to dealers who move it down to Wales where straw is hard to come by due to the lack of arable crops, or keep it to use as bedding for our own animals. A lot of people confuse straw with hay, not helped by the fact that some seem to use the names interchangeably. But they are quite different: hay, as we've already seen, is dry grass used as a feed while straw is the stalk left behind after wheat and barley is threshed out and is used to keep the animals comfortable and warm. It's a useful by-product of the harvest, and means that hardly anything goes to waste and, if needed, we can scrape in a few extra pounds from it.

But we do need to make sure that we're not throwing money away. As the combine turns at the bottom of the field ready to make a return journey I check the straw to make sure that the threshing process isn't throwing out too much grain with the straw. I scoop up handfuls of the stuff and give it a shake, keeping my eye on the ground to see if much grain drops out. Luckily there's hardly any at all, just half a dozen or so individual grains. That's fine, there will always be a small amount lost, so it looks like our combine today is working pretty effectively and the majority of the grain is held in its tank ready to be stored.

It's coming in fast too. Throughout the day the fields are a hive of activity. As the combine works, two tractors pull trailers back and forth between the fields and the farm. Every half-hour a tankful of grain is deposited in one of the trailers ready to be sent back for storage.

As the afternoon begins to wane, it's my shift so I jump up into the tractor cab. You have to concentrate, driving up beside the combine, getting your trailer underneath the spout and hitting the exact right speed, so that the grain pours down evenly even as the combine continues to work. I keep half an eye where I'm driving and half on the rear-view mirror to check on the position of the trailer. The idea is to load the back up first and then slow down slightly so that the spout moves forward and the front

460ml

Buy any 1 Ristorante Pizza or Amy's Ready Meal plus one Haagen Dazs Ice Cream for £5. Offer subject to availability, valid 21/06/2018 – 11/07/2018.

TAKE THIS HOME
AND YOU'RE WINNING

£2

Tetley Tea Bags
80's

£2

Wal

£2 OFF
When you spend £10 or more

(Excluding Cigarettes & Tobacco, Paypoint &
National Lottery services, Baby Formula and Fuel)

Valid 23/07/2018 - 29/07/2018
Participating Blakemore Retail stores only.
This voucher can not be used in conjunction with any other
vouchers and offers

SPAR ⬆

BRING IT
HOME

In-store now

.co.uk

of the trailer fills up. When you're fully loaded, the combine driver stops the gush of grain and you head off back to the store.

It can be a tricky manoeuvre, especially when, like me, you've been up for more than twelve hours. I'll be calling it a day soon, although the combine will keep threshing away well into the night, probably stopping about 11 o'clock. At night the driver will have to keep his wits about him, as huge lights mounted on the harvester illuminate the crop just in front of him.

Back in the yard, before unloading, we check the quality of the grain I've just brought in, popping a handful into a little gizmo that takes a moisture reading. You crank the handle to grind the grain slightly and numbers flash up on the tiny screen letting you know how much water is in there. It comes up at 13.8 per cent. That's actually not bad at all. Much better than I thought it would be and the best thing is that as the sun has played its part we won't have to spend extra money putting the grain through the drier. That's one aspect of a wet harvest that every farmer dreads. There's nothing more downhearting than stepping into your store to see electric heaters blasting away. You know that every watt guzzled is more money off the profit. There is still one niggle, however. In the back of my mind I know that this was one of our better fields. Tomorrow morning, when the combine's out once again, we'll be working on the field that I'm concerned about. But that's another day. All I can think about is unloading this trailer into the store and cracking open the bottle of beer I've been promising myself all day. Hopefully the majority of today's barley will end up being made into beer itself. Each field we've cleared could be worth between five to six grand so fingers, toes and anything else we can get our hands on is crossed. After a year of growing the stuff, we need to reap the benefit.

Fours weeks later, and, even though the last trucks of the wheat harvest are coming in, celebrating is the last thing on our mind. It took us four days to bring in all 198 acres of the barley and, as I had feared, it wasn't all as good as we wanted. Ideally, we'd have wanted all of it to come in at the 14 per cent moisture level, but the majority was reading at 22 per cent. It was like bringing in soggy porridge. And worse of all, most of it had to go through the drier twice. All I could hear was the rumble of the machine blowing heat over the moving beds of grain, accompanied by the sound of money pouring down the drain as the bills for the diesel and electricity the drier needed started to roll in, a cost of around £12 per tonne. Finally, the grain had reached the right moisture level and could be stored in the barn. Of course, in this business you do have to count your blessings. Some people I know have ended up ploughing their crops back into the ground as they have all been ruined. It's a heart-wrenching thought, busting a gut for a whole year and all for nothing. You can't help but think 'there, but for the grace of God, go I'. Looking at the figures, if all goes well, we should make a small profit this year, nowhere near as much as I want, but still a profit. It just shows how much of farming is pure chance. You can be the best agronomist, buy in the very best products, but you can't control the elements.

In the end we brought in around 900 tonnes of barley, which we're storing in three sheds, 300 tonnes in each. The plan was to sell the entire lot for beer, but the rain has wrecked much of the crop meaning that'll it probably have to go for animal feed. That may sound good – after all we're still selling it – but the difference between the two end-uses is immense. In a good year, if all of the barley goes for malting we can easily make a £20,000 profit. However, if it all goes for feed we'll make a £10,000 loss. You can see why a lot's riding on it. At the moment, if things continue going the way they are, we're probably looking at a 50/50 split between malt and animal feed, meaning that we'll just about break even. The barley has spent an entire year growing in the fields, we've tended it, used expensive fertilisers and sprays to keep it healthy and now it's hardly going to make us a penny. Granted, it could be worse – we could be operating at a loss – but it's galling to be knocked back like this.

Even if we break even with the barley, goodness knows how the wheat will do. We hoped to start bringing it in on 7 August, meaning that even if we had a spot of bad weather it would all be done by the twentieth. Plenty of time to combine 346 acres of the stuff. The rains started on 6 August and just didn't stop.

It was demoralising at best and heartbreaking at worse. Every day you'd look out and watch your crop go bad. The idea of a good harvest is to bring in the wheat before the plant has had chance to drop its seed to perpetuate itself. However, it has been so wet that the wheat has started to sprout when it is still in the ear. You run the grain out of the ear only to find little roots popping out of it. Horrible.

At times like this, you try to keep going; we've lived through similar situations and know that the rains will eventually stop. You'll be able to move on. But all the time there's that nagging voice in the back of your mind, 'What state is the crop going to be in when you finally get it in?' You can't help but feel a bit down.

Then you start worrying about the money you've spent on the extra staff for harvest. During the last few weeks they haven't exactly been just standing around doing nothing but there are only so many times you can send them off to tidy the workshop. Thankfully, as we have such a diverse business we've been redistributing them, sending them down to the farm park to help out. Ironically, the rains have meant that our numbers for the park are up, as people are trying to find things to do under cover in the wet weather. It's good that something has gone well.

Fifteen days later the weather cleared up enough for us to finally start getting it in, on 21 August. We should have been done by now.

The news comes that the last of the wheat has been combined and is on its way in and, with a sigh of relief, Duncan marks the date down in the records. Saturday, 5 September 2009. It's unbelievable. What should have taken just a week has stretched on for nearly a month and the effects are going to be felt until this time next year.

Now that the grain is in we still have to dry and bale the straw before the land is cultivated and the oilseed rape can be drilled in its place. We plant our fields in strict rotation, in the same way that home gardeners never grow the same crop in the same part of the garden year after year. Not only does it strip nutrients out of the ground, it can also lead to a build-up of pests and diseases. Ideally, we needed the rape to be in the ground a week ago, but if Duncan's calculations are right we won't be able to sow the seed for five days. That's at least another week we've lost and it means that come December we're going to have a battle on our hands with pigeons.

Any farmer knows two things about pigeons. First of all, they're always hungry. When the little rapeseed plants start to grow, their tasty shoots are absolutely irresistible to our feathered friends. They'll fly in, land on the soil between the plants and peck away till they've had their fill and your crop is decimated. This is when your second piece of essential pigeon knowledge comes in handy. They're nervous little pests and will never land where they can't see the ground. By December, when the pigeons really start to flock, you need a thick canopy of rape, too dense to spy the soil below. A pigeon will take one look at this and think again. As we'll be drilling the rape so late, it might not be thick enough come December.

As the last truck trundled over to the stores, I trudge across the yard to the farmhouse to grab some lunch and feel a spot of rain on the back of my neck. Above me clouds almost as dark as my mood roll over the skies. Great, more rain. Just what we need.

AUTUMN

CHAPTER 10

HAPPY NEW YEAR

We woke up on 6 September to brilliant sunshine. You had to laugh really. We'd just got through two abysmal summer months and the weathermen were now predicting one of the driest Septembers in years. At least it meant that we could bring in our fourth main crop pretty much on schedule and in what turned out to be reasonably fine weather.

We grow only 25 acres of beans, so they don't take long to harvest – a day at most to bring in varieties for both animal and human consumption. As you'd probably expect, the beans destined for our plates can demand much better prices than those grown for animal feed, but they also cost more to produce. You have to keep the crop cleaner, so that means more fungicides, and you have to make sure it's the highest-quality possible. And if it gets too wet or mouldy then it will be downgraded to animal feed anyway.

But both varieties, be they for human consumption or animal feed, do bring some benefits. If at all possible, we try to limit our use of artificial fertiliser and pesticides, primarily because the cost of the stuff is extortionate but also due to the impact they have on the planet. Thanks to our environmentally sensitive scheme, we have to operate under certain restrictions and can't just saturate the ground with chemicals. Broad beans, like potatoes and maize, are especially useful as they are a great 'break crop'. The last thing you want to do is plant season after season of a nitrogen-hungry crop, such as wheat, in the same field. Pretty soon the soil would be stripped of all its goodness. It's best, therefore, to rotate the crops to give the soil the chance to recover. Beans hold a lot of nitrogen in their root nodules, which is then naturally fed back into the ground. The thick roots also run deep which helps break up the soil structure before ploughing. The idea is to bring in your bean harvest, plough up the land and then drill your wheat. If the roots have done their work, you'll get a really strong crop the following year and will have saved on fertilisers too.

I like farming like this. When you plant crops that will help the soil regenerate you feel like you're working alongside nature, not against it. While we're not organic, it doesn't hurt to cut back on as many chemicals as we can.

I'm often asked why we're not organic and it is something we've given a lot of thought to, but there have always been a few things that have kept us from taking the plunge.

The first is the quality of our soil. Cotswold brash is very, very thin, so it's quite hard to build up organic matter. We also have all that old Cotswold grassland that we're in no hurry to plough up. In an organic system, you're required to rotate your grassland and crops, adding clover to the mix to regenerate the nitrogen and put goodness back into the soil. Plus, to meet the organic requirements, a quarter of your arable acreage needs to come out of production and be put to grass. We don't want to do this. We have more than enough grass for our animals.

Then there's the timescale involved. To fully convert your arable crops you're looking at a two-year conversion period. From day one you need to grow everything organically but until you've got your certificate you have to sell your produce to the conventional market – and at conventional prices. If we tried to go organic tomorrow, we wouldn't be able to grow as much as we do now, and our yields would halve overnight. That's why organic food comes at a premium price. The farmer can't grow as much as he would using chemicals, so has to charge more. The snag is that problem of pricing. Until we are officially organic we'd have to sell beans at, say £90 per tonne whereas the organic price is £180 per tonne. There's a massive hit involved in converting. There are government support grants, and we've spent a lot of time looking into it, but always come back to the same decision. At the moment, organic production just wouldn't suit our style of farming and the financial cost of conversion isn't worth the hassle.

One route we could take is to designate just a part of the farm as organic. It isn't the ideal situation, but sometimes it's all you can do. But doing so can be a logistical nightmare. Your organic grain has to be stored in a purely organic shed and you'll need a paper trail that's squeaky clean to prove that you're keeping everything separate. There's always the danger that there will be a muddle along the way.

That isn't to say I'll never change my mind about organic. I try to be very open-minded about these kind of things. There was one point last year when nitrogen pellets doubled in price to £340 per tonne. The pellets, which come as little white granules, are made from refined oil. Every time oil goes up, the price of petrol, and nitrogen, goes up too. As soon as I saw the price rise, I thought perhaps we should go organic after all.

At the end of the day, the decision is driven by financial reasons rather than principles or ethics. Although the way we farm now means that we do have a big carbon footprint, we proceed as sensitively and sensibly as we can. I'm comfortable with the environmental impact we're having on the land.

That being said, when it comes to my family we tend to eat as much organic produce as we can, especially when it comes to soft fruit and vegetables. It's mainly because I do know about the pesticides that are used on this kind of produce and I'd rather Charlie and the kids didn't eat them. When it comes to things like bread, biscuits or milk I honestly don't believe there's a lot of difference between organic and conventional products, especially with dairy and beef. OK, so organic dairy farms do manage the soil differently and don't use chemicals, but when it comes to the animal it's virtually the same process as keeping conventional cattle. You can use practically all the veterinary products that a conventional farmer would use. It's just that there are longer withdrawal periods between the animal being treated and its meat being eaten by humans – roughly twice as long. The organic standards recommend that you use herbal or homoeopathic medicines rather than conventional drugs, although they do allow the use of chemical medicines in order to avoid distress or suffering. So it's the same drugs, but just a longer time between the medicine being applied and the animal being killed – 36 days rather than the usual 12. Once again, there's a cost implication as you have to keep the animal fed for longer before slaughter.

September is one of our busiest times of year. Earlier in the month I'd packed the kids back off to school. They weren't happy, and I can't blame them. I remember what it was like going back to school after a summer out in the fields. The farm is an amazing playground, as long as they're careful, and I used to love exploring the woodlands and playing in the streams. Then, before you know it, you're back in your school uniform and stuck in a dingy classroom trying to get your head around algebra and the complete works of Shakespeare. It seems so unfair.

They certainly didn't look happy when they sat down to their breakfast that first morning of term. Usually they wolf down their eggs, gathered by hand from our new hens, but not that day. We've had eggs for just about every breakfast since the hens arrived and I'm really pleased with the way the birds are progressing. The two flocks – former-battery and former-organic alike – are now living side by side around the house and spend most of the days scratching around under the trees, as nature intended. Within a couple of weeks, the battery hens' feathers started to grow through. Ella and Alfie were so excited when they spotted the little brown tufts coming through the naked pink skin. Each of the organic hens is producing an egg every other day. At their peak they would have laid one a day, but we don't mind – there are more than enough eggs for us and the rest head down to the café to go into the cakes.

September isn't just the beginning of a new school year for the kids; it is, in effect, the beginning of the farming calendar as well. Historically it was the month when new farm tenancies began. It gave the outgoing tenant the chance to bring in his crop before his successor could start ploughing up the ground.

Even after all these years it always amazes me how quickly the landscape of the farm changes. Just over a month ago the fields were full of green and yellow crops blowing gently in the breeze. Now they're brown with cultivated earth or, in some cases, already carpeted with the green shoots of rape and barley. I've never ploughed myself. When I was a lad, there were three tractor drivers on the farm and they were very precious about their machines and doing their jobs. I didn't mind as I was always off with dad working with the livestock. That being said, I always enjoy watching the plough moving up and down the fields behind a tractor. The driver will go into a field in the morning and it's all done by the evening, roughly 30 acres a day. The idea is to bury the heavy grass weed seed deep into the earth and break up the soil, but what you get is a vivid visual representation of the turning year. As the tractor ploughs on the farm is full of nervous anticipation. What is the next year going to be like? Is this a chance to start afresh? Turning the soil is like turning a new leaf, putting the mistakes, difficulties and appalling weather of the previous year behind you. Whatever has happened in the past, the agricultural calendar keeps on rolling. There's one thing you can be certain of – until the day they retire, farmers can never really say, 'well, that's everything done'. There's always a job to do, and, as dad illustrates, even after you retire, there's every chance you'll be back on the farm helping out in some way or another. You can't help it – it's just in your blood.

In days gone by, long before Christianity came to the British Isles, the end of the harvest was a time of celebration. Over the summer, everyone on the farm would obviously have worked their fingers to the bone, so when the last crop was in, it was time for the harvest home – in other words, a great big knees-up. However, there was some important business to be done first. The last cut of the harvest, especially in the case of the last sheaf of corn, was treated with much respect. Historians think that our pagan ancestors used to believe that the spirit of the harvest lived within the crop and when the grain was harvested the spirit either died, or at the very least was made homeless. So, the last sheaf was plaited into a shape to provide a resting place for the displaced spirit. Sometimes these dollies were shaped like humans, or were crafted to resemble horns, hearts, fans or lanterns. In fact, the name dolly is thought to be derived from the word 'idol', which was certainly how the country folk treated their little straw effigy. It had pride of place at the harvest home, where it presided over the revelry as the guest of honour. When the celebrations had passed, it would then be taken into the farmhouse, where a space would be cleared on the mantelpiece for the dolly to reside over winter. Depending on what part of the country you hailed from, the traditions governing what happened to the dolly the following spring changed from place to place. Some folk used to parade it around the freshly sown fields in a form of blessing, while others used to plough it back into the ground so that the spirit of the harvest could be born anew.

These fertility customs continued throughout the centuries, and, like so many of our old pagan beliefs, were even adopted by the Christian Church, adapted slightly to remove any negative connotations of false gods. The influence is still seen at every country fair. You can guarantee that there will always be a craft stall selling freshly made corn dollies.

We don't carry out any such traditions these days on Bemborough Farm, but I have made some decisions that hopefully will bring us a bountiful and profitable crop next year. The barley we've just sown is a new variety for us, known as Maris Otter. It's been grown in England since the 1960s, following its cultivation by Cambridge University expert-breeder Dr G.D.H. Bell, but has in recent years become highly prized in brewing circles, especially the smaller, independent brewers that have grown in popularity over the last decade. Cask ale – beer brewed from traditional ingredients and allowed to ferment within the cask from which it is served – seems to be in the middle of a bright golden age. Cask ale production is currently estimated to be worth £4.5 billion in the UK, four times as much as cider or stout. Almost 9 million barrels of cask ale are supped every year, around a quarter of all beer drunk in Britain. And the barley of choice, according to my maltsters –

Warminster Maltings in Wiltshire – is Maris Otter. The great news is that as the grain is so sought after, they've promised to pay a premium if next year's crop makes the grade.

And so, I'm about to take the *Countryfile* cameras down to the maltsters to film their analysis of last harvest's highly dubious barley. I'm not holding out a lot of hope, and even as the cameras are chucked in the back of the wagon, I'm finding it hard to concentrate.

Last week, Ronnie, my yellow kelpie, began to cough. It's been getting worse and seems to be really wearing her out. We've managed to get an appointment at the vet, but now I have to go to Wiltshire for filming so dad is going to take her for me. It doesn't look good and I have to tear myself away from her when we leave. She's been a companion to me for 12 years now, which is a good innings for a sheepdog, but I can't help thinking that something is very wrong.

In the Warminster Maltings' lab, Jonathan Arnold, the company's malting barley director is shaking his head as the cameras roll.

'I'm sorry, Adam,' he says, running his fingers through the grain, 'but I think you know what I'm going to say.'

I sigh and nod as Jonathan confirms what I had thought. Each individual grain is marred by a gaping black slit down the middle. All you need do is run your finger along it and the barley splits, coming apart in your hand.

'What's happened,' Jonathan explains, 'is that your barley has got very wet, then dried out before getting wet again. It's almost as if it's started the malting process in the fields, before it's even been harvested. If we put this through the malting here, it's going to turn into a black, mushy mess.'

I thought as much, but at least Jonathan has promised to take my barley next year if the Maris Otter makes the grade, and pay that premium. 'We have to,' he tells me. 'We need the economics of farming barley to pick up so that the price is maintained and farmers want to grow it.'

That's music to my ears. This is exactly the kind of place I want my barley to come to. Warminster Maltings is one of Britain's oldest working floor maltings and hand-crafts the malt using the same methods that would have been used when the current buildings opened in 1879. First of all, the grains are soaked in water. Once they've swollen in size they are spread out on the malting floor and left to germinate. Every single day, the barley, which by this point is known as green malt, is turned by hand using what looks like a giant rake. This separates the grain, aerating it so that nature can take its course.

Once the first shoots are seen, it's time to start shovelling it out, dropping it into stores where it stays for five days before being roasted in the kiln so that the flavour starts to develop. The maltsters are careful not to turn up the heat too fast and so the process starts around 65C (149F) and is gradually increased to 95C (203F). The end result is a high-quality malt which can be sent out to brewers. I'm also in talks with my local brewery Hook Norton, located in nearby village of – surprisingly enough – Hook Norton. I'm hoping they will take my malt to brew beer in their shiny copper kettles, which date back to the early 1900s. While there are some other essentials that go into a good pint of ale – most notably the hops which are added to the mixture just before it boils to add that familiar bitterness and distinctive aroma – the barley is the most important element in making beer, the foundation to the entire brewing process.

I already feed my cows brewers' grain, which I get from Hook Norton. This is simply the by-product of barley used in brewing, the mashed-up husks and other material left at the bottom of the kettle after the mixture has boiled. The cows love it and I'd love to complete the circle and have them eating brewers' grain made from my barley. At least the wheels are in motion and the deal with the maltsters is there in principle. Fingers crossed that next year's harvest will be a good one. Perhaps I should start making some corn dollies after all.

The day's shoot done, I give dad a call. He'd phoned earlier to let me know that they were running all kind of tests on Ronnie, culminating in an X-ray. With my heart in my mouth I listen to what he has to say.

'I'm really sorry, Adam,' he begins, his voice cracking ever so slightly, 'but it's bad news. They've found a growth in her lungs. She's obviously in quite a lot of pain. The vet says there's really only one option.'

I ring off after I give dad the permission to have Ronnie put down. Alone in the maltsters' car park, I lean back on my truck and wipe a tear from my eye. When I get back to the Cotswolds

I'll go to the vet and pick up Ronnie's body. She'll be buried in the final resting place of every dog we've ever had on Bemborough Farm, under a clump of old beech trees. I'll do it myself. I always do. And I don't mind admitting that some tears will be shed. How could they not be? Our dogs become part of the family. It's always sad when they leave us.

CHAPTER 11

OUR DAILY BREAD

In the past, most farms were mixed affairs, combining both live-stock and arable operations. Farmers had fingers in lots of pies, bringing in money from this, that and the other. Times have changed and single-purpose farms are now the norm. This means that instead of being jacks of all trades, farmers become masters of one. Specialising has a lot of benefits. You can concentrate your efforts and offer yourself less distractions, scaling up your oper-ation if you're one of the lucky ones.

Bemborough Farm is anything but single-purpose. We're always trying our hands at something new and are constantly juggling the different strands to our business. It's pretty central to our philosophy and I wouldn't have it any other way. I hate having nothing to do, which is a stroke of luck, as around here that never happens.

There are some drawbacks. As our work is made up of a lot of small-scale projects, it's all a bit labour intensive. This morning's job is a prime example. We're moving some Gloucester Old Spot piglets from their nursery to new quarters. As they're around eight weeks old they're now old enough to be weaned from their mum, who in just a few days' time will be put back to the boar to get pregnant again. Mike and I round them up into the back of the truck and get the sow back to the field. It's noisy work. Anyone who's ever picked up a piglet knows what a racket they make, squealing away in your arms. It's a basic survival instinct. They're not in pain, and are usually not that distressed, but are just making as much noise as possible to draw the attention of their mum. As soon as we put them down they shut up again. The little fakers.

It takes a while to gather them all together. A big commercial pig farm, dealing with thousands of pigs, will have highly efficient systems for this kind of thing, but in our small-scale production it's just a case of rolling up your sleeves and getting stuck in.

The first stop is the Old Spots' field so we can drop the sow off. She seems a little unsure at first but is soon making herself at home back in her old place. That is, until one of the older sows notices that she's back, and is over like a shot barging into the interloper and giving her a little nip. The younger pig isn't standing for that and tussles back. This happens every time you reintroduce a sow back into a group. Sows – like the chickens – have a natural pecking order so there's always a bit of a scrap to establish who's the matriarch of the herd. The dust soon settles and although everything looks exactly the same to us, in the pig's mind the status quo has been established once again. Almost as if he's oblivious to the power struggle, the boar trots over to have a sniff of the returning sow. He doesn't really care about the pecking order, he just knows he has to serve all of them. He's also still quite young at the moment and has a lot of growing to do, but I'm pleased with how he's doing. In just a few days' time she'll come into season and will be attempting to seduce him into mating with her – a process called hogging – although, to be fair, he'll need little in the way of encouragement.

The sow's piglets meanwhile are being tagged. I hoist up one of the wriggling pigs into my arms and grab her snout to hold her jaws together and give our ears a rest from all the squeaking. Mike quickly pierces one of her ears with a metal tag stamped with our herd number and the pig's own individual number. While we've got her, we give her a quick wormer injection to kill off any internal parasites she might have picked up. There's no getting away from that fact that tagging the piglets must hurt, but we need to be able to trace them back to the farm and it's by far the most humane method of keeping track of them. Certainly, as soon as we put the little pig down she seems to have forgotten about her short ordeal and is off exploring her new yard, which she and her siblings are sharing with some young Kune Kune pigs.

Kune Kunes are one of the few non-native rare breeds that we have in our collection. The dumpy little pigs, covered in a mop of hair, hail from New Zealand, where they were originally kept by the Maoris for meat. Their name, which is pronounced 'cooney cooney', means fat and round in Maori, and suits them down to the ground. Back in the 1970s the breed was in serious trouble. Their pork had fallen out of favour with the Maoris and hardly any other farmers knew they existed, let alone farmed them. They only exist now thanks to two wildlife park owners, Michael Willis and John Simster, who, after finding out about the pig's plight, drove all across New Zealand to buy every Kune Kune they could find. They returned from their Herculean task with just eighteen pigs. They worked hard to save them and today the breed is in an exceptionally healthy state back home. They first arrived in Britain in 1992 when a couple of farmers, Zoe Lindop and Andrew Calveley, brought them home after a number of years working in New Zealand. They had fallen in love with the little creatures and wanted to ensure that there was a large herd on the other side of the world, in case the worst happened and a local disaster wiped them out in their native land.

The Kune Kunes have now worked their way into British hearts too and have proved to be a favourite choice for small-holders. They certainly go down well at the farm, with their myriad of colours from ginger and cream to black and brown (with plenty of spots in between) and cute little tassels, called piri piri, which wobble about under their chin like a goat. Person-ally, I also think that, like the Old Spots, they make cracking sausages.

Soon all of the piglets are safely transferred and it's time for the next job of the day. While our pork and sausage sideline is going well, other areas of our business are proving to be more problematic.

Across the farm from the piglets, we have over a thousand tonnes of our wheat in the stores. It's a good-sized harvest, but prices aren't at all what they should be. It has cost us about £100 per tonne to produce and currently the price on the open market is about £85. At that rate we're looking to make a considerable loss.

Last year things didn't look half as bad as all this. In fact, at the end of the harvest we were laughing all the way to the bank. The way of the world is that, in agriculture, you often profit from others' misfortune. It doesn't always sit well with me, but that's business for you. Around 12 months ago, market prices for wheat almost doubled over night. There were a number of reasons why. Demand was through the roof, thanks mainly to population growth but also to the fact that developing countries such as India and China were enjoying more wealth than ever before. Higher incomes meant that the Indian and Chinese people were looking to try new things and in this case, that meant eating less rice and more cereals and meat. At almost exactly the same time as all of this excitement, Australia suffered one of its worst droughts on record. Usually the Aussies are the third or fourth largest exporter of wheat but their harvests literally dried up, and their exports soon followed, dropping to 24 per cent of what they usually produce. Suddenly there was a hole in the global wheat reserve and prices shot up. The boys in the City saw this and played the future market, hiking up the prices even more. As a result, we were seeing unheard of prices, selling at £150 per tonne. Encouraged by this return to profitability, farmers around the world increased their plantings of wheat to cash in. You can't blame them.

Then the world shifted. Even as we'd been watching prices soar, the financial pages were full of stories of impending financial gloom. The recession hit, and the speculator withdrew from the commodity markets. Now we're back in the bad old days where we are struggling even to cover the cost of production. To make matters worse, thanks to everyone getting overexcited about wheat, there's a surplus of cereal crops around the world.

And you know that old proverb, 'It never rains but it pours.' We're proving that true this year. As with the barley, the wet summer has meant that the quality of the grain is nowhere near as good as I wanted it to be. To add insult to injury, while I was originally growing it to make biscuits, halfway through the season the Home Grown Cereals Authority decided to downgrade the variety I'd chosen to an animal-feed wheat, thereby slashing its value even more. I don't want to tell you what I said when I read that news in the paper, but needless to say, the air turned a particular shade of blue that morning.

All of this means that we have a thousand tonnes of wheat that the big commercial bakeries won't even look at, let alone touch. It looks as if I'm going to have to just bite the bullet and sell the whole lot for animal feed, taking the hit to the bottom line along the way. Duncan is doing his best. He's constantly on the phone or checking his email to get the latest prices for wheat, watching as the markets go up and down. At the moment it's like a yo-yo. In the City, traders are buying thousands of tonnes of grain on a Monday, resulting in the price creeping up over the period of the week as grain becomes scarce. Then, when it's at its highest at the weekend, they'll sell it, so suddenly there's a glut and the price crashes. I guess it's just playing the game, but what it means in the real world is that farmers like ourselves have to try to feel our way around a volatile market, peaking and troughing left, right and centre.

There is a tiny scrap of light at the end of this particularly dark tunnel however. Duncan has heard of a local, small-scale miller near Tetbury who may be able to grind at least some of our stock into a pretty good flour. Looking at the state of the crop I have my doubts, especially after my disappointment with the barley. I'm not getting my hopes up, but anything's worth trying. Not expecting much, I bag up a sack of grain and head off to Shipton.

There's been a mill here since before the Domesday Book, although unless you knew where you were going you'd miss it for sure. Shipton Mill lies at the end of a very rough and bumpy track halfway between Malmesbury and Tetbury. The current owner of the Victorian building is John Lister who bought the place 30 years ago. It had been a long time since it had last been used to mill flour and was, in fact, occupied by a coffin maker. Lister, a biologist who has spent most of his working life carrying out research in the rainforests of Venezuela, knew immediately that he wanted to restore the semi-derelict place to its former glory. He formed a cooperative, bought the mill and fitted it out with machinery rescued and restored from other old mills.

As soon as he greets me, I know this is a man besotted by flour. He's like an excited child when I open my sack of wheat, bubbling over with enthusiasm. In his presence, I can't help but feel my own bad mood lifting. If someone who knows his stuff as much as John is getting so excited by my wheat then perhaps there is a little hope after all.

He scoops a handful of the grain and, taking it up to his face, inhales deeply, filling his nostrils with the smell of the stuff. He then flashes me a brilliant smile.

'Sorry, forgive me. I do have a habit of getting carried away,' he says, 'but it's always exciting getting your hands on a new bag of wheat. You're never quite sure what you're going to get.'

'And what have you got here then?' I ask, still blown away that he's so taken with a crop I'd all but written off as sub-standard.

'You've got a great-smelling wheat,' he replies, quick as a flash. 'Here, have a sniff.'

And with that he's pushed it under my nose and I can't help but laugh. 'Isn't it fantastic.'

'OK,' I say, 'I admit, it smells good. But can you do anything with it?'

He takes a moment to appraise the wheat again, running it through his fingers.

'Well, it's not the best in the world,' he begins – tell me something I don't know – 'and we'd have to analyse it properly to test how much protein is in there. That's what you're after. Here, let me show you.'

He hurries away and comes back with a smaller bag of grain.

'This,' he announces proudly, 'is an extremely high-grade bread-making wheat, packed with protein.'

He pours some of it into a little pile and makes a similar heap of some of mine.

'As you can see the high-grade stuff is very even, every grain around the same size,' he explains, his expert fingers running through the wheat. 'Yours is considerably paler. That means less gluten, that all-important protein we're looking for.'

'So, it's as bad as I thought,' I say, steeling myself for the worst. To me, the difference between the two crops is obvious. Animal feed it is then.

'Not at all, Adam,' John immediately replies. 'This grain of yours will make fine flour. I know a number of artisan bakers who could happily make big, bold loaves out of it.'

He can see from my face that I still have my doubts.

'If you don't believe me, I'll show you. Come on.'

John has me bring my bag of wheat as we walk through his mill. This is certainly my type of place. It's clean and bright, but you can feel the history of the mill and imagine millers of all generations working the equipment.

'Here,' he says, stopped in front of a metal trough, 'pour your wheat in here.' I do as I'm told and watch as it's taken on to an elevator, which carries it up to the bins that feed the millstones.

'Right,' he says, leaping off once again. 'Follow me.'

The more the afternoon plays out, the more I'm thinking of John as milling's answer to Willy Wonka. His enthusiasm for the process is infectious. We come to the large wooden box that houses the two one-ton millstones. One is permanently fixed in place and the other is rotating, whirring away as it grinds my wheat. We stand there for a while as John points out some of the more intricate technology around us, passing the time until the moment we've been waiting for. Leaning down for a second, John comes back up with a scoop of flour – my flour – which he pours into my hands.

'Go on then,' he says with glee, 'have a smell of that.'

Smell is obviously a very important sense to John and when I take a sniff I can see why. I can smell my own fields in the flour I'm rubbing between my fingers. I'm no expert, but it feels good, far better than I could have hoped for considering what the harvest has been like. I try to think of something to sum up how chuffed I am – the best I can think of is an enthusiastic 'Wow' – but in the back of my mind the pragmatist in me is still wondering if this is all a waste of time. I don't want to get carried away with the excitement of the demonstration. I still need to know if I can make some money back on this.

John just laughs when I ask him. 'I'm convinced of it. At this quality, I reckon a sack like that will produce about 50 loaves. And at £2 a loaf that's not bad.'

Now it's my turn to laugh. John has to be joking. Two quid a loaf from my wheat?

The miller weighs me up as carefully as he would weigh a half-tonne of grain.

'OK, then, if you don't believe me, I'll put my money where my mouth is. Let us mill your flour and I'll put you in touch with a baker friend of mine. He'll turn out some loaves for you. I bet £10 you'll be able to sell at least a hundred loaves at market for around £2 each. Oh, and if I'm right, you've got to come back to see me about your flour. How does that sound?'

It sounds good, and I can't help but shake his flour-covered hand, but I'm still not sure. It's almost too good to be true.

'Adam, you've got to do it.' I'm on the phone to Teresa Bogan, the series producer of *Countryfile*. Teresa has worked on the programme for the entire time I've been a presenter, and stepped up to the top job just before the show went prime-time. I've always liked Teresa. Nothing seems to faze her and even when all around are losing their heads, as the old saying goes, she always seems to find a smile. Ever since we started the 'Adam's Farm' segment on the show, we've been trying to find new ways of entertaining the viewer while also teaching them a little about farming on the way. It isn't usually a problem. With a farm like ours, there's always something going on. But every now and then, it's good to take the action off the farm and explore the Cotswolds a bit. It adds a bit of variety and it also gives me a change as well, getting me out trying new things like I used to when I was one of the band of *Countryfile*'s roving reporters. So as soon as I told Teresa about my little wager with John the miller, I knew what she'd say.

'Have you ever made bread, Adam?'

'No, Teresa. Can't say I have.'

'Well, now's your chance. Get yourself along to the baker's and get kneading dough made from your flour. It'll be great for the show.'

How could I refuse? Besides, it was the prompt I needed to follow up what John had told me. After our meeting he had passed on the details of one of his baker friends – Clive Mellum, a master artisan baker who operates out of Shipton Mill. Clive had agreed to make some loaves for me and I'd been hard at work pulling strings to try and secure a pitch at the Stow-on-the-Wold Farmers' Market. In fact, I'd had to pull strings so hard they almost snapped. It's nigh on impossible to get a stall at the market – one of the most popular in the region – but at the last moment, they invited me to set up as a guest. The stage was set and all I needed was some bread.

And so I find myself in Clive's bakery. He's already made a first batch and now is instructing me, on camera, through the process of making the bread I'll be selling tomorrow.

'You need two kilos of flour,' he's saying, as I try to keep up – Delia Smith I am not – '40 grammes of salt and 500 grammes of your mother straight on the top.'

My what? The mother, it turns out is the active yeast mix that causes the bread to rise. I reach for a plastic scoop, but Clive stops me.

'No, Adam. Use your hands.'

I plunge my hands into the gloopy mess of fermenting yeast. It's like being a kid again, playing with mud pies – but at least this time I'll be able to eat the results.

We're making sourdough loaves, using natural yeast, the type of bread people round here have been making for generations. As we add water and turn the bread out on to the table to knead, I'm really enjoying myself, and have almost forgotten the cameras are there. Kneading bread is quite a therapeutic process, truth be told. It's not something you can rush – if you do, the final loaf will be ruined. You just have to stand there, working air into the mixture with your hands, pulling and pushing until it's elastic beneath your fingers. At times like this, you realise how much we rush through our days, so desperate to get on to the next thing. According to Clive, we're seeing a revival in these very traditional types of bread. People are not only coming to bakeries like his to purchase good old-fashioned artisan bread, they're also rediscovering the joys of making their own, of taking the chance to unwind and relax while keeping old skills alive.

This renaissance in bread-making also brings another benefit to bakers like Clive and producers like me. As we continue to work the dough on the bench, I ask how much Clive thinks I should charge for one of our loaves. His answer is quick and decisive – anything up to £2.50 for a big loaf. I can hardly believe it. That's even more than John reckons. But why would people shell out over two quid for my bread when they could nip in a super-market and pick up a loaf for under a pound?

'They'll be able to taste the difference,' comes Clive's response. 'We're talking about a premium product here and, even today, when we're so used to cheap, disposable food, people will still pay for quality. This bread – your bread – is not mass-produced and is, as you can see, highly labour-intensive.'

He's not wrong. We've been kneading the dough for about 15 minutes now, and after cutting it into individual loaves, pop it in a stack under a sheet of plastic so it can prove, the yeast working merrily away. It'll stay there for two-and-a-half hours before its ready to go into the oven. This is not a job for the impatient.

But if we're going to do this, we've got to do it well.

While Teresa is right, and my exploits in the bakery are making good TV, I'm not playing here. Just going through this process has pushed my costs right up. Milling my wheat into flour has taken the cost of production to around £250 a tonne. Of course, I could stop there, and just sell it on as flour to artisan bread-making operations. But if I want to take it further, to make my own Bemborough Farm bread and therefore hopefully adding real value, it'll add even more costs. The question is whether the final result will live up to the faith that both John and Clive have shown in it so far. Clive has already told me that he's been impressed with the flour. Knowing what kind of wheat it came from, he's been surprised how good it feels and how well it's taken water, the sign of a good loaf. I just hope he's right, because if I come home tomorrow night with a car boot full of unsold bread, I'll be feeding my ducks with it for weeks. Plus, as

I've invited the *Countryfile* cameras along, seven million viewers will watch me walk away with egg on my face.

The following day I am standing in the middle of beautiful Stow-on-the-Wold, a basket of bread under my arm, shouting myself hoarse in the middle of the market.

'Roll up. Roll up,' I cry, trying to ignore the ever-present camera that's in my face to the side. 'Come and get your freshly made bread. Wheat straight off the farm into the mill at Shipton and baked last night. Fresh as you like.'

And fresh is exactly what it was when I arrived in Stow in the first light of day to find my pitch. Clive had done me proud and had baked through the night to turn out enough loaves for my wager. My truck is packed with bread of all shapes and sizes. It's all a bit overwhelming, to be honest. As I picked it up from the baker's this morning, I found myself asking if I would ever be able to shift that lot. But I didn't have time for nerves. I had a stall to set up.

The market had been more than generous with my pitch, giving me a great spot slap-bang in the middle of the square. The market is held here on the second Thursday of every month, near the village green that is still the home of the old penal stocks, the latest in a very long line that date back to at least the fifteenth century. There has been a market of some kind here ever since Henry I first granted Stow its charter back in 1107. By 1330, the town, which, at 800 feet above sea level, is the highest town in the Cotswolds, had become so popular that Edward III authorised a seven-day market, a rare occurrence at that time. The wealth of the town grew, helped considerably by additional wool fairs that were held annually on 12 May and 24 October. By the nineteenth century people travelled from far and wide to come to the fair and it was said that more than 20,000 sheep would change hands in a single day at Stow. Even when the wool trade began to dwindle, the town refused to give up on its fairs. Sheep farmers moved out and horse breeders moved in. To this day, the world-famous horse fairs still take place every May and October, attracting hundreds of travellers to the town, although the action has moved away from the town square to a site on the outskirts.

This is a truly historic place. The last battle of the English Civil War was won just a few yards from where I am standing trying to flog my bread. In March 1646, the Royalist army, led by Sir Jacob Astley, was defeated by Parliamentary forces under the command of Colonel Morgan and over 1000 prisoners held overnight in the parish church of St Edward's. One way or another, this square has seen a lot of action.

I just wish it was seeing more action now. Even though the promised rain hasn't come, the market square is hardly bustling. We do pick up one or two sales, but no one is around. The first hour passes and our tally only just scrapes into two figures. This is not going to plan.

I start to cut loaves up. If Mohammed won't come to the mountain, it's time to take the mountain to Mohammed. Armed with a tray full of samples, I head out to try and lure people over.

As the morning passes, the crowds thankfully start to build. As I wander about offering bread to anyone who gives me a second glance I started to spot familiar faces, people I've quite literally known all my life. I suppose this is one aspect of country life that many people could find claustrophobic. I'm walking around an area where I played as a kid, all those times when mum and dad dragged my sisters and me into Stow so they could come to market. Did I think I'd still be working near here all these years later, living in the very same farmhouse where I was born?

By the time the bells of St Edward's struck noon, the market was heaving and the bread, I'm pleased to say, was going like hot cakes. By the time I'd got back from my last round of market-eering we'd shifted more than 70 loaves and an awful lot of flour, which we'd decided at the last minute to bag up. One hour later, when the crowd had started to thin again and my fellow stall-holders were starting to pack up, I couldn't quite believe it. Four hours ago I'd started with around 120 loaves and a head full of doubts. I was now left with a lot of crumbs and all but two loaves unsold.

All that remained was for me to make a phone call.

'Hi, John, it's Adam. OK, you were right. We sold over 100 loaves.'

I had to sharply move the phone away from my ear to protect my eardrum from John's laugh at the other end of the line.

'What did I tell you?' he asked.

'I think you won your bet,' I replied, 'and I also think we're going to need some more flour.'

CHAPTER 12

A PREGNANT PAUSE

There's a nip in the October air as we usher Inca, my prize Belted Galloway bull, into the race. At first he's not happy about it, but soon he clatters into the cage. Inca has served the farm well and has sired four daughters, but now it's time for him to be replaced as I need to bring new blood on to the farm. There's nothing wrong with Inca, and he's got plenty of years, and offspring, in him. He's done his job and got our cows in calf again this year. But now his daughters are coming into the herd and we can't have him breeding with them.

Before we can wave Inca goodbye he needs to be tested for TB. Even though the entire herd were clear on the last test, after 60 days you need to re-test any cow or bull that you want to move off the farm. It's a sensible precaution – you wouldn't want to unwittingly spread disease on to another farm – but as always, it's a tense time. Gill, the vet, is on hand and my heart is in my mouth when I watch her brush her hand again Inca's thick, powerful neck.

Belted Galloways, or 'Belties' as breeders affectionately call them, are magnificent animals noted for their unique colours. Most Belties are black, red or – like Inca – dun, a light brownish-grey colour, yet all of them have a curious white stripe that completely encircles their bodies between the shoulders and hips. I've heard that American breeders even call them 'the Oreo cow' because of the stark contrast of the white belt between the black, like the well-known chocolate biscuit. It's thought that Belties were originally bred during the sixteenth century in the former Galloway district of Scotland, now part of Dumfries and Galloway. Our Belties must think they're in heaven compared to the exposed uplands and rugged terrain of south-west Scotland for, as you'd expect, the breed is well suited to exceptionally barren landscapes and can survive on remarkably rough grazing land if required. Ours don't have to worry about that, and seem more than happy on lush Gloucestershire grass, but their long hair and dense undercoat comes in handy wherever they are. With over 4000 hairs per square inch, that thick carpet on their backs keeps their body heat in whatever the weather, meaning that they don't need to eat as much as other cattle over the winter and are quite happy to spend the colder months out in the fields. They're a tough bunch and can live up to 20 years, producing the richest of milks for their calves and plenty of well-marbled, excellent quality beef.

'Good news, Adam,' Gill says, after what seems like an eternity. 'He's clear. You can send him off farm.'

Fantastic. And there's no time to lose. Inca's replacement, Hawthorn, is arriving this very afternoon from breeder Denys Shortt's farm in Buckland. When Hawthorn finally clatters down out of the trailer, he is an impressive sight, a ton of pure, unadulterated muscle. Showing him the respect this absolute beauty is due, while also making sure he knows that I'm the boss, we let him into the field with his future wives. It's always interesting introducing a new bull to the herd. Hawthorn is already pretty awe-inspiring, with that distinctive white belt separating a glossy, jet-black coat. But, intimidating as he is, he still puffs himself up as he strides into the field. This is all part of the game. He's trying to establish himself as the alpha male right from the off. He also has no idea what awaits him in the field. For all he knows, there are more bulls in the field and so he has to both make himself look as big as possible but also prepare himself for a fight. Of course, here he has no rivals. The ladies are all his for the taking and as he takes his place at the centre of the herd, his harem are already sniffing around him.

If this were a dairy herd, we wouldn't just let a bull in with the cows. You can't leave the important business of getting their heifers pregnant to chance. Instead, we rely on artificial insemination (AI). Semen is collected from the very best bulls and administered by vets or, in some cases, experienced herdsmen. The reasons for using AI are simple. Primarily, you aren't just limiting yourself to the bulls you own. In fact, if you want to save money, you needn't keep any bulls at all. Frozen sperm can be bought in from all around the world, meaning that you can tap into the finest bloodlines possible. Dairies pay a lot of money to get hold of DNA that guarantees them gallons of premium milk.

It's also a lot more efficient. During normal breeding, a bull will deposit much more semen than is technically needed to produce a pregnancy. Plus, he's had to go through all the effort of approaching a cow in heat, mount her and well, you know the idea. All that effort limits the amount of times the bull will mate. If semen is collected from him, however, it can be diluted and hundreds of doses can be created from one single load.

Most beef farming operations like ours aren't as clinical as this though, and here we usually let the bull have all the fun. Cows come into heat for one day every three weeks – a process known as bulling – and it's pretty obvious when the bull has served her. You can't exactly miss a one-ton bull riding a cow. There's no fancy system for keeping check of what's going on in the field. You simply take a note of the cow's number when you think she's been served and keep an eye on her, checking her in for a pregnancy test about six to eight weeks later.

Talking of which, I need to be elsewhere. I give our new sweethearts a little privacy and head to where I keep the White Parks. While Hawthorn's wives are checking him out, I need to see if his counterparts in the other groups have been pulling their weight.

Gill is back for the second time in one day and the tests she is going to perform are equally nerve-racking as the TB trials. A couple of months ago, we ran routine pregnancy tests on our cattle and, rather worryingly, a lot of the cows turned out not to be pregnant. We have no idea why and so I've decided to test both the White Parks and the Highland cows today. If it turns out that they haven't fallen pregnant in the last couple of months we could have a serious problem on our hands. Either there's something wrong with the cows or, disastrously, we've got a duff bull.

By the time I arrive at the paddock, the first White Park is already in the cattle race and Mike is closing the gate behind her. To the right, Gill is pulling on the long latex glove that reaches to her elbow to protect the cow from any infection and also keep Gill reasonably clean.

This isn't a procedure for the faint-hearted. If you've ever seen an episode of James Herriot's *All Creatures Great and Small* you know what's coming. In a few minutes Gill is elbow-deep in the cow's anus, feeling for the uterus and the uterine horns to see if there is a developing foetus.

I can tell from her face that it's not going well.

'I'm not sure,' she admits, looking doubtful. 'I've got the whole of her uterus in my hand and there's no enlargement at all.'

That isn't the news I wanted, but Gill's not giving up. She tries again, this time not relying on her fingers but inserting an ultrasound scanner inside the cow. It could be that the foetus is too small to feel so if the White Park is in calf, the portable display will show the foetus.

It's not a good start.

'Sorry, Adam,' Gill concludes, examining the screen that I am holding for her, 'there's no fluid within either of the uterine horns. This one isn't pregnant today.'

I try not to get too downhearted. It could just be one of those things. I'd thought that particular cow was quite healthy but for one reason or another, she might not have been in the right condition to conceive.

The next cow is in the race and I suddenly realise I've crossed my fingers without thinking. It doesn't work.

'I'm afraid it's bad news, Adam,' says Gill, 'I can't feel a pregnancy in this one either.'

I can't believe it. Finally we're clear of TB and now this. For a second it feels like the world is against me. When the scan comes up negative, the cow is led out to make way for the third. As soon as I realise what cow it is I can't help but let out a sigh. If those two aren't pregnant, the chances of this particular heifer being in calf are slim.

Gill looks puzzled as she starts the internal examination and I know exactly why.

'There's something a bit abnormal here, Adam. Did this one have problems calving last year?' Gill asks.

Did she ever. I can still remember that night. The cow was pregnant with the most enormous calf and we had to give her a lot of assistance. We had a hell of job getting it out and when it finally came, it was born dead.

When I tell Gill the story, she nods.

'That fits. I can feel that she suffered some considerable trauma during the birth, but I'm sorry to say, she's not pregnant this time either.'

Three cows and not a calf between them. That's it then. If the next one is revealed not to be pregnant, we've got a problem that I could do without – a one-ton problem in the shape of a duff bull. I start doing the sums in my head. The gestation period of a cow is exactly the same as a human's and, like us, they can fall pregnant at any time. However, we try to plan it so that the calves are born in spring, around the same time as the lambs. It means that the spring grass is already growing when they arrive and the cold frosts are passing. There's another bonus for us. By then the farm park has opened for another season and our visitors will be able to see lots of lovely cute babies in the fields. That's always good for business. So, to time things perfectly, we put the bull to the cows around June.

If what I fear is realised and it turns out that the White Park bull isn't performing we'll have to get rid of him and get in a quick replacement. Even if we do that in the next month, the earliest I can hope is for the cows to be in calf by December, or maybe November, if we're lucky. Winter will hit at the earliest part of the pregnancy, raising the risk of miscarriage, but, all being well, the calves will be born next September or October, just as the weather conditions are worsening. We'll need to buy in more winter feed to give them the nutrients they would have got from summer pasture and they'll obviously be ready for beef a lot later. Just from a cash-flow situation, each fully grown White Park can be sold for £1500 and I've worked the budget so that this injection of cash comes exactly when I need it. The knock-on effect of all of this is massive and the implications don't bear thinking about.

I've been so lost in my own, bleak thoughts that I've been working almost on autopilot. I literally jump when Gill suddenly shouts beside me.

'Yip-a-dee-doo-dah! This one is in calf!'

I almost have to ask Gill if she's joking, but the smile on her face as she slips her arm back out of the cow tells me that she isn't.

So the bull isn't infertile? We were just unlucky to get three negatives in a row? Gill nods happily and I let out a sigh of relief. At times like this I remember something my dad told me years ago, 'Adam, whatever happens you need to remember that farming is a roller-coaster ride. Just don't expect many thrills.'

The next cow is revealed to be pregnant, and the one after that. It turns out that six of the nine White Parks are in calf, so all is not lost.

Next up are the Highlands. I'm hoping that they'll bring us five pregnancies out of five to make up for the disappointing results from the White Parks. My hopes are dashed straight away as I watch Gill, now considerably muckier than when she started the entire process, slip her hand into the first Highland. There's the shake of the head I didn't want to see. Once again she has the entire uterus in her hand and there's nothing. The scanner comes out to double-check, but it's negative. Here we go again. Thankfully the next Highland is in calf, but when the tests are finished, we end up with only three pregnant Highlands. Mother Nature has obviously worked against me this season and I can't help but be disappointed. On days like these, you would expect to have a 90 per cent fertility rate. We're looking at 60 per cent. Not the best.

I glance over at the field in the distance, where Hawthorn is getting to know his new wives. I'm sure that, come next season, when he's ready to serve Inca's daughters, he won't let us down.

CHAPTER 13

A TRIP TO
DARTMOOR

My disappointment over the cattle doesn't last. A couple of days later I'm like a kid in a sweet shop, bursting with excitement as I'm heading out to pick up some new animals. I've always been the same. Perhaps it was because, back in the Seventies, I never really knew what dad was going to bring home with him from one of his little expeditions. But these particular arrivals are extra special. It's been 15 years since we introduced a new breed to the farm, but I'm about to do so today. I'm in the car with Mike, driving through the craggy wilderness of Dartmoor. Six thousand years ago this landscape would have looked very different. What we now know as moors would have been covered with trees, with Neolithic hunters darting in and out of the ancient forests, hunting wild animals. Over time the vast woodlands were cleared and, by 2000 BCE, just as primitive man was erecting the standing stones that still dot the landscape, sheep and cattle had been introduced, grazing the new open moorland. By medieval times, sheep dominated Dartmoor and, like my home back in Gloucestershire, Devon became rich on the back of sheep's wool.

Today, shepherds still keep animals on this harsh, unforgiving landscape. It's a very different kind of farming to what I'm used to. This is the world of marginal upland farming, where the elements are fierce and profits are low. It's a wild place, where animals huddle against cold winds and the soil beneath their feet is poor. However, you can't help but marvel at the sheer, austere beauty of the place. I can understand totally why generations of farmers have battled the weather to keep farming this awesome land.

One such man is Colin Pearse who has farmed here for more than 60 years. You can see that in his youth Colin would have been a bear of a man, and must have been tough to tend his flock out here in all weathers, but what has impressed me in the short time I've known him is his easy-going, gentle nature. I could sit and listen to his stories of the moors for hours, thanks to that lilting Devonian accent. It's a good job, too, as we're going to be spending a long time together today.

Colin farms a breed of sheep that was once found all over these moors and still bears its name – The Whitefaced Dartmoor. The Whitefaced is descended from the native sheep that grazed both Dartmoor and Exmoor in the seventeenth and eighteenth centuries. As you'd expect, it does indeed have a brilliant white face and its highly crimped long wool has a good reputation. However, numbers have dropped dramatically since the Second World War and the RSBT has placed the breed in the 'at risk' category, meaning there are less than 1500 registered breed-ing females. All of these animals are based around Dartmoor, so they're particularly at risk. If the West Country was hit by a bad case of foot-and-mouth or bluetongue, it could be game over for the entire breed. We've come down to pick up 16 ewes that we will take back to Bemborough to start a new nucleus flock. This will at least offer the breed a little more protection, and it feels good to once again follow in my dad's footsteps. This was exactly the kind of thing he was up to in the Seventies and Eighties and his reputation for helping rare breeds casts a long shadow. As far as I'm concerned, I want the Henson name to be associated with projects like this for as long as the family is farming.

I'm not the only one thinking of the family name. Mike's great-great-uncle, Cecil Caunter, was the first president of the Whitefaced Dartmoor Sheep Breeders Association and he's keen to re-establish the family connection.

But when we arrive at the farm there isn't a single sheep to be seen. Instead we're greeted by Colin, who shakes our hands warmly and is especially pleased to meet a fellow Devon lad in Mike.

'We've got a bit of a walk ahead of us,' Colin says, with a twin-kle in his eye. 'The sheep are 1200 feet up, about halfway as high as Dartmoor gets.' He pauses a minute to look at the sky, which is slightly overcast. 'It won't be the clearest of days up there, but it's not that bad. After all, you know what they say about Dartmoor?'

I shrug, wondering what pearl of wisdom is about to fall from this farming veteran. Colin fixes me with a smile, 'They say that if you can see Dartmoor it's going to rain, and when you can't see it, it already is.'

The plan is to walk Colin's sheep back from the moor to the farm so we can load them up. We'll have to traipse a good couple of miles and we'll have to take it easy. Colin is recovering from two hip replacements. As we make our way up, he tells me more about the breed.

'I can't tell you how happy I am you've come down here,' Colin begins. 'Back in the 1800s there were as many as 110,000 recorded Whitefaces up here. Now we've got less than 1500. It was foot-and-mouth that finally did for them. Before that, numbers were still around 2000. Not great, but still promising. Foot-and-mouth decimated them and it hasn't helped that all around us, farmers are moving on. These animals haven't altered much over time and the knowledge of how to care for them has been taught from father to son. That information is being lost now. It's Dartmoor's saddest story, if you ask me.'

By the time we've made it to the flock, Colin's son Paul is rounding them up from the back of his quad bike. It's an emotional day for Colin. These animals really have been his life.

'I've lost track of the sleepless nights I've had when the snow has closed in on the moor. All I can think about is my animals. I lay there wondering if they're all right and whether they have enough food? Then you get up at first light and look out of the window, to see if you can get through the snow to check on them.'

By now we're walking back down to the farm, guiding the flock down roads and across fields. I wonder what Colin is going to do with his time now that he's decided to start scaling back his flock in the autumn of his career.

'Don't get me wrong, Adam,' he says. 'It's been a privilege to have these sheep. We owe a great debt to them around here. But I have to face facts. I can't walk as fast as I used to and time is moving on for me. I'm looking forward to having a little more of it so I can concentrate on some of my other passions.'

It turns out that Colin tries his hand at photography and is also a bit of an amateur poet.

'You can't help but be a poet when you wake up and see Dartmoor around you every morning,' he says, throwing up an arm to point out the surroundings. I can see what he means. The views on the way back to the farm are awe-inspiring.

Back in the yard, we inspect the ewes that Colin has picked out for us, checking their teeth and udders, and when we're happy with them, load them into the trailer. I can't help but notice that Colin is a little choked. This is a historic moment. The first flock of Whitefaced Dartmoors to leave their homeland in hundreds of years. As we turn to leave, I give Colin a friendly pat on his shoulder, promising that we'll look after them.

'I'm sure you will,' he says pushing a piece of paper into my hands.

As we drive off, I watch as the figure of Colin leaning on his farm gate shrinks in the rear-view mirror. He's rapidly reaching the end of an era, but hopefully it's the beginning of a new one for his sheep. I open the paper he gave me and see that it's one of his poems.

I feel like I'm touching winter again,
It must be the darkness and the rain,
Brief is the sunset light and daytime bright,
The moor's all washed, it's not surprised
As it puts on its overcoat disguise.
Water pumping over granite rock,
Confining the wandering flock,
Old walls of stone, weaved and shaped, unseat,
Fall and slip, sinking into sodden peat,
A gap spotted by an indigenous sheep,
Leads into another piece of barren waste
Too damp upon to sleep,
Where the stepping stones of a bygone race
Are eroded and displaced.

A few days later and the Whitefaced Dartmoors have made themselves at home, along with a ram that we'd bought from a farm in Widecombe-in-the-Moor in Devon. We had the choice of two rams, but dad has always told me that if you're going to buy a sheep, buy a good one. The best out of the pair was twice as expensive and cost me £300. But I'm a true believer that you get what you pay for and in this case it's all worth it. I've spent the best part of £1500 on my new flock, but it's very satisfying to know we're helping keep the Whitefaced bloodlines growing. I'm hoping that these ewes will have lots of lambs next spring and we'll be able to start to trade with other breeders. The Dartmoors make great mothers so, all being well, the future looks bright for Bemborough's first Whitefaced flock.

The Whitefaced ram isn't the only new tup on the farm. I have 18 in total, both commercial and rare breed, and between them they'll hopefully father about a thousand lambs over the next year for me. When it comes to rare breeds like the White-faced or the new Herdwick ram that I bought a month or so ago it's all about instinct. You look for good teeth, a straight back and all the qualities of the breed, but most of the time you rely on your gut instinct and your experience.

With the commercial flock that's not enough. It's big business, so science plays a major part in choosing the right ram. Not long ago, Mike and I travelled to Melton Mowbray, home of those famous pork pies, to bring home a couple of Charollais rams from award-winning breeder Charles Sercombe. The Charollais were first brought into the UK from the Saône-et-Loire region of France in 1976. They are hard-working rams who are exceptionally good at serving ewes and can work six or even seven seasons, meaning that if you get a good one you'll be looking at plenty of lambs during the ram's lifetime. I've always found the Charollais incredibly easy to lamb as well, which is a bonus come spring time and the lambs they produce are quick to get on their feet and suckle, and grow exceptionally fast, reaching weights of 40 kilos in just eight weeks.

This year we decided to go for the best, and that means Charles's rams. When we were there we performed a few manual checks. First, the teeth. Our rams are going to have to work hard, mating with around 75 ewes each, and so you want to know that they have good strong teeth in order to be able to eat well. The jaw formation and quality teeth will hopefully be passed on to their lambs too, so that the little ones can graze well when they are putting on weight.

You also check that they've got plenty of meat around the bum – after all, their offspring will need good meaty gigots, in other words, fair-sized legs of lamb. Finally, there are another couple of things to check and there's no need to be shy about this. When buying rams you need to get personal, grabbing between their legs. Those testicles are going to have to work hard in the next month or so, so you need to get your hand on a nice, firm pair with no deformities – and when I say get your hands on, that's literally what you do.

These manual tests are only the beginning however, and before we hand over our hard-earned cash, it's time for a spot of science. The final selection is made using something called the Signet recording system. We want to know how well the ram will perform genetically and so an estimated breeding value (EBV) is calculated by number-crunching some key data. The breeder takes note of the ram's sire and dam (another name for its father and mother) and then weighs the lamb at both 8 and 21 weeks. At the time of the last weigh-in, an ultrasound is performed, checking its muscle depth and fat coverage. All of this raw data is then run through a computer that grades the ram and assesses its chances of performing well in future. It's a bit like the old 'Top Trumps' games I used to love playing when I was a kid. You're looking for the best figures you can get for each animal. The two rams cost me £450 each– but my experience in the past tells me that I'll reap the benefits in spring. Each of the rams I bought from Charles earlier this year will hopefully provide me with 130 lambs a year, which will sell for around sixty quid a time. It's not a bad conversion rate, and as I only buy rams from the top 25 per cent of the breed the lambs should make good stock and will all go for meat. That is, all except for the very best ewes. We breed all of our replacement females, selecting them by going carefully through the record to find those bloodlines with the best maternal traits – the ease of lambing, willingness to raise the young and good feet among others.

About now I have to make sure that the ewes are ready to conceive. It's also a great chance to put Millie, my rookie sheepdog, through her paces, training her to get the sheep in pens so I can check them over. I've been really happy with the way she's getting on and over the last few weeks have been given a helping hand training her. We've got a visitor to the farm who hails from the other side of the world. Katie Dickison is a sheep farmer from New Zealand and is used to dealing with far more sheep than our flock. I can still remember catching my first glance of a New Zealand flock when I travelled around the region after college. They are simply massive, averaging around 1400 per farm. It's said that there are roughly a dozen sheep for every person in New Zealand and I can believe it. Katie runs six dogs back home, and really knows what she's talking about, so I'm glad when she tells me that she's impressed with Millie.

'You've got a good dog there, Adam. She's a natural,' she says the first time she sees Millie do her stuff. 'Your only problem is that when she's out in the paddock, she doesn't stop quickly enough when you call, meaning that she's a little out of control at the moment.'

I can't argue with her. I've noticed exactly the same thing and have been hard at work training Millie with a gaggle of geese back in the farmyard. She's been doing well, but it's a different story when she's in a field with a big mob of sheep and is a hundred yards or so away from me.

Between us we soon get the ewes together in a pen and Katie has one last training trick to show me before she heads off to spend time on one of my neighbours' farms.

'Millie needs to show those ewes who's the boss,' Katie says, matter-of-factly, before getting me to pick up Millie. 'Right, now throw her on to the back of the sheep.'

If anyone could see us, they'd think we've gone mad. We spend the next ten minutes chucking Millie – quite gently I should point out – on to the back of the ewes. The idea is that she'll get used to being in the middle of them and, more importantly, superior to them. The last thing we want is for Millie to resort to biting the sheep to get their attention and this way she starts to build her confidence. She also loves every minute of it. She's a tough working dog and loves a bit of rough and tumble.

It also gives me a chance to look at the ewes. I keep a close eye on them as they try to walk away from boisterous Millie. Almost immediately I spot one with a problem. She's nodding her head as she's walking and lifting her front left leg. I single her out to see what's making her lame. I clean up the foot, trimming away part of the hoof and see that she's got an abscess under the skin. That needs to be cleaned up before we put the ram in with her. It's a pretty simple cause-and-effect lesson, really. A ewe who finds it too painful to walk won't forage to find food and will start losing weight, making it more difficult for her to be likely to become pregnant. If we're lucky and she conceives anyway, there's every chance that she'll have only one lamb because she's so skinny and poorly. I give this one a quick jab of antibiotics to clear up the infection and, along with the rest of the flock, walk her through a foot dip containing diluted chemicals that kill off the bacteria that cause foot rot in sheep.

Once the ewes have walked through the dip they're supposed to stand on the concrete at the far end while the chemicals soak into their feet, but as I guide the last sheep into the race I look up to see the flock disappearing over the next field. How have they got out there? Katie has the answer. Some idiot forgot the golden rule of the countryside – and left the gate open. There's no one I can shout at however, as it soon transpires that the idiot was me. Rolling my eyes, I call for Millie. At least she'll get a little more training this afternoon and luckily there are no hazards that I can think of in that field.

A couple of weeks later and the ewes are being gathered together again. This time I make sure that all the gates are well and truly fastened as we're about to unleash the Herdwick ram I'd bought earlier in the season. He's a huge beast, with a typically long-haired fleece. Herdwicks hail from the fells of the Lake District where they survive in the wettest part of the country on scant grazing, some 3000 feet above sea level. According to legend the Herdwicks, who start off with a dark grey fleece that gradually becomes lighter the older they get, came to these shores with the Spanish Armada. When a galleon went down off the Cumbrian coast, the hardy sheep saw a chance to escape and swam to freedom. It's a charming story that no one has ever been able to substantiate, but I can certainly believe that the Herdwicks of legend wouldn't have given up without a fight. They're survivors, born and bred. And I'm hoping that this ram's survival instincts will be passed on to his young in the spring.

Elsewhere, the other rams have already been put to work. My Romney ram has been in with the ewes for a week now and we've been keeping an eye on how he's been getting on, thanks to a special harness we slip on to his chest before we let him loose with the ladies. Fitted to the harness is a crayon known as a raddle. As the ram mates with the ewe, the crayon rubs against the wool on her rump, leaving a coloured mark on her back.

As a ewe comes into oestrus, or heat, about every 18 days, shepherds change the colour of the raddle in a corresponding 18-day cycle, starting with a light colour such as yellow, then working through a rainbow of green, red, blue and finally black. The ewes with all the same colour mark can then be separated out at lambing time for ease of management. Also, if you find that one of your ewes is plastered with a lot of colours it means that she's probably infertile. On the other hand, if every ewe's rear end is constantly changing colour as the tupping season continues, it's the ram who's not performing, although that's a problem I'm praying we won't have this year after spending so much money on the boys.

Of course, Bemborough is not your average farm. We have 20 different breeds to manage during tupping. Plus, as we want our ewes to lamb in front of the public, we have to make sure that the lambing season is spread out as evenly as we can. This means that Mike heads out to change the raddles every nine days rather than the usual 18. It's a massive job.

We also need to make sure our records are kept up to date and that we note which ewe was put to which ram. This means that when the lambs are born, we can record the lineage as well as match up the ewe and lamb numbers.

It's a good job Mike likes paperwork.

Things have just become a lot easier, though. The laws have changed meaning that every animal now has to be tagged with an electronic tag that contains a tiny microchip. That chip records all the information you ever need about the animal from the moment it's born. It helps speed up everything. In the past, if we had to check all of the ewes' records we'd get them into the sheep race and, one by one, have to rub mud off the old plastic tag to get to the number. You'd then shout each number over to your workmate who'd write it down in the book. You can imagine how fun that was in the pouring rain.

These days you simply run a handheld scanner over each ewe's head and it reads the information, ready to download back at the office. It's proved to be a hugely useful step when it comes to registrations, speeding things up no end. Granted, it has been expensive to implement, costing us a couple of thousand pounds, but it soon pays for itself, especially at this time of year when we're getting the ewes ready to conceive. One scan of the chip tells us that this or that ewe had difficulty lambing last year, or proved to be a bad mother. In the old days that kind of information was either buried away in ring binders or locked in your memory. Now, it's all available at the touch of a button and means that you can remove problem ewes before you even begin. They say that 10 per cent of your flock is 90 per cent of your work. If you can weed out that problematic 10 per cent, then life becomes a lot easier.

CHAPTER 14

FREE-RANGE OR NOT FREE-RANGE. THAT IS THE QUESTION

Dad comes walking towards me with an apple picker, a simple contraption that is basically a small net at the end of a large pole. I immediately know what he's after. The back garden of the farmhouse has a number of huge apple trees that dad first planted 40 years ago. He's persuaded mum to bake one of her famous blackberry and apple pies and wants some of the juicy apples that have been ripening in the tall, upper branches. I don't mind helping – after all, chances are I'll be able to scrounge a slice or two of the pie myself. As I reach up to clip the apples some fall to the ground. They won't go to waste – I know a lot of hungry mouths that will love them.

I'm glad of the break. This morning has been hard work. Mike and I have been in the nursery yards where we keep our piglets. They are taken from their mothers at about eight to ten weeks when they are weaned and let out into open straw yards. Here they get as much food as they can eat, a concoction of grain and my mate Bean's apple pulp, so that they start to put weight on. We're looking for them to get to about 50 kilos, when they can be taken on to the next stage of the system that separates the pigs according to size and weight. This morning we had about twenty pigs to move out of the nursery so Mike could take them to the main pig sheds. Most of the pigs we want to move are Tamworths, with a few Iron Age pigs to boot. As soon as we walked over to the yards we knew we were going to have trouble. Pigs, especially Tamworths, are lively creatures with a healthy amount of curiosity and today they all seemed full of the devil himself. Getting them out of the yard and into a trailer involved constructing a run using metal hurdles so we can guide them into the back of the vehicle. Before we knew it, the pigs were around us, wanting to know what we were doing. If I were a gambling man, I would have put good money on the fact that as soon as we got our twenty pigs into the run, they'd try to escape. It turns out I would have won my bet. Give a pig the chance to wriggle through a gap and it'll be off, its little legs scrabbling away nineteen to the dozen and squealing so loudly you'd think it's trying to wake the dead. There's no way you can be dignified when moving pigs. The trick is to prod them here, stop them pitching an escape bid there and hope that they don't suddenly run and take your legs away from beneath you, so you land with a crunch in a pile of pig muck.

Today we actually managed the entire operation quite well and pretty soon all of the pigs were in the back of the trailer.

And then I took my eye off the ball. With a squeal of triumph one of the large black Iron Age pigs had leapt over the hurdle and was tearing across the field. I could kick myself, but one pig out of 20 isn't actually that bad. Usually they don't go too far anyway, as they don't like moving away from their mates. I set out after him only to find the large porker snuffling away around an old outhouse. If I didn't know better I would have said that he had a smug expression on that face of his as I guided him back to the run, as if he was thinking, 'Ha! And you thought you were the boss around here.'

The prodigal pig returned, the trailer's back gate was shut and Mike was soon driving them over to their new home.

Later on, with a basketful of windfall apples, I head to the pig shed. At the moment this is a little bit of a make-do job. The pig operation has taken off faster than we thought. It's a great position to be in. The demand from the butcher is now greater than we can produce so if we want him to keep coming back to us, we need to scale things up quickly. Last year we had 9 sows and now we're up to 18. The next step will be to escalate it to around 40 to 50 sows. But where will we keep them? At present, the pigs are living in a former sheep shed that we've adapted by blocking up any holes which would allow the pigs to escape. We're always having to go back and patch up this place or that and it's a constant struggle to keep them in the place.

Saying that, I'm happy with the environment we've created for the pigs here. The hard floor is covered in a lovely, deep carpet of straw and it's warm and dry. They certainly seem content as

I watch them tuck into dad's apples. But when we start getting more pigs, this would soon become overcrowded. Also, I'd prefer to market them as free-range and while they spend their early days outside in the yard, we have to bring them in for the rest of their lives. It's not what I originally planned.

The problem is that, while I'd love to give all our pigs the freedom to wander where they please outside, it would be disastrous for our fields. Stick a pig outside and it will immediately begin to snuffle around in the soil. That powerful snout makes short work of the ground and before you know it, it will have their nose right under the turf, turning it over as it searches for a tasty meal of worms and roots. They can't help it – the habit is hard-wired into their brains from birth. This can cause all kinds of problems, some of which I've experienced recently. Many of our traditional breeds, such as the Old Spots, are kept out all year in their own special paddocks, but I've experimented by keeping a number of our porkers in one of my grass paddocks near the house where I also graze sheep. In just a few days the pigs had turned the place into a quagmire, much to the disgust of the sheep, and water has started to pool in the furrows. I don't want these to become stagnant, or start to attract bacteria. The entire paddock is going to have to be cultivated and seeded next spring to return it to its previous state.

For centuries farmers have countered this by putting rings in pig's noses. The rings, which are clipped to the rim of the nose rather than through the nostrils, consist of open copper wire bands, around 2.5 cm in diameter, which put pressure on the sensitive areas of the nose. This stops the pig rooting about by making digging uncomfortable for the animal. Typically, an adult pig will be given three or four rings in its lifetime as they often become dislodged, but it's not a route I want to go down. After all, why bother to put pigs outside if you then stop them doing what comes naturally?

I need some advice, so I jump in the car with Mike and head off to an organic pig farm near Cirencester to see a man who may have some answers. Richard Hazell has been keeping pigs for more than ten years and, crucially, all of his animals are kept outside. Even as we drive up we can see that the fields are littered with semi-circular pig huts made from corrugated metal. Everywhere you look sows are running this way and that, with piglets hopping around on their trotters. A few minutes later, we're being given a tour of the paddocks. The pigs certainly seem in their element.

As Richard is fully organic he runs his farm to the strict guidelines set by the Soil Association, which is based in Bristol. Many of the conventional pig-keeping practices are banned. Many producers, for example, dock pigs' tails at birth. Piglets are born with sharp incisor teeth that Mother Nature has provided for them to fight for the best teats on their mother's body. Young pigs quite often use these to nip at each other's tails, a process that can lead to infection, or even the development of abscesses in later life. To combat this, most of the tail is removed. The idea is that without a tail, a docked pig can get away faster from an attempted bite. Many welfare organisations object to such measures, claiming that poor living conditions cause pigs to become aggressive in this way. Organisations like Compassion in World Farming suggest giving pigs lots of stimulus that will satisfy their inquisitive nature, be that toys or wood and straw to play with. Under the EU 2001 Pig Directive, which became British law in 2003, docking can only be carried out as a very last resort and for organic farmers like Richard it's a complete no-no, along with teeth clipping, when for the same reason the incisors are cut off almost as soon as the piglets are born.

In Richard's system, sows that are ready to give birth are kept together in groups of four, each group given its own straw-filled hut where the sows will suckle their piglets after they are farrowed. Four weeks after birth the smaller huts are replaced with larger communal ones, with water and feed on tap. At eight weeks the piglets are weaned and a month later are moved on to separate-sex finishing fields, where they stay until they are big enough to go to slaughter.

I'm impressed and, more importantly, the pigs are nowhere near as muddy as I thought they would be. I talk through our own operation with Richard and, as I hoped, he's full of advice.

'I think your best bet,' he says, after giving it some thought, 'is to put your pigs into your arable rotation. After you've had them in a field for a season, you can plough it afterwards and then drill the follow-on crop – wheat would be a good choice. Even though pigs like to root, they're only churning the surface. All it'll take is one run of a cultivator and you'll be left with a pretty level seed bed. You won't even know they were there.'

As we drive back to the farm, we've got a lot to think about. Richard spoke a lot of sense. I certainly can't afford to give grasslands over to the pigs. It's too valuable for grazing the commercial sheep flock to watch it being churned up. So having the pigs as part of the arable rotation makes sense. We drive past some of our wheat fields, still full of the stubble left by the harvest. They will be ideal. The soil is light and free draining, but can I afford to take them out of production for a year to house the pigs? Like most decisions on the farm, it's a solution I will only find by breaking out the calculator. We have to ask whether the field will make more money from growing wheat or rearing pigs for the table. At the moment, at least, I've decided to keep the herd at its current size. Unfortunately, Itchy and Scratchy haven't exactly worked out. Love did blossom between them and the boar, but Itchy failed to conceive and Scratchy's litter was small and weak. Both sows have now gone off to slaughter; harsh I know, but a fact of life. Their job was to produce healthy piglets and, therefore, profit. If they couldn't do that I couldn't afford to keep feeding them. Thankfully the boar performed better on our other sows, so for the meantime I've decided to stick with the numbers we've got, possibly keeping a number of gilts to build up the herd slowly. I've talked to Bob the butcher and we've upped the number to three pigs a week. We can manage that easily and look to invest more in the spring.

There are other issues involved here as well. The only reason we have a commercial flock of sheep is that we would never make enough money from our rare-breed lambs. It's the same with the pigs. There's certainly more money in rare-breed pigs these days, but would we ever consider going over to a more modern commercial animal? After all, while it's all very idyllic seeing little Tamworth piglets hopping about in the mud, there are modern breeds with more teats than these old breeds, able to produce litters of even-sized bountiful piglets, perfect for cheap pork. It's a road that I can't see our farm going down, but you can see why people do. It's the reason that rare breeds became rare in the first place. I've always said that no matter how much I love Gloucester Old Spots, there's no way they could feed cities the size of say, Birmingham or Manchester. Whether we like it or not, thanks to an ever-growing population, mass production of farm animals is here to stay, but at least, thanks to farmers like Richard, and hopefully one day us as well, people have a choice of what kind of meat they want on their plate.

CHAPTER 15

TESTING TIMES

Stretch smiles when I get out of my car, but his eyes are cold. It's not that he's not pleased to see me, but today is a bleak day. I've known Stretch for years. He's one of the hardest-working dairy farmers I know and I hate seeing him like this. A couple of days ago he had his compulsory bovine tuberculosis test, and failed. I've come here today to help him get the cows that have to go for compulsory slaughter off to the abattoir.

It's sickening. Stretch's herd has been closed down with TB for two years now and he's lost hundreds of cattle. But there's another sting in the tale. To produce milk, dairy cows need to have given birth. If they give birth to females all is well and good, those can go into the future herd to produce milk themselves or to be sold on. If they give birth to males it's a different story. The meat from a dairy cow isn't ideal for beef, although you can produce good-quality veal. But the market for veal calves in the UK is small, thanks mainly to the welfare scares about Continental veal in the 1980s. Thirty years ago, you couldn't move without images of pathetic-looking calves peering out of tiny crates. It's true that the conditions these European animals were

– and in many cases still are – kept in are far from ideal. The crates may have finally been banned in 2007, but the animals still have hardly any space to move, are fed the bare minimum and are kept on bare floors. Things are very different here in the UK. Baby calves are fed twice as much as their European cousins, are allowed much more space and have to be kept on straw. They also have access to natural daylight. The conditions can be even better if you're talking about organic veal. All of these improvements mean that the meat produced in the UK has a slight pink tinge to it, hence its name in the beef industry – rosé veal.

However, only 1 in 100 families in the UK buy veal, so most dairy bull calves are killed. According to the Meat and Livestock Commission, around 170,000 calves were shot at birth every year for the last two decades. As long as I've known Stretch he's thought this was a waste and so used to rear as many calves as possible for breeding purposes. That was until he was hit by TB. In the two years he's been shut down he's had to have 250 bull calves shot at birth because he wasn't allowed to move them off the farm to sell. As he tells me this I can see the anger in his face. It's such a waste.

To try and cut down the number of bull calves born, Stretch buys in highly expensive so-called sexed semen, which is used to artificially inseminate the cows. Created in a lab, this semen has been treated to favour the female chromosome to such a level that if you use it there's a 90 per cent chance the cow will give birth to a heifer.

Not that this has helped Stretch today.

The harvest now over,
the fields are ploughed ...

... and drilled with seed.
The cycle begins again.

Modern technology keeps chemical spraying to a minimum,
which is better for the planet – and our pockets.

Walking Whitefaced Dartmoors back to Colin Pearce's farm. They'll soon have a new home in the Cotswolds.

Kate Humble with her Kune Kune sow and litter. 'Kune Kune' means fat and round – appropriate, isn't it?

An Iron Age piglet. The breed originated on our farm when dad crossed a Tamworth with a wild boar from London Zoo.

Taking apple pulp out to our free-range pigs.

Gloucestershire's third county breed, the gorgeous Gloucestershire Old Spot.

We wake in early January to find that the Farm Park has turned white.

It may look pretty, but the snow on the farm brings nothing but problems.

We walk into the sheds to see over two dozen cows waiting for us.

'All of these have TB, Adam,' he says, his voice strangely flat, 'and if that's not enough, these ten over here are in calf with females.'

There's nothing I can say. The loss Stretch is feeling isn't just financial, it's deeply emotional. I've had people outside of agriculture say to me that they can't see what the problem is. After all, the farmer gets compensation from the government for every cow that's killed because of TB. They're right of course, but that's not the point. Stretch knows that after filling out all the paperwork he'll get a cheque, courtesy of the taxpayer, for £24,000 dropping through his letterbox. Replacing these animals will cost him around £36,000, so immediately his business has been hit by another £12,000 loss. But then there's the human cost. I know how depressing it is to watch your business stagnate because of something you can't control. It's completely out of your hands and the sense of helplessness is extraordinary. Stretch has weathered the storm of low milk prices for years and now, when the market finally looks like it's improving, he gets this next kick in the teeth. Thankfully, he can still sell his milk as the pasteurisation process eradicates any danger of TB being passed on through dairy products. That is small comfort on a day like this. We hardly speak as we herd the cows on to the waiting lorry, save for a few encouraging words to the cows we are sending to their wasteful deaths. The last is loaded up, the doors are shut and the lorry drives off leaving another eerily, silent shed.

*

The sight of that shed haunts me for the next week, playing on my mind day and night. I am just a couple of days from my next compulsory TB test. We've been clear for over half a year now, but can we hold on to that? Stretch's farm is only a few miles away and so many of my neighbours have TB on their land. The Cotswolds is riddled with it. Do I really think I'll be lucky enough to escape it once again?

As always, the more I worry, the less sleep I have and the more my mood worsens. The night before my test it's almost unbearable. The *Countryfile* crew have turned up to film the test and after a few drinks in the evening we all head off to bed. In my heart I know I need to sleep. Tomorrow is going to be long enough as it is and everyone is going to be on edge. The last thing they need is a tired and ratty boss. But sleep won't come. My mind is reeling with trepidation. Will I find myself in Stretch's shoes, unable to control the destiny of the herd?

That's enough, I think decisively and swing my legs out of bed. Pulling on clothes, I make my way to the room where Dan, the *Countryfile* director is staying. A rap on the door soon reveals that he's not asleep either. Good. I've got an idea. 'Have you got your lights for a night-shoot?' I ask. When Dan says he has, I tell him to get dressed. We're going on a little expedition.

Badgers are an important part of Gloucestershire's wildlife but they're an animal I view with mixed feelings. One the one hand, I love seeing them. As they're nocturnal, spotting a badger is a rare treat, especially if I'm out with the kids. Both Alfie and Ella love to watch these wild animals snuffling about in the under-growth of the farm woodland.

However, for beef farmers such as myself, old Brock brings another problem. Like cattle, badgers can be infected and carry bovine TB from place to place. DEFRA claims that there is no single proven source of TB, but every farmers' newspaper you pick up, or television report you hear confirms that there's plenty of evidence to show that badgers are, at the very least, an impor-tant piece in the TB puzzle. Political battles surrounding the disease have raged, with some farmers calling for a cull of badg-ers in TB hotspots while animal welfare groups campaign for vaccinations instead. This has been going on for years now and there's still no solution in sight. The government has said there will be no culls in England, but over the border in Wales the Welsh Assembly is preparing controlled culls to see if these will solve the problem.

I don't know what to think, personally. All I can see is the effect that this awful disease is having on the local farming econ-omy, and on my friends and neighbours.

I walk carefully in the dark, my torch highlighting the path that Dan and I are taking. If there are badgers here I don't want to disturb them. Then I spot something and crouch down. Yes, I thought so. Badger prints in the soft soil. There are some here. I knew that there used to be a sett down this side of the farm but didn't know how active the creatures were. These tracks are fresh. They've been out tonight. I shine the torch around, reveal-ing more. Lots more. And then, before we know it we are on top of the sett. It's huge, a massive amount of soil dug up all around the entrance. There's no sign of the badgers – they would have heard us coming. I've been chatting to the camera all the way, hardly keeping quiet – but looking at the size of the thing I can guess there's at least one fair-sized badger family down there, maybe even two. As soon as I see the sett, the butterflies hit my stomach again with a vengeance. I continue to deliver my lines to the camera but my head is spinning. Obviously, I know that badgers are active on the farm, they're all over the place, but this sett is so close to my cattle sheds. It will be winter soon and at night the badgers from here will be foraging around for any scraps of cattle food that have been spilled. Is this sett a TB reservoir? We're bang in the middle of a TB hotspot with Gloucestershire consistently boasting the highest concentration of herds shut down because of the disease. Even if we get through the test without incident tomorrow, can our luck really hold throughout the winter?

Morning comes and the dark clouds in the sky match my mood. We start going through the motions as if on autopilot, heading out to get the first batch of cattle in, manhandling them into the narrow cattle races so Gill, the vet, can see if any have reacted to the injections she'd given them a couple of days ago. Almost immediately it looks like my worst fears have been founded. Gill is running her hand down the side of a Dexter steer. 'There are lumps there,' she begins, and I can't help but sigh, 'but it's fine.' I shake my head, not quite believing what I've just heard. Is she sure? Yes, the top lump is much larger than the bottom. The animal has passed.

Is this what it's going to be like all day? I'm on tenterhooks already and there are hours to go. At least I've got another job to occupy my time. As all the cattle are being brought into the race, I might as well take the opportunity to treat them for worms and parasites. As Gill passes the Dexter, I spray a line of the treatment along its back from the canister I'm wearing like a back pack. We'll also give them some extra minerals to keep them healthy. Of course, I'll wait until each cow is given the all clear. There's no point wasting expensive medicine on an animal that then is found to be a reactor and sent to slaughter. I hope it won't come to that, but with farming it always pays to be pragmatic.

And then it happens. I spot the problem as soon as the Gloucester is guided into the race, even before Gill has checked its neck and know what the result will be.

'I'm afraid it isn't good news, Adam,' Gill says. 'We've got two lumps. Eighteen on the bottom and just 10 on the top. I'm afraid that's a reactor.'

So that's it. Not even a year after we'd been given the all-clear we've got TB on the farm again. I want to scream. I want to swear. I want to run away. Instead I have to hold it together and deliver a piece to camera. Through clenched teeth I report what's happened. To add insult to injury I realise at the last minute that this is one of our cows that is in calf. So that's two lives being extinguished because of TB and no chance to sell any more breeding animals until we have two clean tests, 60 days apart.

Gill apologises, even though it's not her fault and I turn my back on the camera. Dan is still filming as I announce that I won't bother worming the cow then.

'There's no point,' I say bitterly, 'because she's going to have her throat cut.'

I don't care that the camera's still on me and I don't care how harsh that sounds. The truth of the matter is that the situation is harsh and completely unfair. I watch her being led out and wonder for a moment why we even bother. Like Stretch, it's a case of two steps forward, three steps back.

The mood plummets around the farm as the news goes from bad to worse. The next reactor is a White Park heifer born earlier in the year. I jump into the race and feel for myself. The top lump on her neck is like a pea and the one on the bottom is like a plum. My guts feel like a lump of ice as I read out her number so a record of the infection can be made and her rear is marked by a dot of spray paint. Red marks the spot. Another cow to the slaughter.

Now that we know that TB has reared its head again it's a case of damage limitation. A Belgian Blue calf is the next to react positively to TB and so we immediately put it into isolation, to limit the chance of it infecting the others. It stands lonely and confused in its box, not knowing why it's been removed from the rest of the herd. In just two years' time, that calf would have been ready for beef and worth anywhere between £800 to £1000. We'll be lucky if the compensation comes in at £400.

The final straw comes when a shaggy Belted Galloway is found to be a reactor. That's four animals with TB from four different herds kept on four different areas of the farm. How could we have gone from clear to this? I think back to a phone call I had received from DEFRA a few weeks earlier. They were looking for people to take part in a pilot vaccination scheme. Would we take part and help vaccinate the badgers on our farm? Of course I said yes. Even though I didn't know that the TB has returned it would give me a chance to do something, feel like I'm taking control again.

But after today, you can't help but wonder how it will help. We're not just talking about one sett here. There are badgers all over this farm and then there are the deer – they can also carry the bacterium and I've got plenty of those as well. Today has proved it. At one point we had to drive three miles to get from one herd of cattle to another, and yet TB has spread, even across that distance. I've no idea how we'll vaccinate all of those badgers.

The last cow is tested and the herds returned to their fields and sheds, minus the four that will be sent off to be killed. Fittingly, the heavens open as we trudge inside. Dad looks as broken-hearted as I feel. 'This would have never happened in your day, would it?' I ask, but don't expect an answer. What can anyone say? It's happened now and the business of the farm must continue. The cattle will be housed for winter and it won't be until spring that we will have a chance to go clear again.

WINTER

CHAPTER 16

WINTER WONDERLAND

It's nearly Christmas but as the world prepares for the festive season there's no let-up on the farm. It's the time of year when cash flow is at the foremost of a farmer's mind. In winter you're running on your reserves. The grass has stopped growing and some of the animals have been brought in, meaning that you're relying on animal feed more than ever to get them through to the spring. The farm park is now out of season and will remain closed until Easter, so that's one steady stream of income that has come to a halt for now. That being said, we've got plenty of maintenance to do on the place to keep up standards and have it all ready for when the gates open again.

My first job of the day is to shift some of the barley that is still sitting in the shed. A grain lorry has arrived to take the better stuff off for malting. The problem is that the good grain, which is currently commanding around £110 a tonne, is sitting behind piles of the barley that's only good enough for animal feed, which is only worth £80 a tonne. So it's time to jump in a digger and start moving grain from one place to another. A few hours later the lorry, safely stocked with around 30 tonnes of grain, is trundling out of the farm. It's a haul worth around two and a half grand, which may seem like a pretty good morning's job, until you remember that we're not making a scrap of profit from it.

At least we can put the animal feed barley to good use. While we're selling most of it on to cover costs there's no point buying in cattle concentrate when we have our own supply of feed on our doorstep. No sooner than the lorry has got on its way, I'm driving up to the cattle sheds to give them a midday snack. It's a blustery day and the wind blows the barley, which I've mixed with some of our wheat and beans, back in my face. As the weather starts to turn this is one of my favourite places on the farm. We bring the cows in to over-winter to keep them dry and warm, and also to protect the pasture. While the grass is dormant, the cows' hooves would constantly churn up the ground, meaning that the field would have to be turned over and re-seeded come spring. I've already had to do that in one of the sheep's grazing fields, thanks to the pigs, and don't fancy an extra job. Winter is going to be hard enough as it is. And it's so much easier to care for the cows here. We have plenty of our straw on standby. If it looks like they need more bedding, you simply turn it on its side, cut the wrap and roll it out like a new carpet. Most of the food they survive on is also here in the yard, as that silage we cut in the early summer comes into its own. Today I notice that it's a little too tightly packed together, even though it's out of the plastic wrap, meaning that the cows can't get to it, even with their long tongues. Using my forklift I pick up the stack of silage and give it a little shake, loosening it up for them. As soon as it drops to the ground, the hungry cows descend on it, eager to fill their bellies so they stay warm. This is what life will be like for the next few months. It's a time for remaining vigilant, keeping an eye out for little quirks like this that could have a real effect on the animals' welfare. There's another good reason, too. We've got heifers here we're preparing to go to the bull next year and steers that we're fattening for beef. The farm may be shut down with TB but the business of the herd continues all the same. And no matter how miserable the bleak midwinter gets, and how tough working conditions become, heading up to these sheds always lift my spirits. The cows, warm and safe in their little winter retreat, always seem so glad to see you.

The dogs are keen to work whatever the weather so I take them out to round up the remaining lambs that were born in the spring. I'm really glad how Millie is getting on. The first time I give her the stop command she drops obediently to the floor and is learning to use her natural kelpie talent of barking on command. Maude is still working, but is now happiest when she's travelling around on the back of my truck. She still enjoys being out with me, but can't quite keep up with the rest now. Even Pearl is beginning to react more quickly than her old mum now. Maude's served me well, and I'm determined that she is going to have a nice easy retirement although I can't see it happening anytime soon. Come the spring, I'm going to continue working with Millie and start looking for a new puppy to train.

I love to work the dogs even though it can be quite a challenge at times. We keep hitting obstacles such as the odd muddy ditch between gateposts. Trying to get a flock of sheep to walk through sticky mud is one of the toughest things a shepherd will ever try to do. The dogs circle them, Millie speaks up on cue, barking like mad and even I rush towards them, but still they hold their ground, looking at the muck as if to say 'You don't really expect us to walk through that, do you?' The good thing about sheep is that, most of the time, you only need to get one to move and the rest will follow. Finally, one of the ewes decides that she's had enough of this silly farmer and his noisy dogs and tentatively steps forward. Now one has made the move, the rest of the flock decide that following her is the best option and are soon squelching their way through.

Once safely at the pens I start sorting through the lambs, working out which are ready to go to the butcher. It also gives me a good chance to count them all, seeing how many we have left – an end-of-year stocktake if you like. There are 194 lambs left on the farm, all of which need to be gone by the time the first ewe goes into labour in March. That's a good number. They've certainly done us well this year – one of the farm's best operations in the last 12 months. We just need to get the stragglers to put on some weight, to get up to that magic 40-kilo live weight. Of course, now that the grass is going, we'll have to fall back on concentrate, but it's all been accounted for.

As the sun sets, I feel an enormous sense of well-being. The cows may be away for the winter and the stored crops may be moving out, but the next few months won't give us much time to relax. However, there's a real sense of closure in the air. The year is coming to an end and a new one is around the corner. Tomorrow, the *Countryfile* presenting team are all arriving on the farm to film our Christmas special – something a few years ago we would never have dreamt we'd have. Surely Christmas specials are the domain of *Only Fools and Horses* and *Doctor Who*? No one could have thought that the show would go from strength to strength in the first year of its new format and that my farm would be such a big part of it. I'm actually looking forward to the day. The new gang will be together for the very first time – the guys I hardly know, James Wong, Katie Knapman and Jules Hudson, Julia and Matt, who are becoming real friends and, of course, dear John. Back at the farmhouse, the kids will be getting out the Christmas decorations and tomorrow the *Countryfile* team will be sitting down for an early Christmas dinner. I'm sure it's going to be fun – for us at least. The director may have her work cut out. As we don't get to see each other too often, it's always a bit chaotic when the entire team gather in one room. It's like directing a bunch of kids – albeit highly professional ones, of course.

Before I head over to the house, I meet up with dad who has come bearing gifts, a bottle of sloe gin he'd made a couple of years ago using berries from the farm. That'll keep the cold out over the next few months. We take a little wander around the barley fields, so he can look at the Maris Otter crop. As we walk he points out plants and fruits in the hedge we keep untrimmed on the edge of the conservation area. We've done this for years and I never tire of the little bits of country lore he imparts as we walk. In front of us the gorse has flowered, adding a welcome flush of yellow in the barren hedge.

'You know what they say, Adam,' he says, pointing with his stick, 'kissing's out of fashion when the gorse is out of bloom.'

I'm confused for a second. 'But gorse is always in bloom. It flowers all year round.'

'Exactly,' says dad with a twinkle in his eye, 'that means we can kiss all year round. Charlie better watch out.'

We stop in front of the same blackthorn bush where dad had picked his sloes for the gin. It is absolutely laden with fruit. It's not alone. I've never seen so many berries. At least the farm's wild birds will have plenty of food for the winter. The sight also prompts another proverb from dad.

'If berries do grow, you're in for some snow.'

'It looks like we'd better batten down the hatches then, dad,' I say. 'By the look of this lot we're in for a blizzard and a half.'

Just a few days into the New Year, I couldn't help but recall dad's words. Perhaps I should take more notice of his quirky proverbs in the future. As the country recovered from the excesses of the festive season, Britain was plunged into its coldest winter for 30 years. Extreme weather warnings came thick and fast, but not as thick as the blanket of snow that awaited us on the morning of 6 January. We were told to prepare ourselves for up to 40 cm in some areas while the news was full of scary reports that Britain only had eight days' worth of gas left and that councils had only just realised that their stockpiles of gritting salt were running thin.

The weather warnings were right. All over the country, cities come to a standstill and in rural areas the length and breadth of Great Britain farmers suddenly find themselves with a lot more work on their hands. There is perhaps nothing so stunning as the snow-laden Cotswolds, and the slopes of our farm become a real winter wonderland for the kids, whose schools are closed due to adverse conditions. They head off, head to toe in ski gear, pulling sleds while I head off in the other direction in a truck heavy with animal feed and my ever-present companion in the form of Maude. A week in, the snow is starting to wear a bit thin now.

In the fields surrounding the farm, the winter barley is safe and sound. Although the ground itself will be frozen, the barley is in the best possible place, buried away and protected from the heavy frosts that would snap off all of its leaves in an instant. The biggest problem we have is keeping the animals' water supplies available. I've already had to break through the ice in the chicken trough and clear a path through the snow so they can get over to the food, but I've heard there's a bigger problem over by the cows. I stop off at one of the yard's water butts to fill some large containers with water, but even then have to put my foot through the ice before I can do anything. The sheep will be OK, as they are able to get enough liquid by licking the snow, but both the cattle and pigs will need water. Finally I lug the containers of water into the truck next to Maude and head off to the cattle shed. It is these little extra jobs that take up all of your time when it snows. Usually I wouldn't be expecting to have to cart water back and forth, but these aren't normal conditions. According to the radio it's –10C (14F) at the minute, and parts of Britain are colder than Moscow.

I'm trying not to complain though. Compared to farmers elsewhere in Britain, we've got it easy here in Gloucestershire. Horror stories are already doing the rounds. In Scotland, a dairy farmer in Huntly, Aberdeenshire spotted that his cow shed, sheltering 400 animals, was about to collapse under the sheer weight of the snow. He started to move the animals out, but just as the last calf was ushered out of the shed, the roof buckled and the entire structure came down on his head. Miraculously, he was saved thanks to the layer of soft cow dung that covered the shed's concrete floor. He sank into the muck, which cushioned him from the rubble. Already more than a hundred other farmers in Scotland have reported collapsed farm buildings. In Wales, dairy farmers are having to throw away thousands of gallons of milk as the tankers can't make it down slippery, frozen farm tracks while many are struggling to get feed delivered, meaning that their animals are starting to go hungry. For the first time since the harvest, I'm actually grateful we have plenty of animal feed in the barley stores. All over the place things are freezing solid. There are the usual problems with water pipes but I've also heard of eggs freezing before they're collected and in some areas it has been so cold that diesel is freezing in the storage tanks.

Of course, farmers aren't the only people who live in the country and a lot of remote communities have been badly affected by the bad weather. I felt a real sense of pride, the day after the snow started falling, when I heard Hilary Benn, Secretary of State for the Environment, Food and Rural Affairs, praise farmers across the country who were helping locals, clearing roads and rescuing stranded motorists. 'As well as being the custodians of our countryside,' he said, 'farmers have shown over the last few days that they are also an extra emergency service.' A lot of farmers worry that we are expected to wear too many hats these days – from food producer to environmental steward – but I don't think anyone will complain about the extra label of hero.

When I finally reach the cattle shed, I realise that it isn't actually a huge job that needs doing. A water supply pipe has frozen and while it needs immediate attention, it's a simple problem to solve. First of all I break through the ice in the trough, pulling out the biggest blocks so that it doesn't immediately freeze again and then, by running a blowtorch along the side of the pipe, melt the blockage within.

The mercy missions continue all day. The concrete pad where we throw the pigs grain and apple pulp needs clearing of snow but the pigs themselves seem as happy as can be. As soon as I appear they're tearing across the field, great plumes of snow erupting around them as they stampede over. As long as they've got enough water I'm not too worried about the pigs. They're such a hardy bunch that they'll soon shrug off these temperatures and those who are a little more sensitive to the weather will hide themselves away happily in the straw-lined metal arks and the wooden shed. Even so, I'm glad I didn't expand the herd as much as I'd originally planned in the autumn. I would have been worried sick if I'd had 50 or more sows outside in all this snow, especially if there were piglets out here.

As you'd expect, the primitive sheep also don't seem to know what the fuss is all about. Even though some of the North Ronaldsay, Soay and Castlemilk Moorit ewes are heavily pregnant they can easily survive conditions that would finish off a conventional commercial sheep. When one of the Castlemilk Moorits nuzzles against me I realise that she even has icicles in her fleece. The wool is such a good insulator that it's keeping in all of her body heat, rather than melting the snow and ice on her back. Here I am, wrapped up in layer after layer of waterproof clothing and thick synthetics to protect myself from the elements and she doesn't even care. The Castlemilk Moorit is interesting because, although we class it as a primitive sheep, it's one of the youngest breeds on the farm. Its bloodline only dates back to the early 1900s when Sir Jock Buchanan-Jardine of the Castlemilk Estate in Dumfriesshire began a breeding programme using Moorit Shetland, wild Mouflon and Manx Loaghtan sheep. He was simply after a breed that would satisfy his romantic vision for the estate, an animal that would beautify his parkland and produce a light tan-coloured, quality wool. However, when his descendant Sir John Buchanan-Jardine died in 1970 the flock of unique sheep with their wide-spreading horns and long legs was almost entirely culled. Dad heard about this impending tragedy and immediately bought six ewes and a ram, sparing them from extinction. Today, all Castlemilk Moorits are descended from dad's sheep.

The Soay, on the other hand, is a completely different kettle of fish. If the Castlemilk is one of the newest breeds we own, the Soay is one of the most ancient. In fact, many scholars believe that the Soay is the ancestor of all modern sheep breeds. Originally from Soay, in the St Kilda group of islands off the north-west coast of Scotland, the name is a corruption of the old Norse for 'the island of sheep', seeming to indicate that when the Vikings came to the islands there were sheep waiting for them. Archaeological digs have confirmed that the sheep kept by Neolithic shepherds are almost identical to the Soays we keep on the farm today, meaning that the breed has remained largely unchanged since the Stone Age. It's an exciting thought. The scene I'm seeing today – small, short-tailed sheep with quizzical chocolate brown faces standing unfazed in a brilliant white snowdrift – is one that our distant ancestors would have recognised instantly. But those early shepherds would have been puzzled by one aspect of almost every other breed of sheep we keep on the farm. Most sheep flock together, which is why we can round them up using a sheepdog. The Soay is completely different. Instead of flocking, they scatter, heading off on their own in every possible direction.

Seeing these primitive breeds here, in these conditions, following their natural instinct to dig into the snow using their feet to find the grass below, it's hard to imagine that in just a couple of months they'll start to lamb in this very same field. Here's hoping that the snow has passed by then and life can get back to normal.

But for now, I think I've deserved a break. As I head back from checking Butch and Sundance, I hear the sound of Charlie and the kids still enjoying those sledges. All day I've kept myself warm and dry. It's probably about time I got thoroughly covered in snow. After all, as a dad it's important to entertain the kids and everyone loves a bit of sledging. As an old friend of mine often reminds me, we're here for a good time, not for a long time.

CHAPTER 17

PORTLAND BILL

Even as the snow begins to disappear around the country, the tops of the Cotswolds are still covered. It looks beautiful. The winter sun catching the blankets of sparkling crystal, while snow-covered trees dot the white rolling hills. A Christmas-card-maker's dream. However, it's also been an exhausting time, chasing around the farm and trying to make sure everything is OK, so I'm glad to take a break and hit the open road. I'm on the road down to the Isle of Portland, a four-mile-long island that juts into the English Channel off the Dorset coast. It's home to around 12,000 people and is heavily quarried, its limestone having been used for some of Britain's most famous buildings including St Paul's Cathedral and Buckingham Palace.

Once it was also known for Portland sheep and behind me in the truck I have five Portland ewes that I am taking back to where the breed originated. The Portland is unique as, unlike the rest of Britain's indigenous breeds, it has a long tail and the ability to lamb all year round. This makes it likely that the breed is descended from Mediterranean stock, as these are common characteristics on the Continent. Maybe they were brought over on trading ships and then bred with a local Wessex breed to create the Portland. No one really knows. Like the Herdwick, there's a legend that they are survivors of a wrecked ship from the Spanish Armada. Hardly anyone actually believes that though, and you have to wonder how many sheep the Spanish had on their galleons to give birth to all these myths.

The Portland is quite a primitive sheep, horned in both sexes and incredibly thrifty, able to live on poor forage. It has a tanned face and the lambs are delightful, born with a foxy-red colouring that fades the older they get. They also have a fleece that is prized by hand-spinners as the wool is so fine and has a lovely natural colour. The fact that it has stayed so unchanged for so long is because Portland is an island, albeit one still joined to the mainland. Its isolated nature has kept the sheep from too much inter-breeding over the years. The Domesday survey of 1086 puts the number of Portlands on the island at around 900, although by 1840 those figures had swollen to 4000, most probably because the Dorset gentry had a fondness for Portland lamb and mutton. I've been told that King George III would eat nothing but Portland mutton if he was travelling around Dorset.

The decline began with the expansion of Portland's limestone exports. Farmland began to be – literally – swallowed up by the quarries and the flocks started to dwindle. The situation wasn't helped by the usual rare-breed problems. Portlands are small sheep who rarely have more than one lamb and you have to wait until they're around 18 months old before there's enough meat on them to take to slaughter. The last Portland stock left the island in 1913, heading off to Dorchester market. Some remained nearby, on the Dorset mainland, while the others were taken to other places in the countryside. By the time dad heard about them in the early Seventies, they were on the brink of extinction. Once again, he got out his chequebook and bought every Portland he could find, establishing the flock that we maintain to this day.

That's one of the reasons I was so chuffed when Su Illsley phoned me a few weeks before Christmas. She runs a small concern known as Fancy's Family Farm in Southwell on Portland and already has a flock of 22 Portland sheep, which she took over with her husband Jon last summer in an attempt to keep them on the island. She told me on the phone that the sheep were in a quite bedraggled state when she first got hold of them, but the small flock I witness when I drive up to the farm looks exceptionally well. As I finally meet Su in the flesh, both of us wrapped up like Michelin men to protect ourselves from the bitter wind, her Portland ram regards us with what could be mocking eyes, as if to say 'Look at you wusses. I'm out here all the time.' He had some of the most magnificent horns I've seen on a Portland. The older they get, the more a Portland tup's horns grow, spiralling down. Like many rare breeds, the horns themselves are in high demand from button- and stick-makers and a good pair from a four-year-old that's gone to slaughter is worth £20.

Su is getting impatient as I stand there ogling her ram's horns. She wants to meet his new wives and, when I open the truck, the ewes themselves are keen to stretch their legs. They look at home almost immediately, trotting off to make friends with Su's other ewe lamb. And what a view they'll have for the rest of their lives. The sea stretches in front of us, waves crashing towards the shore and to the right, the famous lighthouse at Portland Bill stretches into the grey winter sky. There's been a lighthouse here for 300 years, keeping vessels from running aground. It's a major landmark in the area, and Su hopes that, thanks to her efforts and those of other enthusiasts, the Portlands will become the same.

'Look at them,' she says happily as her latest arrivals explore their new field. 'This is a sight I never tire of. They belong here, they came from here, and they've just got to remain.'

It's a sentiment an old friend of mine agrees with. What Norman Jones doesn't know about Portlands isn't worth knowing. I couldn't travel all the way down to this part of the country without visiting Norman, who has written the definitive history of the breed. A former navy man, Norman worked at Portland and became aware of the small flock of sheep that was once kept on the Portland Prison farm. Unfortunately, due to cutbacks, this flock was sold in 1995 but twelve years before Norman had approached the prison and bought a couple of in-lamb ewes. His flock has grown since then and he's become a passionate advocate of the breed. It's in better shape than it's ever been, but there are still some concerns.

'When your dad stepped in back in the Seventies,' Norman tells me, 'there were only 73 Portland sheep left in the county. He took on half of that number and took them back to the Cotswolds. It's better now. There are just under 2000, but while those are reasonably healthy numbers, the future's still uncertain. A lot of the breeders are reaching the kind of age – myself included – when we start falling off the edge. And quite often, we're the ones with the biggest flocks. Overall numbers are still under threat.'

Norman's words are ringing in my ears as I set out for home. There must be hope, however. After all, young farmers like Su are springing up, trying to maintain breeds such as the Portland. Granted, Su's the first person to admit that what she is doing is a hobby, but the more smallholders who start keeping rare breeds the better, if you ask me. As far as I'm concerned, selling part of my stock to the likes of Su is what it's all about. It's part of dad's legacy and a tradition that I'm immensely proud to continue.

I have just one more stop before I leave Dorset. Steve Gould keeps a great flock of Portlands at Milton Abbas and his mutton sandwiches are second to none. Well, if it's good enough for George III, it's good enough for me.

A couple of days later, I'm back among my own Portlands making sure that they have enough fodder as the snow continues to blanket the ground. When I'd returned from Dorset I'd been on a bit of a high, but have come back down to earth with a bump. News reached us that yesterday one of Su's pregnant ewes was attacked by a dog. She'd received a call from a traumatised woman who admitted that her lurcher cross had attacked one of the sheep after getting into the field. Su and a nurse friend of hers patched up the ewe and gave the sheep some antibiotics. It's apparently touch and go whether she will survive and there's also a worry that the other ewes, who were quite spooked by the attack, may begin to miscarry.

Thank heavens the dog owner did the right thing and phoned Su immediately. It's quite soul-destroying when you hear this kind of thing. People are working so hard to save these animals and then incidents like this happen. Su must be heartbroken. I know I would be.

It's amazing how attached you become to your animals. Su and her husband are discovering this bond quite late in life but dad ensured that myself and my sisters connected with the animals on the farm as early as possible.

When we were young, my father gave all four of us a different breed of animal. His plan was to pass on his lifelong passion for rare breed conservation. As always, dad proved himself to be a wise man. His plan worked, as we all developed a real attachment to the beasts we called our own. Even better, when we sold them, half the money went into our own individual savings, while the rest was reinvested into the flock or herd.

For me, dad chose a wonderful Exmoor pony. These Neanderthals of the equine world can survive even the harshest of conditions. It's thought that the very first ponies arrived in Britain around 130,000 years ago, originally coming from Alaska at a time when the continents were still connected, and what would become the British Isles was attached to the European mainland. The ponies flourished in their new home and soon spread all across Europe. This ancient ancestor of the modern horse would have shared the Earth with woolly mammoths and would have provided a tasty snack for the sabre-toothed tiger.

It wasn't only tigers that found sustenance in the form of the pony. You may have used the expression 'I could eat a horse', but for our Stone Age forebears the phrase was slightly nearer their natural diet. Pony meat was on every Stone Age hunter's menu, and in order to survive these early men and women made sure nothing went to waste. The skins of the ponies were used as clothing and the animal fats were mixed with vegetable dyes and coloured earth to create paints for rituals or recording events in wall paintings. Over time, as Britain's climate changed, the numbers of ponies began to fall, eventually becoming more isolated on uplands around 9600 years ago. The British hill pony was born.

When Celtic tribes settled in Britain, these wild herds were seen as a wonderful natural resource. Tribesmen headed out to the hills to bring back the skittish and independent creatures and, amazingly, the ponies were broken in and used to pull chariots. They are even believed to have pulled the Iceni chariot of none other than Queen Boudicca herself.

At the time of the Domesday Book, when Exmoor was officially designated as a royal forest, we start to see the first written records of ponies on the moor, and by the sixteenth century the pony population was around a thousand. The pony reigned supreme on Exmoor for hundreds of years until the 1940s, when war came to Europe. Numbers plummeted for all kinds of reasons. Some perished as there was no one to care for them with their owners off to war; there are some records that many were actually shot by troops in training operations. A large number also ended up in the pot. Nearby city folk, desperate to supplement meagre rations, headed out to the moor to bag themselves a pony and plenty of tasty meat. It's thought that by the end of the war, and after sharing these islands with humans for more than 25,000 years, there were no more than 50 Exmoor ponies and four stallions left. If things weren't bad enough, Britain suffered one of its worst winters in 1947 and numbers dropped further.

Today, the fact that the Exmoor pony came so close to extinction seems amazing, especially as they are such a staple of the North Devon and Somerset tourist scene. The fact that we have any at all is mainly thanks to a woman called Mary Etherington. Realising that the situation was grim, she set about replacing all of the gates on Exmoor with cattle grids, set up a firm boundary to the common ground so that ponies couldn't wander off, or be easily taken, and started working with breeders to build up the numbers once again.

While numbers are much healthier now, there's still much work to be done. About 3000 of the breed exist worldwide, with just a few hundred found in Britain, most, as you'd expect, in the west of England. Once again wild ponies can be seen wandering the wide expanses of the moor, but are only wild in the sense that they have freedom to roam – every pony on the moor is actually owned by someone. The Exmoor National Park Authority owns two herds, while six other herds are in private hands. Every autumn the herds are driven down to their home farms so that the foals can be weaned and branded before heading back up to the moors to live through incredibly challenging conditions throughout the winter.

Up on the moor, they live off moor grasses, rushes, heather and gorse. Their heavy brow shields the driving West Country rain from their eyes while their coat of downy underlayer and longer surface hair offers the kind of protection that a mountaineering jacket designer can only dream of.

When the wind blows these thrifty ponies, standing 12 hands tall, turn their backs on the elements, their tales fanning out like a protective shield. Thousands of years of evolution have done their job, giving us an intelligent, strong and hardy creature.

I'm extremely proud to have six breeding mares and a handsome stallion on my farm. As always, part of the job is to keep selling our animals to breeders, helping to increase the numbers of a breed so that the national herd is spread out to help avoid disaster if disease strikes. A week ago a couple drove up from Bedfordshire, braving the snow to buy two of my Exmoors, which they hope to halter train and enter for horse shows.

I chose two of my best ponies, but I think the buyers are going to have their work cut out for them. My ponies, while fine animals, are even wilder than usual. We hardly handle them, meaning that they can get really worked up when we try to work with them. To make it worse, this particular pair had never even been near a horsebox, let alone a lorry, meaning that even loading them up was interesting to say the least.

The challenge had started early in the morning, when we'd got the ponies in to identify the two that we were going to sell. As Exmoors look almost identical, you can't always work out who's who by sight. When they are weaned, we brand them, using a hot iron, with a number that ties them into their equine passport, but as they age, that coarse hair soon covers up the mark. So, on a particularly cold morning, I arrived at the ponies' field to be greeted by the sight of Mike shaving a patch of hair from each pony to find the right one. I wasn't sure if the ruddy nature of his cheeks was down to the bitterly cold weather or the fact that getting the ponies into a race to check them would have been quite a monumental task.

He certainly sighed in relief when the number 54 was revealed after his little barber's work. Both ponies had been found.

But that was only half the battle. As our buyers drove up in their shiny expensive lorry, we worked out how we were going to get the ponies on board. It can be absolutely nerve-racking working with lively animals like the Exmoors in close corners. They can easily kick out and hurt you or themselves. That's the last thing you need when you're completing a sale.

As the lorry backed up and came to a halt, I hit upon an idea. We'd never persuade the ponies to clatter up its ramp, so it was time for plan B. I shot back to the farmyard and returned 10 minutes later with my daughter's horsebox. Mike and I are so used to working together that he soon clocked my plan. I parked the horsebox at the end of the race and with a little bit of prodding and pulling between us, we got the ponies into the box. Then

Getting ready to check whether our commercial ewes are pregnant …

… All those coloured rumps mean our ram has been very busy.

Two of our Exmoor ponies, Tia Maria and Vicia.
They went to a new home in Bedfordshire in January 2010.

I backed the box up to the lorry, opened the gates and watched satisfied as the ponies, eager to get out of the horsebox, charged out, only to find themselves in the back of an even bigger vehicle. As we shut the doors behind them, they already seemed to be calming down, but I mentally wished the buyers' luck in training them to be show ponies. They, however, were determined that the next time I'd see these two ponies they would be being led into a ring and into the Exmoor pony hall of fame.

I really hope that's the case, but in the meantime it did prompt me to make a phone call to see if I could call in some help to manage the ponies. After all these years, I had to get a better handle on them.

So a week later, on an equally cold morning, help arrives on the farm. Kelly Marks has been around horses all of her life. Her father was a Lambourne racehorse trainer and after becoming a championship showjumper as a girl, Kelly went on to become a jockey, only retiring in 1995 after winning the Ladies European Championship. Two years before, she had a chance encounter with a man in a French petrol station – Monty Roberts. Now in his seventies, Monty has lived the most remarkable life. He's trained championship horses and the Queen's equestrian team, been a Hollywood stuntman, fostered an amazing 47 children and created one of the most revolutionary equine training techniques he calls Join-Up, but which the press has dubbed 'horse whispering'. Because of their mutual love of horses, the two struck up an instant friendship and Monty asked Kelly to work on his first book about his methods – *The Man Who Listens to Horses* – and eventually to put together training courses based on his experiences training troublesome and temperamental horses. If anyone can help me communicate with my ponies better, it's Kelly.

Kelly starts by watching the Exmoor ponies running through the snow-covered grass, asking me questions about how we interact as they dart back and forth.

'How often do you handle them, Adam?' she asks, to which I have to reply, hardly at all. They run with their mothers all year and only really come in when we wean them off and brand them.

Kelly's eyebrows rise.

'And there you have your first problem,' she says, without any condemnation in her voice but firm enough to let me know that she doesn't approve. 'It's no wonder that Exmoor ponies get such a reputation for being difficult. Think of their first experience of human contact. It must be such a traumatic event that many of them never forget it.'

It's a dressing-down I don't mind as I actually agree with her. I've already decided that we will move away from branding this year. It's a process that has already been banned in the UK for sheep and cows, and from this year all ponies must be microchipped anyway, a chip injected just under the pony's skin that contains all of the animal's history and data. In my mind that makes branding unnecessary. It's also a view held by the British Veterinary Association, which has described branding as 'unacceptable' in terms of animal welfare.

Not everyone agrees, however. Many farmers, especially those who still keep their ponies on moorland, say that microchipping is useless unless you can read it at some distance from the ponies. Until the technology is available to allow that, they believe that branding is a necessary evil. I've also heard many pony breeders relate stories of ponies being knocked down on Exmoor. Holidaymakers or passers-by have found the distressed animal and have been able to phone the number branded on the pony's skin, so that its owner can give immediate aid. This, of course, would be difficult if the owners relied on microchipping alone.

In Scotland, branding is already en route to being banned. At present, it can only occur if an official permit has been issued by the Scottish parliament. In 2009 nine permits were sent out and this year, the Scottish Rural Affairs and Environment Secretary, Richard Lochhead, announced that he will no longer be authorising branding. I suspect that a legal fight is on the cards, but here on my farm the procedure just isn't needed. My ponies never go far, so it's not like we have to identify them from a distance.

This news seems to please Kelly and I take her to meet my newest Exmoor, a young filly called Venus. I have her in a shed and we can hear her whinnying as soon as we cross the yard. Glancing over the door, its obvious that Venus is almost climbing the walls. She's visibly shaking and almost presses herself against the far wall at the sight of us.

'She's beautiful,' Kelly comments, 'but obviously very stressed.'

'That's an understatement,' I reply. 'She was weaned about four or five days ago and is still very much missing her mum. She won't let me near her.'

'It's going to be a challenge,' Kelly says, before breaking into a huge smile. 'Luckily I like a challenge.'

Kelly lets herself into the shed and Venus immediately lets out a concerned whinny, kicking up the straw around her hooves. Kelly describes what she's doing for me, keeping her voice nice and calm. I feel like I should be taking notes. After all, if this works, I want to be able to try the same techniques on all of our existing and new Exmoor ponies.

'I'm going to start by approaching Venus,' Kelly begins, inching slowly across the floor towards the frightened pony. 'I want her to know that I'm not going to hurt her. At first, my presence will be quite intimidating for her but...'

Venus's head suddenly snaps around to fix Kelly with a stare.

'There you go,' she says, backing away back to the door. 'When she looks at me like that, I'm going to back away and wait for her relax again.'

After a minute or two, Venus looks away again and Kelly moves in once more.

'She'll start to appreciate that I'm not as dangerous as she first thought if I move away whenever she looks directly at me.'

Again, Venus turns and Kelly retreats. But this time she got closer. Again Venus glances away and Kelly tries again. She's keeping her body at an angle to the pony, in order to make herself less threatening. The dance continues, Kelly moving back and forth, getting closer with every attempt. And all the time, Venus seems to be relaxing. It's almost hypnotising to watch.

'Do you see that, Adam?' Kelly asks. 'She's started to lick and chew. That's exactly what we want. It's a sign that her adrenalin levels are starting to come down and that she's looking at me in a new light. She's no longer seeing me as threatening.'

Kelly is now close enough to touch Venus and I ask her if that's the next step. She says no; at first, she needs to get Venus used to her being near and then they can move on to touching, helped by a simple tool.

This turns out to be nothing more than a long pole with one end covered in soft pipe lagging. Kelly asks me to hand it over and I watch as she approaches Venus – something that half an hour ago would have been impossible – and gently place the pole on the pony's back. I would have thought that this would cause the pony to buck, but instead Venus stands there, chewing merrily away.

'What I'm going to do now will take some time, Adam,' Kelly says, 'I'm going to rub the pole against Venus's back to get her used to being touched and then, inch by inch, pull the pole away and replace it with my arm. After a while she'll barely notice when it's not the pole, but me.'

Kelly suggests I leave her for an hour so I head off to carry out some little jobs around the farm. One of the first is giving the rest of the Exmoor ponies a new bale of hay in their feeder, using my forklift. Usually the ponies graze on some of the roughest terrain on the farm and help keep the gorse from growing out of control, but when it's as cold as today, I like to give them a little treat that they don't have to work so hard for. As I cut away the binding string and the hay tumbles out, the rest of the herd trots in from the next field. Most of them hover about, waiting for me to leave, but one brave creature walks over and even nuzzles against me, allowing me to stroke her neck. This is May, the only quiet Exmoor we have. I wouldn't call her tame but she's friendly and relatively easy to handle. She's also the mother of Venus. Is it too much to hope that Venus may follow in her mum's hoof-prints?

Just over an hour later I get my answer. I head back over to the shed and gently open the door. I can't believe what I'm seeing.

'Adam, just in time,' Kelly says, 'I've got a job for you.'

Kelly is standing beside a chilled out and totally relaxed Venus. The pony has even allowed Kelly to get a rope around her neck. Extraordinary.

'I was just about to slip a head collar on Venus, Adam. Would you like to do it?'

I take the collar and slip it easily over Venus's head. The young foal even lets me scratch her neck in the same way I was fussing over her mother not long ago. It's amazing. In just the space of a few hours, Venus has gone from problem pupil to top of the class. Kelly does point out that this is just the beginning, but assures me that things can only get better. I'm totally made up. If these are skills I can pick up myself, controlling the herd shouldn't be half the problem it is now. As I stroke Venus's neck, my mind goes back to that first pony dad presented me with all those years ago. As always, he'd got it right. The love he encouraged all those years ago has certainly stood the test of time and, as Kelly has proved this morning, you're never too old to learn something new about caring for your animals.

CHAPTER 18

FUN IN THE SADDLE

Even though I love our Exmoor ponies, I was never one for jumping on the saddle when I was young. That's dad's doing, really. My sisters were mad on horses and he knew how expensive keeping ponies could be, so he must have rolled his eyes the day I came in and announced that I wanted to learn to ride. In my six-year-old mind, I wanted to be a cowboy, the John Wayne of the Cotswold hills. So dad, quite mischievously really, bought me a little spotted pony called Domino. I was so excited. We saddled Domino up and I'd trot off across the farm. The trouble was that Domino was quite a nasty little thing. Two miles from the house he'd buck me off and trot happily home by himself. I used to trudge back crying my eyes out. After it happened a few times, I decided that I didn't want to ride horses after all. I'm sure I can remember dad smiling happily at the thought that he wouldn't have to buy me horses. His face soon fell though.

'Don't worry, dad,' I said, 'I'm still going to be a cowboy. I'm just going to do it on a motorbike. You'll have to buy me one of those instead!'

Years later, *Countryfile* found out about my dislike of riding and so decided it would be great fun to send me on all manner of riding reports. Sadists! I couldn't really complain. Some of the assignments were magical, such as the riding holiday I covered in Sligo, on the west coast of Ireland. Absolutely stunning.

I wasn't so happy the day I was told that I was going on the Golden Horseshoe endurance ride. Anything with the word 'endurance' in its title is pretty off-putting in the first place, but the colour must have drained from my face after I did the initial research. The Golden Horseshoe is said to be the toughest endurance riding event in Britain, a 50-mile route across the rough terrain of Exmoor. There are four different classes. You can choose to do 50 miles in just one day, or spread it out over two days, while the hardcore riders go for 100 in two days. I was down for 25 miles a day and had to throw myself into training. The first hurdle was losing weight, as I was apparently too heavy for my faithful steed. Dad had more than one chuckle as he watched me return bandy-legged from a hard day building up my time in the saddle. My horse, Murphy, didn't buck me off, but there was a little of the spirit of Domino in him, and he tested me a couple of times as I struggled to keep him under control. Thankfully, an eventer friend of mine, Chris Hall, was on hand to give me some tuition. After a rocky start, I started to build up confidence.

The day came and the *Countryfile* cameras were there to see me off. OK, I have to admit that it was actually quite fun – and Exmoor is, of course, a wonderful part of the country to see from the back of a horse – but my muscles soon started to complain.

At the end of the first day, we'd done quite well and had completed the 25 miles but I had to report to the *Countryfile* viewers that we had a problem. My horse had gone lame as we'd traipsed across the moor and we'd have to pull out of the second day. I looked suitably disappointed on camera, but inside I was jumping up and down in glee. After a day in the saddle I could hardly walk.

On the farm, horses have served us incredibly well. Back in 2001, after foot-and-mouth, we were looking for new ways to make money. One morning, after we'd been racking our brains for ideas, I went for a walk to clear my head. I bumped into one of our neighbours, Kevin, who was riding around our farm with his children. It was an old arrangement, a favour to a friend, and most Sundays you would see them trotting around our land. We got chatting and I'd told him of the need to make some extra cash.

'The answer's staring you in the face, Adam,' he said. 'Why don't you let people ride around your farm? I mean, why do you think we keep coming back. Look at this place. It's beautiful. Lovely Cotswold hills. Limestone streams. Fabulous old woodlands. People would definitely pay to ride here.'

'Should I start charging you then?' I teased.

'Not if it turns out to be a money-spinner, no,' Kevin replied. 'You can consider it my commission.'

Kevin's suggestion got me thinking. At that time, fun rides happened regularly, but they were usually run by the local hunts as charity events once a year. Could we throw one every month? It could certainly be a nice little earner. Chris Hall was on hand again, this time to give us advice about how to set up a course and plotted a 12-mile ride with 70 optional jumps that we built from wood around the farm. Well, when I say we, I mean Dunc. As well as being a business wizard, Duncan is also pretty handy with a hammer, thanks mainly to lessons from his dad. I shy away from such things. There was a time when my dad couldn't even change a light bulb, and I'm not far from that. I'm always amazed how history repeats itself. Like dad's partner John Neave before him, Duncan looks after the arable and can turn his hand to any repairs or building that's needed and to a certain extent, I'm the front man just like dad was, heading up the livestock and farm park, and nipping off to do the odd bit of telly to boot.

Our first fun run was a real success and we've been doing them ever since, although we now manage to squeeze in one every three weeks. They were one of the things that really helped us dig ourselves out of the hole that foot-and-mouth dropped us in and now are just a regular part of the working calendar.

Which is why this morning, I'm out in the snow with my eleven-year-old daughter, Ella. Even though the farm is still covered in snow, we're hoping to be able to hold this weekend's fun ride and need to set up the course. Ella's a bit of a whizz at helping me prepare for the rides now and earns herself some extra pocket money in the process.

The first step is to mark out the course. The jumps are still out at various points across the farm and we need to plant flags – or arrows as they are called – at each end of the logs. The red arrow goes on the right and the white on the left so that the riders know which direction they're supposed to be jumping in. We also need to hammer in posts complete with signs pointing out the way. With Ella working alongside me, it's taking no time at all.

I love doing stuff around the farm with the kids. It takes me back to helping dad when I was a young lad and, even though it's still absolutely freezing and the work is quite monotonous, you can't help but be in awe of the view as you travel around the course. Dusted with snow, the Cotswolds look amazing. We need it to start thawing off, but the odd scrap of snow should make for an idyllic ride on Sunday.

I'd really like Ella and Alfie to follow in my footsteps and take on the farm, but at the moment neither of them are showing much sign. Sometimes they'll pull on their wellies and come and help me with the animals and at other times they won't. I don't want to push them though. Dad was always supportive with me. He used to say he'd support me whatever I wanted to do. He was the same with all of us as kids. I feel the same way about my two. The only slightly sad thing would be that if they didn't want to take on the farm, the tenancy would come to an end on my death. I'd still like to think there was a Henson here when I'm gone.

When we're happy that everything is marked out clearly, it's time to turn our attention to the animals. The last thing the fun riders will want is to keep having to dismount and open and shut gates to get through field after field of livestock, so we move the animals out of the way, giving them a change of scene for the weekend. The Exmoor ponies are the first to be moved, and I take a moment to give Venus a friendly rub under her neck. I still can't quite believe how calm she now is.

Once the rare breed sheep and the Highland cattle are moved on, our job is done and Ella can call it a day. As I drive her back to the farmhouse, she asks me if I think the fun ride will go ahead.

'I can't see why not,' I reply. 'It is getting slightly warmer and if the snow melts the ground should be soft enough. We just need to hope that Mother Nature is kind. If she sends a hard frost, we'll end up with a frozen course. But I don't think that'll happen.'

I shouldn't have tempted fate. Two days later, on the morning of the fun ride, we woke not to find frost, but a brand new flurry of snow. I immediately pull on my wellies and coat and head up to the highest points of the course. Duncan's waiting for me and I know we need to decide whether to cancel the event, but from the look of things, it's a decision that's already been made for us.

'It's not good, Adam,' Duncan says as I crunch through the snow to reach him. 'We've had a couple of inches overnight and it's worse on the top of the hill. You can't even see the take-off and landing on the jumps. Even if anyone does attempt to drive here, and I wouldn't on the roads around the farm today, we ought to put them off. It's just not safe.'

And so that's it. There's no point in getting angry – there's nothing you can do about it and no one to blame – but it's frustrating. In a foul mood, I head back to the office to update the website and change the answerphone message.

Afterwards, to cheer myself, I head down to the sheds. In all of this snow it's hard to think about spring, but it is just around the corner and our first arrivals have started to make their appearance. The sheds are currently full of our goats, and kidding is in full swing. About 13 have now given birth, with about 15 to go.

As goats have two teats we ideally want a nanny to feed two kids, although this morning a Boer nanny has given birth to triplets. The lovely Boers, with their white bodies and chocolate-brown heads, were first developed in South Africa in the early twentieth century. Their name comes from the Dutch word *boer*, meaning farmer. The Boer goats were primarily bred for meat, although here in the UK goat is quite a long way down on our menus. It's not so elsewhere in the world. It's thought that goat meat, or chevon, accounts for 80 per cent of all meat consumed around the planet and it's a favourite in many of the world's poorer countries. We Westerners have largely turned up our noses at it over the last couple of centuries. Personally, I think it's delicious. It's certainly gamier than lamb, needing to be slow-cooked, with the slightest hint of beef. And with a fraction of the fat and cholesterol you find in lamb, and plenty of protein and iron, it makes for a healthy dish too.

The triplets are looking healthy enough, so I quickly check the nanny to see how much milk she has. A quick feel reveals that she's still got plenty. Usually we'd adopt one of the triplets on to a nanny who'd only had one kid, but in this case it doesn't seem to be a problem. She may be able to nurse all three.

Elsewhere in the shed, I need to step in to stop a potential problem before it happens. One of our small Bagot goats has just given birth to a lovely nanny kid. Bagot goats are beautiful animals with a black head and forequarters, a white body and sweeping, curved horns. According to legend, they took Richard the Lionheart's fancy when he was fighting the Crusades in the twelfth century, and he brought a herd back to England. Around 1390, Richard II was invited for a day's hunting on the Staffordshire estate of John Bagot. The king so enjoyed his time at Blithfield Hall that he gave the royal herd of goats to Bagot, hence their name. Certainly, when John received his knighthood in 1387 the goats appeared on his coat of arms, with two of the animals standing either side of a shield. There are plenty of other stories about how the Bagots ended up in this country, and DNA profiling has suggested that the breed may have originated in Portugal, perhaps travelling back with John of Gaunt when he returned from battle in the Castile region, but wherever they're from, they have lived semi-wild at Blithfield for centuries. In 1970, a trio of Bagots was given to dad by Nancy, Lady Bagot, to establish our own herd. Unfortunately, Bagots are extremely rare – with only around 80 breeding nannies left – and will never probably recover totally as they aren't that good for either milk or meat, although they can cope with incredibly rough scrubland, meaning they can be used in conservation grazing. As they're so rare, every female born is an extremely precious thing.

This one could soon be in trouble though. A large Angora crossbreed is trying its best to pinch the kid from her mum. This happens every now and then. The Angora hasn't had her kid yet, but her maternal instincts have already kicked in. She can't wait to have her own kids, so has decided to go for the easy option of stealing someone else's. As she is so much bigger than the Bagot nanny, she's easily muscling the poor mother out of the way and trying to bond with the kid. If that happens the kid is in real danger. As soon as the Angora's own kid is born, the wannabe-mother will reject the Bagot in favour of her own offspring. By that time, however, the real mother won't want anything to do with her kid and won't have it back, meaning that we'll have to hand-rear the kid if it's to survive.

I need to break them up, especially as the Bagot nanny had started trying to butt the Angora out of the way. If she's not careful the kid-snatcher could end up losing an eye to one of the Bagot's long sharp horns.

Picking up the kid, I back out of the pen slowly, making little kid noises to attract the real mum's attention. The idea is for her to follow me so I can leave her to bond with her kid in her own private little pen. The Angora isn't having any of it. She's still barging the Bagot out of the way, keeping her from following me. There's only one thing for it. I go in and capture the real mum, leading her into the pen to properly meet her kid. Before I leave them be, I just check her stomach to see if she's pregnant with any more kids. There's nothing there, so it's time for them to get to know each other and for the kid to have the all-important colostrum, the extra-rich first milk.

The drama is averted and the Angora is off in the corner of the pen. If I didn't know better I would say she was sulking. She looks as miffed as I was when I saw the new snow this morning.

CHAPTER 19

TO MARKET,
TO MARKET

Thankfully, as the next few weeks pass the snow clears in most places on the farm and all over the country the agricultural business begins to get back to business as usual. Scotland continued to be the worst hit by Britain's cold snap and the bad weather will have long-lasting effects for many. Over 3000 barns collapsed under the weight of the snow, causing millions of pounds of damage to property and, unfortunately, some livestock. The Scottish Government has raised £3 million in emergency funding to help struggling farmers cope with the damage and even the design of farm buildings north of the border is said to be undergoing a rethink due to the lessons learned. Down in the Cotswolds, the snow brought us inconvenience, but at least we had no structural damage or loss of animal life. We consider ourselves lucky.

In the first few days of the snowstorm, many livestock markets across the UK were forced to close their doors due to treacherous travelling conditions, but are now back in full swing.

I've popped over to Cirencester market to sell a couple of old troopers from our farm. Our gigantic Tamworth boar, with the kind of tusks you wouldn't want to find yourself at the wrong end of, is first up, accompanied by a Saddleback sow. Both have served me well for a couple of years now, but in the case of the boar, his usefulness has come to an end, as he has now sired most of the Tamworths on the farm. So that we avoid him mating with his own daughters, I've bought in a younger replacement and earlier this morning guided the old boy, rather reluctantly, across the yard to the trailer. Whereas sows are usually rather lovely and affectionate, moving boars can be tricky, as they can turn quite aggressive at a moment's notice. Using the trusty old pig board, I manoeuvre the boar to exactly where I want him.

When we got the Tamworth to the market, the first thing we did was to weigh him and it soon became clear why I take so much care when moving animals as bulky as this. He weighs in at a whopping 283 kilos. That's a lot of boar. But it means that he should bring a pretty decent price. As he's getting on a bit, the boar won't be used for prime cuts and instead will probably be destined for the processed food market. Pigs are sold according to their live weight on a simple pounds per kilo basis. At the weighing the auctioneer told me that I could expect between 50 to 60 pence per kilo, meaning that I could expect around 150 quid for him. The sow, which is in slightly better condition, will probably go for a little bit more. The British Saddleback is a fairly new breed, first official recognised in 1967 when two different breeds – the Wessex and Essex Saddlebacks were amalgamated. Both breeds shared similar colours but had quite different characteristics. The Wessex was originally from the New Forest, although by 1914 had spread across the south and south-west of England. It was completely black, save for a belt of white hair than ran over the forelegs and shoulder. The Essex, on the other hand, hailed from East Anglia. Like its Wessex cousin, the Essex had the band of white around the neck and forelegs, but also had a white tip to its tail and white feet. The amalgamated breed enjoyed massive popularity during the Second World War and in the early 1950s made up around 22 per cent of all pigs registered in Britain. Their good fortune continued right up to the 1970s when they were often bred with white breeds to create so-called 'blue pigs' – white pigs that had grey-blue markings along their back. These 'blues' were often destined to be used in swill feed systems. However, an outbreak of a disease much like foot-and-mouth disease, known as swine vesicular disease meant that such practices became highly restricted and the bottom fell out of the blue pig market. Around the same time, the growth of intensive pig systems meant that the Saddleback soon joined the ranks of those on the RBST rare breed watchlist. It is currently classed as a minority breed, meaning that there are around 1000 breeding sows in the country. British Saddleback sows make excellent mothers, producing around 10 piglets per litter, and it's good to see them growing in popularity, especially in organic operations. This sow has certainly done me well over the last few years and produced dozens of healthy little piglets.

The market is already buzzing as the boar and sow are led into the pens. Sheep are being sold first and before long, money is already changing hands. When it comes to my turn, my boar and sow are among the first pigs to sell, bringing in £150 and £180 respectively. It may not sound a great deal, but when you consider how well they've worked for the farm it's a nice bonus at the end of their working life.

When I arrive back at the farm, pigs are still high on my list of priorities. I check Rusty, a lovely young Iron Age sow who I'm expecting will start to farrow her first litter of piglets any time now. You can usually tell when a pig is about to give birth. Her udder grows in size and she becomes quite loose around the back end. There's another trick of the trade. If you can draw milk from the sow's teat then you can usually expect the piglets to arrive within the next 12 hours. Gently I bend over Rusty and apply some pressure to one of her teats. I'm immediately rewarded with a little gush of white liquid. That's it then. We're soon to have some new arrivals.

Iron Age pigs originated on this very farm, when my dad crossed a Tamworth with a wild boar from London Zoo back in the 1970s. As such, they're the only animals that we show in the farm park that aren't a true breed. As their name suggests, they're a reconstruction of the kind of pigs that would have been herded through the forests by our Iron Age ancestors. Originally they were needed for the Butser Ancient Farm project in Hampshire, a recreated Iron Age farm complete with three examples of the kind of roundhouses folk back then would have lived in. The historians behind the project had wanted the farm's animals to be as authentic as possible, and so no relatively modern breed would do. Dad's Iron Age cross was the answer to their problem and he was soon able also to hire out the new variety of pig to broadcasters and filmmakers. One programme which used dad's pigs was the BBC's *Living in the Past* series which, in 1978, saw 15 plucky volunteers living in roundhouses equipped only with the tools, plants and animals that would have been available back in the second century. The Iron Age pig remains one of our more popular animals in terms of filming. After all, wild boars are temperamental and quite dangerous animals. Why not replace it with a pig that looks almost identical but is docile and actually quite lovable?

Rusty isn't the only one expecting. The rams have done their work and most of the ewes should now be in lamb. I drive over to the Whitefaced Dartmoors to pick up the ram. Now that all of the ewes are marked, and should be halfway through their pregnancy, he needs to be removed from the flock. Most of all, he needs to get his strength back. He's been an exceptionally busy boy over the last few months and his exertions have seen him lose a lot of weight. It's definitely a much skinnier and tired ram that I grab by the horns and wrestle into the trailer.

He's going to spend the winter, together with the other horned rams on the farm, out in a field where they will be able to feed on the grass. After a while they'll live together quite well, but I am expecting a bit of trouble at first. For the last few months they've been masters of all they survey, the heads of their flocks and now, put together, they'll soon be jostling to be the top man. It's quite usual for them to spend the first day scrapping and, even in their slightly depleted state, they're still strong creatures and those horns can be vicious. If you're not careful two rams will back away and then run at each other at full pelt. The force of the collision can cause considerable damage to their heads and, in the very worse case, even snap their necks. So when I get the ram to the shed where I'm getting them all used to each other again, I segregate the space off using metal hurdles, reducing the amount of space they have to move around. Almost as soon as the Whitefaced goes in, he has a little tussle with the Norfolk Horn tup, but as they have a fraction of the room they'd usually need to cause trouble, the fight amounts to just a little pushing back and forth. They'll stay in here for the next 12 hours at least, getting used to each other. As they rub together their various scents will become mixed up and the chances of clashes will diminish.

Once the boys are all secure I head across the yard to the piles of packed silage which continues to ferment in its plastic. I need to take a sample to see how it's doing and so plunge in a long rod-like tool, which extracts a core of the maturing grass. This will be deposited in a plastic bag and sent off to a lab to be tested. This is the second batch that has come under the microscope this season and, sadly, the first results back haven't been good. While, on the surface, the silage that we've been feeding the cattle and sheep looks, smells and feels fine, the wet summer has had yet more damaging effects and the nutritional levels of the grass has turned out to be right down. You want silage that is packed with protein for energy but also trace elements of minerals such as magnesium, cobalt, phosphorus and selenium. This isn't welcome news at all. In the middle of the winter, especially one as bitter as this, the grass has stopped growing and its nutritional value is next to nothing. The ewes need to be getting all the minerals and vitamins they can in order to remain healthy throughout their pregnancy and so that their unborn lambs grow well. We had thought they were getting it all from the silage, but that appears not to be the case. I hope that the next batch of results come back more positively. Not all of our silage can be under par, surely?

The afternoon sees me constructing portable sheep pens in the fields where the pregnant ewes are grazing. At this sensitive time in their cycle I don't really want to be moving them around that much and at least this means that they are not too far to be rounded up. Once in the pen I give them a drench, a dose of vitamins and minerals that will hopefully make up the silage's shortfall. It's administered via a small gun fed by a pack of medicine that I wear on my back. Carefully, I slip the nozzle into the corner of their mouths, lying it just on top of the tongue. You have to be gentle, as you don't want to bruise their mouths, making it painful for them to eat. A little squeeze of the trigger and the drench is delivered. The ewes automatically swallow and the job is done. Drenching costs around 80p a head, but while it's an expense I'd rather not have, it's worth every penny if we're going to have healthy lambs in the spring as each of the lambs they are carrying should bring me £70. After a few hours I'm done, drenching the last of the Whitefaced Dartmoors. I've become very attached to my new arrivals and can't wait to see the first

Dartmoors born on Bemborough Farm in just a couple of months' time.

Of course, the sheep aren't the only animals to feed on the silage. It's the main component of our cattle's diet too, so I also need to supplement their meals. These minerals are incredibly important. While they probably amount to the smallest part of an animal's diet, they are the foundation stone on which every beast's health is built. I need the cattle to be as healthy as possible, especially with our next TB test on the horizon, and so I set up licks around the cattle sheds – buckets containing a mixture packed with the missing minerals which the animals can snack on. Back in the old days I used to keep these on the floor around the sheds, but I can't risk it now. It isn't just cows that like sampling the licks. Badgers will seek them out too and the saliva they leave behind could pass on TB. Instead, the licks are held out of the reach of a badger, in bucket mounts attached to the hurdles. It's better to be safe than sorry.

Whereas we plan for our lambs and calves to arrive in the spring, pigs are constantly being born, all year round. With a gestation period of three months, three weeks and three days, the average sow gives birth twice a year. On a commercial intensive system, the sow can be put back with a boar just three days after her piglets are weaned. Quite often the weaning period itself is brought forward, cutting it down to just three weeks rather than the full six so the pigs are ready for slaughter as quickly as possible.

My pigs are weaned at six weeks and are ready for pork at six to seven months and for bacon at eight. It all depends on the weight, but if your pig weighs in between 70 to 80 kilos live weight, you're looking at a porker. On a commercial operation they'd probably reach the required weight within just five months.

After a busy day, I pop into check on Rusty and soon have some exciting news to tell the kids – she's started to farrow. My children have certainly inherited my love of piglets, especially when they're newly born. Ever since Ella and Alfie were young, I've never been able to resist picking up a little piglet, popping it up my jumper and smuggling it back into the house. I sit down with a little lump wriggling under my top, much to the kids' delight. I guess that one day they'll get sick of this little ritual, and will probably just find their old dad embarrassing. The problem is, I never tire of it. I used to love it when my dad pulled the same trick with his original Gloucester Old Spots when I was three.

As Rusty seems relaxed and is quite happy giving birth, I leave her to it, returning the next morning to give her some well-deserved pignuts. I'm greeted by the sight of nine healthy piglets huddled together, while mum tucks into the afterbirth. This is all part of her natural instincts. In the wild, a sow will start clearing up the birth site to get rid of any pungent odours that may attract predators. When it comes to the placenta, the most convenient way of disposing of it is for the sow to digest it. I want to have a closer look at the new arrivals, but am always a little wary of approaching a new family unit like this. Even the most friendly sow can turn nasty if she thinks you're going to take her piglets away and so I slowly clamber over the gate, ready to skedaddle if Rusty begins to appear twitchy. Instead the dopey thing snuffles around me affectionately as if to say, look what I did. I drop a little apple pulp in her trough to distract her and inch over to her litter. I can't help smiling when I see them properly for the first time. Back when I put Rusty to the boar nearly four months ago, I didn't want to mate her with the hulking great Tamworth boar I've just sold. He was almost twice her size and could have quite badly injured her. So instead I opted for a Gloucester Old Spot. The result is an amazing array of piglets. Some look exactly like little Old Spots, while others resemble Tamworths, a throwback to one side of Rusty's heritage while the rest look like wild boar, with their distinctive stripy backs. It's a perfect little selection, three of each. Not wanting to chance my luck, I give Rusty a pat and nip back over the gate. As I leave, the piglets are streaming over to mum ready to seek out a tasty teat.

CHAPTER 20

TB TIME AGAIN

It's been two months since we failed our last TB test and no breeding cattle have been sold since that day. Yes, we've been able to send some to slaughter for beef, but that's not where we make our real money. Being shut down like this is now costing me thousands.

Before we know it, it's testing time again and this time the vet carrying out the procedure is Robert Broadbent. He arrives bright and early, in time to see us bringing our Highland cattle over the field. They're the first ones to face the needle as, unlike the rest of the herd, they've spent the winter outside.

Robert gives them those two injections in the neck that we'll be examining in three days' time. If they've turned into lumps, and the bottom one's bigger than the top, we've got another reactor on our hands and we'll continue being shut down until we pass two consecutive tests.

Working with the Highlands is difficult when you're trying to get them through the race. Their horns are so big and sharp that one false move could lead to a nasty slash on your face, or an eye being poked out. Such thoughts are morbid, but they match my mood today. I don't know what to think about the tests. I don't want to get my hopes up, but at the same time I'm praying that we'll be clear. It's crippling this side of our business.

The rest of the cattle are still under cover for the winter so at least I haven't got to round them up from miles about. Using hurdles, we improvise a cattle race to get them in the crush. They say that animals can pick up on how you're feeling. Today I can believe it. All of the cows are skittish and just don't want to cooperate. There's no way we're going to get them into the race. We step back for a while, let them calm down and try again. Finally they quieten down, so we get them in and Robert gives them the jabs. It doesn't help that many of the cows, such as the Gloucesters, are heavily pregnant. Finally they're all done and we move on to our last shed, where we keep the bulls.

Later in the day, I'm joined by Robbie McDonald from the food and environment research agency. He's come to the farm to be interviewed for *Countryfile*. The subject is one that is very close to my heart – the plan to vaccinate badgers against TB. I show him a typical sett on the farm and he says that a location such as this will be ideal for the trial, which will happen in the next year.

At the moment the agency is trying to survey badgers in the area. It's a good time of the year as the grasses and plants haven't started to grow back yet and you can get a clear view of the badgers' workings. The idea is that they catch the badgers and vaccinate them.

'There's no magic number of how many we have to catch,' Robbie tells me, 'but we're aiming for about 80 per cent of the population. If we can get near that sort of number we're pretty sure that this is going to have a big effect.'

I nod for the camera and ask the appropriate questions but I can't help but wonder if vaccination is a hopeless venture. All the efforts are being focused on vaccinating the badgers, not the cattle, so that the source of the infection can be reduced. Of course we'll take part – any positive action is better than none at all – but vaccinating half of the badgers on my farm, let alone the whole of Gloucestershire, is going to be a mammoth task. And they want to hit 80 per cent?

It's so hard to remain positive. Perhaps it's just the winter blues but I haven't got a great deal of hope pinned on this latest TB test. Most of my friends and neighbours have been shut down for months now, years in some cases. Why should we be any different?

Then there's that little devil who is whispering in my ear more and more. Even without TB we always struggle to make money from our cattle. Perhaps it's time to cut our losses and reduce the size of the herd. After all, we could make far more at the moment from lamb for the table. Is that the long-term answer? To scale back the cattle and ramp up the sheep operation?

Three days later and we're in the middle of the process all over again. The Highlands are first again and I herd them across a field using my truck. I've already overheard Robert being interviewed for the camera saying that the chances of us being cleared today isn't good. They've had more and more cases in the last few months and the entire herd is riddled with it. Brilliant. Just what I want to hear. And to think I've got to go through all of this on camera too. I've heard people in the past say that *Countryfile* offers a rose-tinted view of the countryside for urbanites. If that were the case, we wouldn't be showing this, would we? This is the stark reality for cattle farmers today. A terrible disease that ruins your business and saps your will. Hardly cuddly, country-side TV. But that's why I keep agreeing to have our test filmed. I want people at home, eating their tea, to realise just what we're going through out here and also, how much this crisis – for that's what it is – is costing the taxpayer.

Robert starts checking the Highlands for lumps and while he's there, gives them the once-over to see if they're pregnant as well. Dad's on hand to keep a record and give me some support. I need it. I'm churned up inside.

But it's good news. Our bull has done well and all of the Highlands are in calf. Even better, not one of them has reacted to the injections.

The bulls and steers are next and first up is one of our stars of *Robin Hood*, Sundance the Longhorn oxen. A shadow passes over Robert's face immediately and my heart sinks. He's explaining to the camera what he's doing and for a second I feel like I've stepped outside of myself, watching it all from a million miles away. This can't be happening, I keep telling myself, this can't be happening.

But it is.

'What we *don't* want is a big bottom lump,' Robert is saying, 'and we've got something here that looks like a goose egg.' He measures it and the look in his eyes tells me everything I need to know.

This is the last straw. We've worked so hard on Butch and Sundance, getting them to take the yoke and pull a cart. Hours and hours of work and for what? Sundance is now going to be destroyed.

The rest of the day passes in a blur. A week later, when the report is due to be shown on TV I don't know if I can watch it. I see myself standing in front of the two oxen, having been asked by the director to let the viewers know what I'm thinking. I hardly recognise myself. I look so tired and beaten. It was one of the hardest pieces to camera I've ever had to do.

'It's such a crying shame,' I hear myself say, 'I suppose you just become hardened to it in a way. I feel a bit blank inside.'

I still do. At the end of the test, only Sundance completely failed, although one White Park was borderline and was sent for slaughter just in case. And here we are, still stuck in the nightmare of being closed down.

What we need is some good news and I'm hoping that today is the day for it. In just a few hours we find out exactly how many lambs are going to be born on the farm in March and April. It's the shot of excitement I need to get myself out of the funk I've been feeling ever since the TB test, and it works every time. No matter what else is going on in my head, the thought of all those new lives cannot help but raise my spirits. I've always been the same. This has to be one of the best moments in the farming calendar, that point when you realise that the cold, hard slog of the winter is waning and spring is on its way.

A few weeks back now, Richard Chantler arrived to check half of our flock for pregnancies and he's back today to scan the other half. Talking about watching a master at work. Richard has been doing this for more than 30 years and is held in such high regard that he travels the world to ply his trade, flying to destinations as far away as New Zealand or Canada. He reckons that in the course of his career he's scanned the wombs of around two and a half million sheep. Today he gets to add another 325 to his tally.

It's a slick operation. We've separated the sheep that need to be scanned into three groups of about a hundred sheep in each of the locations. As a contractor, Richard is paid for every sheep scanned, getting 55p per head, so he needs the sheep to keep moving as quickly as possible. The more sheep he can scan, the more money he can make. I know he's already got two more farms lined up after us today. We help him speed things up as much as possible, hurrying the sheep through the race, up on to a platform where Richard scans them with an ultrasound, using the same kind of equipment that is used on pregnant women. He tells us how many babies are inside and then the ewe is out the other end. It's a quick in and out job and I must admit I'm always stunned at the speed Richard works. On average we crack through 125 sheep in just half an hour. It's staggering.

As Richard shouts out the number of lambs inside the ewe, Mike is on hand with a can of spray paint. If there's one lamb, he sprays a quick dot of red paint on her back before she skips off the platform. However, if she's carrying two lambs then we don't bother with the paint. Twins are the norm and so we don't spray those to save valuable time – and paint.

In fact twins are exactly what we're hoping for with our commercial sheep. Every sheep has two teats and so, using simple mathematics, it's obvious that the most effective model is for each ewe to nurse two lambs. Because of this, as we scan the flock, we work out a percentage to help us keep tabs. If every ewe is having one lamb then the percentage for the flock will be 100, two lambs per ewe is 200 per cent and so on. What you're aiming for is 200 per cent. One hundred isn't good enough – you'll struggle to make that work financially – while getting 300 per cent means that your ewes are over-producing and you're going to be left with smaller babies and more hungry mouths to feed by hand. We are getting a few cases where ewes are scanning with triplets and quads. It's not ideal. Of course, when breeding commercial sheep you're always looking to up their prolificacy, to have them producing as many lambs as possible, but in the cases of quads that's going far too far. Amazingly, I hear Richard say 'five' at one point. That's not good. The ewe is going to be shattered by the time she gives birth. I hope we don't get too many of those.

It's different when it comes to our rare breeds. Unlike the commercial sheep, they only usually have one lamb each. It's purely a survival tactic. The Herdwicks, for example, would struggle out on the wet fells of their native Lake District habitat to find enough food to produce the milk they'd need for more than one lamb.

Before we know it we're on to the last batch. To make Richard's job just that little bit trickier, the sun has decided to make an appearance and is hanging low and bright in the sky. So that he can still make out the screen, Richard sets up a tarpaulin tent that he darts beneath to give himself darkroom conditions. He's a real pro.

The last hundred ewes start filing through.

'This one's empty,' comes the muffled voice from beneath the tarpaulin. Mike reaches for the purple paint can. This colour indicates a barren ewe and seals her fate. In just a week's time she'll be in market and will hopefully be earning me about eighty quid, which will go some way towards paying for Richard's services. Her ejection from the flock will also mean that we save money by not feeding her over the next six to eight weeks. That may sound a harsh way of thinking about things, but it's the way you have to operate if you want to make a profit, especially with the cattle side of the business frozen. This entire process isn't just a case of curiosity. We want to work out, in advance, how many lambs are likely to arrive so we can start working out cash flow and also how much we have to feed each ewe to make sure she is as healthy as she can possibly be for the rest of her pregnancy.

The last ewe hops off the platform. We've just done 73 ewes in a quarter of an hour. Richard runs through the results so we can double-check.

'So that's 7 empties, 31 singles, 31 twins and 4 triplets. Seventy-three sheep at 144 per cent.' In less time than it takes to tell, Richard has cleaned up, packed up and is off to his next appointment. How he lives his life at such a pace I'll never know.

Back in the farm office I go over the numbers. Overall, the result for the entire commercial flock is 170 per cent. It's slightly down on last year so we'll have fewer lambs to sell, but I'm not worried. The drop in numbers is probably due to the low quality of the autumn grass, just another result of last year's bad summer. However, as the day draws to an end I find myself walking back across the yard to the house with a spring in my step. In eight weeks we'll be preparing to meet 966 new arrivals to Bemborough Farm. I, for one, can't wait.

CHAPTER 21

LAMBING LIVE

It's February and I find myself sitting in *The One Show* studio in London's White City clutching a fake sheep. The lights glare in my face and cameras zoom in and out.

'Tell us what's happening to the sheep, Adam.'

That's the director coming through my specially made earpiece.

I nod and launch into a spiel about twin lambs and the many problems of pregnancy.

'Camera two, Adam. Link to next section.'

I do what I'm told. This is absolutely terrifying. I'm being trained to do live television using a cuddly toy on one of the most recognisable sets on TV. What have I got myself into?

It all started six months ago when I received a phone call. It was Lisa Ausden, a BBC producer. She had been reviewing tapes of my lambing footage from last year's *Countryfile* and wanted a chat.

'We're planning a new series, Adam, and we want to run something by you,' Lisa explained. I sat up in my seat. The prospect of a new series is always interesting.

'Do you watch *Springwatch* or *Autumnwatch*, Adam?' she asked.

'Yes, when I can. I'm quite often busy on the farm when they're on,' I replied.

'Well, we're looking at a similar type of programme based around farming, specifically sheep farming. It's called *Lambing Live*. We're looking at a week-long series, with a one-hour-long programme every night live from a lambing shed. We want to show the viewers what a week on the farm in lambing season feels like.'

OK, now I was interested. Were they phoning because they wanted to do it here?

'We want to ask your opinion, Adam. Do you think it's a sustainable format? Could it work?'

Now that was a good question. Of course, we'd been lambing live on the farm for years so I knew that the general public was interested, but would they be interested enough to follow it every night for a week? I wasn't so sure.

But the phone calls kept coming. They weren't looking to do it here, but had found a sheep farmer in Monmouthshire who had agreed to invite the cameras in, and things were starting to move quickly. The production team were asking me lots of questions about the biology of sheep, when they lamb, what timescale they could be looking at. The thing was, I still didn't have a clue if I would be actually working on the show.

'Lisa, can I just ask you something?' I finally asked during one of our conversations. 'I'm giving you a lot of free consultancy here. Am I going to be presenting this?'

'Well, at the moment it's between you and Kate Humble.'

Brilliant, I thought, I haven't got a hope then. Kate had been presenting *Springwatch* since the beginning and knew everything you need to know about live television shows. I'd never done one in my life.

'OK then,' I said, feeling a little crestfallen, 'I doubt you're going to choose me over Kate Humble to do live telly. Look, I'm happy to give you some of my time, but if you want me to stay on the phone for hours talking through things, I think we need to talk about employing me as a consultant.'

A few days later they phoned back to talk through the consultancy term, or so I thought.

'Adam, we'd love you to be part of the show. Would you present it alongside Kate?'

Of course I said yes. Who wouldn't? They'd pretty much persuaded me that the format would work, and what an honour. To present a live show on prime time TV with Kate. And then the realisation sank in. A *live* show.

'OK, everyone. Live in two minutes.'

If I thought practising in *The One Show* studio was scary, it was nothing compared to this. In two minutes we would be going live to the nation.

It's day three of *Lambing Live* and even though the barn is full of lights, it's an absolutely freezing March evening.

The first two shows have gone really well. We've been broadcasting from Great Tre-Rhew farm in Llanvetherine, near

Abergavenny. It's one of two farms owned by the Beaven family, a sheep farming dynasty that spans three generations, born and bred in the foothills of the Brecon Beacons. The two farms are run by the two Beaven brothers. Jim Beaven runs the 300-acre Great Tre-Rhew while Huw runs the Skirrid, just down the road. Jim has 550 sheep in total, with 130 cattle, 19 pigs and 50 chickens.

And today, in the middle of his busiest time of the year, he also has 60-odd BBC crew members on site making a programme.

The response has been better than we could ever have imagined. Over the last few days we have shown recorded footage of Kate working with Jim as they prepare for lambing, along with short films I've made about the wider issues of sheep farming. The one thing we haven't shown is an actual lamb being born on camera. I think the producers are slightly worried about showing so much blood and gore at teatime.

'One minute.'

OK, now I'm really nervous. For the last two episodes, Kate has introduced the show, welcoming the viewers to *Lambing Live*. Today it's my turn. We've practised it, blocked out exactly what we're going to do and what we're going to say, but I keep getting my line wrong.

It's stupid. All I have to say is 'Welcome back to *Lambing Live*, here at the Beavens' farm in Wales...'

A simple, simple line, but I'm so nervous I'm getting nervous. The voice continues in my ear.

'Live in 30 seconds.'

Kate looks at me and smiles. She's been brilliant. So warm and friendly and has already helped me find my way around the pitfalls of live TV. Now she's being incredibly patient with me. We're 20 seconds away from going live and I can't get my mouth around my line. I know other presenters who would have panicked or got cross with me. Not Kate. As the countdown starts, she rubs my back.

'OK, Adam, say it to me one more time.'

'Fifteen seconds.'

I deliver the line perfectly, not a single fluff.

'Brilliant,' she says, 'then off you go.'

'Five, four, three and cue Adam.'

I smile at the camera.

'Welcome back to *Lambing Live*, here at the Beavens' farm in Wales.'

Two days later and the first-ever *Lambing Live* has been a complete and utter success. The only snag was that members of the public had started to email in asking why they hadn't seen a lamb born yet. They didn't have long to wait. It all kicked off on the third show. Whether the producers were worried about blood at teatime or not, they got it as lambs started being born left, right and centre. All the time, we had more emails flooding in, people asking about all kinds of things. Prolapses, castrations, stillbirths. My years of lambing live in the sheds back home certainly came in useful. By the end of the week, we were in the middle of a gynaecological and biological feast.

As we bring the last programme to a close, Kate is standing holding Humble, the first lamb she helped deliver. Unfortunately, Humble turned out to have slightly wonky legs and when she was out in the field couldn't keep up with her mother. The poor little black lamb was wasting away in the fields, so Kate had brought her in and bottle-fed her, falling in love with her in the process. Jim had said that she could take Humble home to her smallholding in the Wye Valley, and Kate has one last surprise for me on live TV.

'Adam, could you look after Humble for me on your farm?'

How can I refuse while I am being watched by millions of viewers. And Humble is a particularly cute little lamb.

The credits roll and I start preparing Humble for the journey home. I've promised Kate that I'll look after her, but I'm worried. The little lamb is really ill. I'm not convinced she'll make the journey. There are lots of hugs and kisses as the crew start to pack up and then we're off, heading back to the Cotswolds, with me praying all the while that the little lamb is still OK when we get home.

CHAPTER 22

NOW OR NEVER

I've known neighbouring farmer Pat Quinn for almost of all my life, and went to school with her son, Michael. I always like popping by to see her, but today is a visit of mixed emotions. I'm looking to replace Butch and Sundance, the oxen I spent most of the last year training to take the yoke. Since Sundance was destroyed after contracting TB, Butch has been lost without his companion. It's heartbreaking to see him, especially after putting so much work into the pair. However, life on the farm must go on and one remaining oxen isn't much use, so I'm preparing Butch to go for beef now. It's just another sting in the tail in our ongoing TB saga. My mood isn't as bleak as that moment a month or so ago when I considered calling it a day with the herd, but I'm still under a bit of a cloud. But if in the past I've questioned allowing the *Countryfile* team on the farm during testing, it's a route I now know that I'll continue to go down in the future. The other day I was talking to a prominent industry leader who told me that a senior minister at DEFRA had admitted that watching my TB test on *Countryfile* helped him realise just what cattle farmers are going through. It's quite telling that it takes something like a

Sunday evening TV show to get this message across to the powers that be, but it justifies my decision to let the TV crew film the business of the farm.

Pat has bred Longhorn cattle for more than 30 years now and her herd is considered one of the best in the country. Longhorns have been a real success story for the rare breed movement. When Pat started out in the Eighties the breed was seriously endangered but Longhorns are now flourishing in farms across the country. I can't think of a better place to buy young replacements for Butch and Sundance than Pat's farm, but it all depends on two things. Today, on this bright April afternoon, Pat is undergoing her latest TB test and, back on my farm, I'll be doing the same in just a few weeks. If Pat passes hers, she's be able to sell to me, and if I pass mine, I'll be one step closer to being able to buy in new stock. Of course, I could buy them in and set up an isolation field, keeping the newcomers well away from the rest of my cattle, but that's a real gamble. If I remain closed down for years, I'll be left with cattle that I can't integrate into the main herd for all that time.

Pat got into Longhorns thanks to dad. One day at the school gates, as they waited for me and Michael to come running out, they were chatting about the farm park and Pat mentioned that she'd always wanted to keep some livestock. Dad logged the information away and when an auction for some Longhorns came up, gave her a call.

'Are you serious about keeping livestock,' he asked, to which Pat said that she was. 'Right then, Pat,' he continued, 'get your coat on. We're going to auction.'

Pat came back with a small herd of Longhorns and hasn't look back since. Her love for these creatures is evident as she walks me around her sheds. I spy a couple of new heifers that were born a few days before.

'They're beautiful, aren't they?' she says, before turning back to me, 'but I guess you'll be after males, won't you?'

'Usually Pat,' I reply, 'but with the TB I'm wondering if I should try and train up heifers to take the yoke. That way if I lose one of them in the future, I won't have to sell the other for beef. At least, I could keep her for breeding then, if the worse happens.'

'We'll have to see what happens after the test, Adam,' Pat comments quietly. 'I have to admit, I can't really concentrate this morning. My brain is melting at the thought of the result. If I lose any more...'

It's hard to see an old friend of the family trying to hold it together. I can feel for her. I know how conflicted she must be feeling. But, the moment passes and she slips her arm in mine.

'No point standing around worrying,' she says. 'It's now or never.'

An hour later and the test is in full swing. It's the same old drill. The vet is checking the cows' necks and Pat is standing behind a wooden lectern taking down the results.

'She's 20 over 15,' the vet shouts over. 'This one's fine.'

Pat, standing so calm and composed behind the record books jots down the figures. I notice a sheet sticking out from between the leaves of the book and ask Pat about it. She draws out the paper, which is full of pictures of beautiful Longhorn cattle.

'These are the cows I've lost this year to TB,' she explains, and the sadness in her words is palpable. There are a couple that are with calf in the pictures. That makes the tragedy all the more unbearable. At the age of the calves in the pictures, the babies are absolutely dependent on their mother's milk. With the mother gone, caring for the young calf becomes a nightmare both logistically and financially, pushing the costs of being closed down even higher. Pat rests a finger on the picture of two cows at the bottom of the sheet, identified in the captions as Harford Florence and Harford Fen. Just looking at them, I can see what's coming. 'These two were in calf – around seven months into their pregnancies. They went in February.'

Four lives, extinguished just like that.

Even though I know what Pat's going through, I still don't know what to say.

'It's just so indiscriminate, isn't it?' I finally manage. 'You never lose the skinny, horrible ones, do you? The ones who look ill. It can be any of them.'

Halfway through, and the test is all-clear. I ask Pat how she's holding up. Her response makes me smile despite the tense atmosphere, it's so typically her. 'I get very stressed, Adam, but one has to be very disciplined about not allowing it to get you down. It's not just about the money, you see. This is my life and these animals are like family.'

Luckily it's good news for Pat's extended family. The vet calls out the result of the last animal tested – her mighty bull.

'14 over 12. It's a pass.'

The all-clear. Pat allows herself a moment of emotion, the first she's really shown since she took her place behind the lectern.

'Brilliant,' she exclaims, punching the record book happily. 'Thank goodness.'

I give her a hug.

'Congratulations, Pat. That's it. You're clear.'

Pat smiles, but can't help adding a few cautious words.

'Until the next time, Adam. Until the next time.'

Pat wasn't just being gloomy or downhearted. She really was overjoyed that she wouldn't have to send any more animals to slaughter, but every cattle farmer knows that your stock is only as good as their next test. The trick is to start working as soon as you hear those wonderful words, 'You've got a clear test.'

I wonder if they're the words I'll hear from my own vet, Gill, today.

She's going to be here any minute, but I take a moment to get away from the preparations in the yards for our latest test. I need to clear my head and so I've popped up to a field where ewes and new lambs are resting in the sun. I've come to check on the first-ever Whitefaced Dartmoors to be born on Bemborough Farm. I find one immediately, a gorgeous male, and can't resist picking him up. All of the Whitefaced Dartmoors that I brought back from Colin Pearse's farm lambed perfectly and I haven't lost a single lamb. This one will be reared for breeding. I pop him down and watch him scamper back off to find his mum. I think it's fair to say that the Dartmoors have worked their way into my heart, just as they did Colin's. They're officially my favourite sheep now.

It isn't just the Dartmoors that have done well this season. We're about two-thirds of the way through lambing and all the rare breeds have now given birth. Of the commercial flock, we have 244 ewes turned out with 438 lambs. I'm really pleased with that number – which means we're operating at around 180 per cent so far – and we still have about a hundred ewes in the shed ready to lamb. It's going to be a good year for Bemborough Farm lamb.

Feeling slightly calmer than I did when I couldn't eat my breakfast this morning, I jump in the truck and make my way back to the cattle yards. Last night, I couldn't resist visiting the cattle and running through my own highly unscientific test. I walked among them, brushing my hand along their necks for lumps. I couldn't see any, but don't want to count my chickens before they're hatched.

When I get to the field where we're carrying out the first test, Gill's already waiting for me.

'I don't want to get your hopes up, Adam,' she says as we shake hands, 'but I've just come from another farm near Stow. They've been under restriction for a year now, and I've just been able to give them the all-clear.'

'Brilliant news,' I say, but half wish she hadn't said anything. What with Pat's all-clear a few days ago and now the news that another of my neighbours is out of the woods, I should be feeling positive, but I have to be realistic. There's no guarantee that good news for them will mean good news for us.

We start to lead the Highlands into the crush, watching out for those wicked-looking horns. It's always dangerous dealing with horned animals, which is why, in a commercial herd, the horns are always removed at birth.

They trudge in and out and, thankfully, are all given a clean bill of health. The Highlands are clear, so we head over to the bulls and the steers. First up is Alfie, my prize bull that we tried to sell after the last all-clear. I desperately need to be able to sell him soon, if only the results go our way. He passes and so we continue to work our way through, until we get to a Belted Galloway steer.

'Unfortunately this chap has got a lump.'

Oh no. Gill pulls out her callipers and we all wait for her to speak again.

'It's fine. He's clear.'

Gill is one of the best vets I know. She has to be thorough, but she really puts me through it at times.

When the last of the steers is cleared we move on to the last yard, housing the majority of our heavily pregnant cows. This is the moment I've been dreading. Some of the cows have already given birth, but most of them are still due any time now – some literally in the next 12 hours. If anything goes wrong, they could easily lose their calves. I'm not sure who's more spooked – Mike and me, or the cattle – and they prove to be immensely jumpy as soon as we arrive.

The first cow in – a Belted Galloway, extremely near her due date – panics as soon as we put her in the crush. She leaps up, getting her legs over the front of the cage. This is exactly what I didn't want to happen. Caught for a minute, she crashes about in the crush, before propelling herself through the narrow gap and running off. I head after her to make sure she's OK. There's no sign of external damage and I'm just praying that the babies inside are also fine. I leave her to calm down while I feel my own anger rising. This disease is costing the country millions and farmers need to work together to rid us of it, no matter how long that takes. Dairy farmers need to keep badgers out of their silage pits and we all need to be vigilant and stick to the law of the land when it comes to things such as pre-movement testing of animals. It's no good arguing and going up against each other. We need to work together to help beat this thing. A few days ago, a new coalition government was formed. Will they be able to do something about all this? Will they make a difference? I hope so, but even if they do, we could be looking at another 10 years, at least, of having TB hang over us. And all the time I'm having to do things like this, having to handle cattle that I want to be able to leave alone. It's driving me bonkers. In tests like these, the cows can hurt themselves or their unborn calves. What if this Galloway had kicked Gill in the face as it tried to escape the crush, or landed on Mike as she jumped forward? It's just too dangerous for everyone involved.

I remember the still, stoical presence of Pat at her test and try to keep a check on my emotions. Everyone is already stressed to high heaven. They don't need me to lose it. Eventually, the Galloway calms down enough to be led into the crush again. This time she stays there and is soon given the all-clear, so she can be let out again.

One more to go. Is it too much to hope that we're clear?

Gill punches the air.

'Adam, that's it. You're clear.'

You can hear the sigh of relief from everyone and there are hugs all round. Thank goodness for that. The cows can relax now, and carry on calving. Personally, I won't be able to relax myself until 60 days have passed and we receive that all-important second pass.

But this isn't the time for doubts about the future. At the minute it's looking pretty good. We have hundreds of new lambs, the Maris Otter barley is growing well and the summer is predicted to be a scorcher (although we've heard that before, of course) and for now, we've won a battle against TB. Will we win the war? I've no idea, but I can't help but feel that good times are coming.

EPILOGUE

Looking back now, I can't believe what an eventful year it has been, full of ups and downs.

The best news of all came 60 days after we went clear from TB. We sailed through the second test, not a reactor in sight. Of course, the fear is always there, in the back of your mind, that the disease can return but, for now, it's not something I should allow myself to lose sleep over. I just hope when the inevitable happens, and TB rears its nasty little head again, I can get through it without throwing in the towel. I don't think I ever will. After all, dad's been keeping cattle on this farm for 40 years and I don't want to be the one to make the decision to turn our back on them.

There have been some important developments in the fight against TB. The government has proposed a series of controlled badger culls across England and have launched a year-long consultancy period. This doesn't mean that it will actually happen. The English cull proposal was announced the same month as Welsh campaigners managed to halt the cull in Wales by appealing to the Court of Appeal. A trial to vaccinate badgers has kicked off near Stroud, but it'll be a few years before we know if it's a success. In the meantime, we'll continue to go through the nightmare of TB testing, knowing that it could return at any time.

The current all-clear came at just the right time for Bemborough Alfie, my prize bull. A month before the test, a guy phoned me up and told me he was interested in buying Alfie and so I walked the bull out and gave him a good lather down and a wash. It was quite therapeutic and hopes were running high that I could sell him for breeding as long as the movement restrictions were lifted.

Alfie always enjoys a good wash, too. There's an old farming saying that a wash is a good as a feed and it does always seem to perk the animals up, making themselves feel happy about themselves.

I'm happy to say that as soon as we were given the all-clear, the deal was done and Alfie was sent to his new home to sire a whole family of young cattle. It was a good job too. At two-and-a-half years old, he needed to go for breeding soon, otherwise he was destined for beef. While the difference for him is obvious, for me it meant I could sell him for £1800 for breeding rather than the £800 to £1000 I could expect for beef. A happy ending there.

We've also heard some fantastic news from Portland Bill and Su Illsley. Sadly the ewe that was mauled by a dog had to be put down, but Fancy's Family Farm has been blessed with 14 new Portland lambs and a couple more are on their way. They're the first Portland lambs to be born on the island for around eight years. You have to admire Su. She's so dedicated to helping promote the

Portland breed that she's launched a publicity campaign for the new arrivals. She's got herself interviewed in the local paper and asked readers to write in and give the lambs names. Here's hoping that she has many more lambs in the years to come.

It's not just Su who has had something to celebrate. Finally, after years in the doldrums, the price of British wool has started to rise. The outright winner is the Cheviot sheep, which produces one of the softest fleece varieties on the market. As I'm writing this, Cheviot wool is commanding prices of £1.70 a kilo, meaning that larger sheep can bring in around a fiver a fleece. This level of pricing would have been unheard of even a couple of years ago. The main reason is a shortage of supply. Around the world the numbers of sheep are plummeting. Even New Zealand has lost around 50 per cent of its national flock. So, in the short term, prices should stay reasonably strong. At the moment, Britain is the seventh-largest wool producer in the world and we've now got the chance to build on our historic foundations once again. Even Prince Charles has got behind the industry, launching his Wool Project that promotes wool's green credentials as well as encouraging manufacturers to develop innovative woollen products. So far, it seems to be going well. Wool-based insulation – finally a use for the Herdwick's wool – is on the rise, and one of the most unique products launched has to be a woollen coffin, which turns the clock back to those days when it was against the law to be buried in anything but wool. The coffins, made by the West Yorkshire firm Hainsworth, are made from wool and cardboard and come with an embroidered nameplate. They're seen as a greener alternative to being buried in wood. I've always said we need to learn from the past, and it's great to see that principle in action.

That being said, I had to smile when I read about a new breed of sheep that hit the headlines this April. Developed by Peter Baber from Christow, Devon, the Exlana sheep produces 500g of wool, which it sheds naturally come spring. The papers went crazy over the so-called self-shearing sheep. Obviously no one had told them that if it wasn't for our demand for wool, all sheep would probably still moult. What's that they say? The more things change, the more they stay the same.

Elsewhere on the farm, all is going well. Our spring barley has been a little disappointing, thanks mainly to an unusually cold spring and a drought (where is that rain when you need it?) but the Maris Otter is doing really well and we've already organised a fixed-price contract on that harvest with Warminster Maltings.

And, slowly but surely, we're building up the pig herd. We're up to around four pigs a week now, and have also done a deal with Gary Wallace from Butts Farm Shop in Cirencester who has taken some of our meat. Gary supplies a lot of meat to the restaurants in London, including John Torode's, so I'm hoping that will go well. It would be good to have a local retailer, as well as sending our meat further afield.

I've also had a new arrival on the farm in the form of a new Kune Kune boar. My old boar had picked up some lameness in his front left foot. I had the vet in to see him and an animal osteopath, but neither could work out what he had done. The problem was, as he was hobbling around he couldn't serve the sows, poor fellow.

While he's in rehab I've bought a 12-month-old from Hereford-shire breeder Wendy Scudamore, who has been breeding Kune Kunes for ten years. He's a little fellow but fuelled with testos-terone, and raring to go. I'm hoping he'll sort my girls out as well as a couple of sows – Delilah and Duffy – that I'm looking after at the moment for Kate Humble. The idea is that when I return the girls to Kate's smallholding in the Wye Valley, they'll be in pig. If they're not they're probably destined for sausages, although I'm convinced that Kate will persuade her husband to keep them as pets if they can't conceive. They can keep Humble the lamb company. Despite my fears, Kate's little lamb did survive the jour-ney home and is doing really well. I'm going to miss the sweet little thing when she goes to live with Kate in Wales. The only snag is that the little boar is much smaller than the girls, but he's quite a boarish little guy who definitely fancies himself, so I'm hoping that the course of true love will run smoothly.

Oh, and while we're on the subject of pork, I'm pleased to report that in June 2010 the mandarins in the European Union granted the Gloucestershire Old Spot its Traditional Speciality Guaranteed status, making it the newest of 42 UK products on the Protected Food Name scheme. I told our sows the news when I fed them their apple pulp, but they didn't seem that bothered. We've actually teamed up with Bean Benson to help promote our sausages. Every year, Bean goes out to the summer festivals sell-ing his juice and lollies. The trouble with summer, as we have seen, is that you don't always get good weather and so he's started sell-ing our sausages from his wagon, even using bread rolls made from flour from the mill at Shipton. We're now investigating whether next year, the rolls could be made from our flour. So far, we haven't decided to go down the artisan bread route, but this could be a nice way of breaking into the bread market.

And so now it all begins again, the constant cycle of life on the farm. Of course, I don't expect everything to go perfectly. After all, this is farming.

It's not the easiest life. It's still difficult to make money and can be really tough at points. But the highs outweigh the lows. I'm not a rich man, but live the life of one. As a tenant farmer, I live in a six-bedroom house in the middle of a beautiful 1600-acre farm. What's not to love about that? It's an amazing opportunity that I absolutely appreciate and I know many, many farmers who feel the same. I just wish more of us would shout about it. Farming has changed, there's no doubt about that, and these days you need to be more than a whizz at growing things or being good with animals. You need to know business, take a step back and take a hard look at what you're doing. The problem is there are so many of us that are stuck in a rut, with our heads so far up a cow's arse that we can't see the bigger picture. The cold, hard fact is that the average age of a farmer is now 59 and we desperately need to be attracting fresh blood into agriculture. At the last-ever Royal Show, the Royal Agricultural Society of England said that farming needs to attract 60,000 new farmers over the next ten years if the industry is going to survive. I couldn't agree more. I took over the farm when I was in my thirties, but I'd been lucky. Dad included me in the farm from such a young age.

My kids are still a little too young to get really involved, but I try to do my bit. Recently we took on a young apprentice, Nick Menjou, who is just 18. Nick grew up on a farm and is going to be with us for about 12 months and his apprenticeship is part of his studies at Warwickshire College. We get some help on the farm and he gets some real-life experience while earning a basic wage. So far it's going well. We have had a few sticky moments, like the time he almost demolished the drystone wall of my log shed with a heavy bag of fertiliser, but he's picking up the ropes. Watching him loading grain on to a 29-ton lorry in one of our big JCBs reminded me of how daunting farming must be to an 18-year-old lad. After all, he's driving a highly expensive piece of kit that could do a lot of damage to another expensive vehicle – and that's before we even consider the chance of dropping all my wheat on the farmyard floor. It's no wonder he's nervous. At the same time, though, I'm pleased to see the excitement in his eyes as he takes on a new challenge and masters a new skill, from something as simple as giving the sheep a drench to handling a huge tractor.

It's certainly true that we need new blood, but the important thing is that it can't just be the same old, same old. Those 60,000 new farmers need to be the kind of people who are good at marketing, at promoting their businesses. It's what we lack at the moment. We're good at producing, but rubbish about selling our products and ourselves. If we're going to attract young people away from other industries we need to do something about it, shout about the good moments, explain why the bad moments happen and show everyone that farming is a fantastic way of life.

It's slowly working, too. Agricultural colleges are getting fuller and more people than ever are experiencing farming first-hand, through schemes such as Open Farm Sunday and farm diversification. With a growing world population, who will all need feeding, there's such potential. It's an exciting time. All we need to do is shed the mantle of the underpaid, overworked, whining farmer, lording around in our Range Rovers collecting subsidies that no one understands. It's time for us to show real clarity and bring the last remaining barriers down.

I hope this book has gone a little way into making that a reality. As you can see, life is never dull when you're working the land and looking after livestock, but, as far as I'm concerned, whatever the weather, disease and Fate throws at me, one thing never, ever changes – I love this farm.

INDEX

ACKNOWLEDGEMENTS

First and foremost, I'd like to thank my mum and dad, Joe and Gillian Henson, for all their guidance over the years, and also dad's business partner John Neave and his wife Joanna. The farm park and farm wouldn't exist now if it hadn't been for the work of dad and John and their passion to save rare breeds. Thanks to my business partner, Duncan Andrews, for his support and to all the staff at the farm and farm park for their dedication, even when times have been tough. And finally, thanks to my family – my partner Charlie and our children Ella and Alfie.